The 614th Tank Destroyer Battalion

The 614th Tank Destroyer Battalion

Fighting on Both Fronts

Samuel de Korte

Pen & Sword
MILITARY
AN IMPRINT OF PEN & SWORD BOOKS LTD.
YORKSHIRE – PHILADELPHIA

First published in Great Britain in 2022 by
Pen & Sword Military
An imprint of
Pen & Sword Books Ltd
Yorkshire - Philadelphia

Copyright © Samuel de Korte, 2022

ISBN 978 139900 868 6

The right of Samuel de Korte to be identified as the Author of this work has been asserted by him in accordance with the Copyright, Designs and Patents Act 1988.

A CIP catalogue record for this book is available from the British Library.

All rights reserved. No part of this book may be reproduced or transmitted in any form or by any means, electronic or mechanical, including photocopying, recording or by any information storage and retrieval system, without permission from the Publisher in writing.

Printed and bound in England
By CPI (UK) Ltd.

Pen & Sword Books Ltd. incorporates the Imprints of Pen & Sword Archaeology, Atlas, Aviation, Battleground, Discovery, Family History, History, Maritime, Military, Naval, Politics, Railways, Select, Transport, True Crime, Fiction, Frontline Books, Leo Cooper, Praetorian Press, Seaforth Publishing, Wharncliffe and White Owl.

For a complete list of Pen & Sword titles please contact

PEN & SWORD BOOKS LIMITED
47 Church Street, Barnsley, South Yorkshire, S70 2AS, England
E-mail: enquiries@pen-and-sword.co.uk
Website: www.pen-and-sword.co.uk

or

PEN AND SWORD BOOKS
1950 Lawrence Rd, Havertown, PA 19083, USA
E-mail: uspen-and-sword@casematepublishers.com
Website: www.penandswordbooks.com

Contents

Foreword		viii
Chapter 1	The Sources, History, and Criticism	1
Chapter 2	Activating the 614th Tank Destroyer Battalion	9
Chapter 3	The 614th Tank Destroyer Battalion	34
Chapter 4	Three-inch Fury	49
Chapter 5	Getting out of the Northern Wind	74
Chapter 6	Fighting and Resting	87
Chapter 7	Racing through the Alps	102
Chapter 8	The 827th and the 679th Tank Destroyer Battalion	114
Chapter 9	The Dusk of the Tank Destroyers	136
Appendix A: List of men in the unit		155
Appendix B: List of casualties		181
Appendix C: Medals and citation		184
Literature and sources		202
Endnotes		207
Index		220

This book is dedicated to the segregated soldiers of the tank destroyer branch. Not all of them fought in combat, but all of them helped the Allies to win the Second World War.

Foreword

I became acquainted with the author, Samuel de Korte, through Bob Scherer in the course of his work to recognize the African American soldiers in the Second World War. Samuel instantly became a subject matter expert. He previously wrote a book about his great uncle who took part in the Dutch resistance and who was betrayed, captured, and executed along with four other men. That book is entitled *Tragedy & Betrayal In The Dutch Resistance*. Samuel majored in Cultural History of Modern Europe at the University of Utrecht in the Netherlands. He completed his thesis on the representation of African American soldiers during the Second World War.

Before Nazi Germany declared war on America, the U.S. Army felt the necessity to adapt to the Blitzkrieg rapidly sweeping across Europe. One response was the tank destroyer concept, a hurried, daring, and somewhat flawed answer to the unstoppable panzers. The tank destroyer units were organized as towed battalions equipped with anti-tank guns, or as mechanized battalions equipped with self-propelled anti-tank guns. The 614th Tank Destroyer (TD) Battalion was a towed unit with 3-inch (76 mm) high velocity guns as their main weapon. The TD concept envisioned independent battalions that could respond rapidly to enemy tanks. In this role, they were mostly attached to infantry divisions. The 614th TD Battalion served with the 103rd and 44th Infantry Divisions. Shortly after the war the entire TD force disbanded when supreme headquarters deemed it militarily illogical.

You are about to read the 614th TD Battalion's initiation, i.e. the fight for their right to fight. It will take you through racial friction. OK, I get it. There are those who are weary of being reminded of the rigors of white supremacy. But what if those weary individuals had to live with it?

Moving on, this work will take you through the 614th TD's training. Generally, the tank destroyer units practiced their skills against tank battalions at Camp Hood, Texas. This became a rivalry like college football on a Saturday afternoon along with cheering fans and trash talk. If you let the 761st Tank Battalion tell it, you will hear something like: 'We out maneuvered the TDs at every turn. We set up a diversion and they would think we are coming from one direction and we came from another. The TDs have a motto – Seek, Strike, & Destroy. But when we came up, it became: Sneak, Peek, and Retreat.'

The 614th TD performed superbly in combat. You are about to vicariously experience their uncommon valor. The 3rd Platoon, Company C, 614th TD was the first African American World War II unit to receive the Distinguished Unit Citation; also known as the Presidential Unit Citation, it is the highest decoration bestowed on a military unit. Additionally, Lieutenant Charles Thomas was awarded the Distinguished Service Cross that would be upgraded to the Medal of Honor (MOH) in 1997. His niece Sandra Johnson accepted his posthumous MOH. Charles Thomas departed this world in 1980.

Now for a miserable shard and smear on this service's reputation – brace yourself. On 1 September 1944, before the 614th TD sailed to the Europe Theater of Operations, a unit member from an adjoining TD unit, the 827th, robbed and murdered a fellow soldier. He was tried, convicted, and executed – judicial asphyxiation (hanged), seven and a half months after committing the heinous crime.

Moving on, the images you are about to view are astounding. Most have never seen the light of day since their initial archival. These never-before published images make this work unique. Rather than being generic, they relate directly to the units and the men being discussed. These images come from a wide range of sources including personal family archives, the United States Army Heritage and Education

Center, The Donovan Research Library at Fort Benning, and many other repositories. Every image will tell you a story.

Now, you can look forward to a scholarly work that is profusely illustrated, well-researched, and well-written. It is a labor of love.

Joe Wilson Jr.
Author of various works on African Americans in WWII

Chapter 1

The Sources, History, and Criticism

History is an ongoing process where people examine past events and use them to explain the present. During this process selections are made from within these events as understood from the sources that a person has at his or her disposal. The primary goal of this project is to provide a detailed account of a battalion that fought during the Second World War: the 614th Tank Destroyer Battalion. To a lesser degree, the goal is to provide insight into the experience of the segregated Tank Destroyer Battalions during the Second World War and to give insight into the black American perception of the Second World War.

To achieve these goals, various sources have been used. Beyond doubt, the most important source was the booklet 'Three Inch Fury', the unofficial history of the battalion written in 1946. Although no author is credited, the battalion commander Frank Pritchard is the most likely compiler. Pritchard's past as a journalist and newspaper editor, combined with the focus on the battalion officers, provide plausible explanation of his role. 'Three Inch Fury' was intended for members of the battalion and is dedicated to their fallen comrades. The book provided a lot of interesting information and funny anecdotes.[1]

Written in a less amusing fashion but equally valuable were the official documents that the examined units produced during their existence, such as the battalion journal, or monthly reports. More information is acquired from documents to which the units were attached or which fought together. To this were added legal documents from court martials, providing insight into issues of that historical period. All of these sources mention different aspects of the units and what happened at various moments. In some cases, they provided context to events and happenings that are mentioned in 'Three Inch Fury'.

Further information is retrieved from interviews which were conducted at one time or another with one of the men involved. Especially significant were the ones conducted by Mary Penick Motley for her book *The Invisible Soldier: The Experience of the black soldier, World War II*. Among the men interviewed were three officers from the 614th Tank Destroyer Battalion: Christopher J. Sturkey, Charles L. Thomas, and Claude Ramsey. Thomas Saylor conducted an interview in 2003 with James G. Kirk, who was a member of the 679th Tank Destroyer Battalion. Charles Branson, who served in the 827th, did an interview with David Gregory in 2000.[2]

Equally valuable were the stories of the men that served in the 614th, or one of the other tank destroyer units, written by themselves, in newspapers, or narrated to me by their descendants. Patiently, they told me what their fathers had told them, or what their fathers had left behind. Many pictures were also acquired through them. Thanks to them and their enthusiasm, this project became much larger than originally intended.

Other important sources dealt with the examined time period or with specific aspects of the past. As for insight into the Tank Destroyers, the study *Seek, Strike, and Destroy: U.S. Army Tank Destroyer Doctrine in World War II* by Dr Christopher Gabel was extremely valuable. This was combined with the book *Mobility, Shock, and Firepower: The Emergence of the U.S. Army's Armor Branch, 1917–1945* by Dr Robert Cameron, which provides a larger scope of the struggles of the Tank Destroyer branch in relation to the other services.[3]

The 614th Tank Destroyer Battalion was attached to the 103d Infantry Division for almost the entire time it served in combat. To examine the 103d Infantry Division, the book *Report After Action: The Story of the 103d Infantry Division* by Ralph Mueller and Jerry Turk was used.[4] It gives a lot of information about the places where the men fought. The division was officially known as the 103d and will be referred to as such in the work throughout.

The book *Riviera to the Rhine* by Jeffrey Clarke and Robert Ross Smith, part of the official U.S. Army in the Second World War series, examines the front in Eastern France, where the 614th performed most of its operations.[5] Two books detailed the service experiences of black American troops and racism: *A Historic Context for the African American Military Experience*, especially the chapter by Robert Jefferson, and the study *The Employment of Negro Troops* by Ulysses Lee. The latter book is also used for the research about the 827th Tank Destroyer Battalion and the 679th Tank Destroyer Battalion.[6]

The Medal of Honor, which was eventually awarded to Charles L. Thomas, and the process in awarding it are described in the study *The Exclusion of Black Soldiers from the Medal of Honor in World War II: The Study Commissioned by the United States Army to Investigate Racial Bias in the Awarding of the Nation's Highest Military Decoration conducted* by Elliott V. Converse et al.[7]

In the historical material of this project there will be instances of implicit and explicit racism. In the sources, words or abuse will be encountered that are hurtful, insensitive, or ignorant. These words can still offend readers to this day. They are kept in the project as they give insight into the social climate that existed. The usage of those words in this research is not to hurt or insult a contemporary public, but to present an accurate image of the past. Some words were controversial even at that time, but they are present in the source material, uncomfortable as they might be. They are part of history, and historical research must also examine the unpleasant aspects of our historical past.

In a similar vein, it's also wrong to erase or ignore uncomfortable aspects of history, as this would give the impression that certain problems might not have existed or weren't such a big deal then or now. Thus, in this research the material might offend some readers, but to deny or remove it would also be wrong. The men of the 614th Tank Destroyer Battalion, and the other examined units, such as the 679th and 827th Tank Destroyer Battalions, experienced racism, and discrimination. They were called degrading names and the discrimination that they endured at that time, which will be presented here later, would be staggering by any accounts today.

While respecting the history, the liberty has been taken to make small changes in the source material. These are all intended to improve readability. Minor grammatical or spelling errors have been corrected and some words updated to a modern spelling. Most place names, as far as possible, have been updated to their appropriate spelling. Ranks, and most abbreviations, have been written in full. So Cpl. would become Corporal and Lt. would become Lieutenant.

In the research material there are also conflicting reports or minor errors in dating events. In each case, the most likely, or accurate, version is chosen. For instance, an event dated in the unit journal takes precedence over the same event in the battalion histories. Sometimes clerical errors slip into the material, either in the archiving process or at another stage. Mistakes could even be made in the researching and writing of this book. Such errors are entirely my own fault.

To complicate matters even more, it could be that the original writer, or compiler, had access to material which is no longer preserved or has since been lost. Similarly, other source material, such as the Morning Reports, were only temporarily accessible, due a variety of reasons. This also includes a movie of the 614th when it served with the 95th Infantry Division. History can be fickle in that regard.

To give an example, William L. Tabron earned the Bronze Star Medal, but is not mentioned in the list in 'Three Inch Fury' as having received it, despite his citation being available. He is also mentioned as a casualty twice in 'Three Inch Fury'. First as KIA and then as MIA. While listed as killed-in-action, he had only suffered a foot injury. Later he was taken prisoner.[8]

The Sources, History, and Criticism 5

The so-called 'fog of war', ever present during combat, prevents the participants from always knowing everything. Yet it lingers on in the sources long after the smoke has dissipated from the battlefield, obscuring the historical past from sight. Besides differences in the source-material, there are other important aspects to keep in mind, or rather, related to the human mind. The human brain is far from perfect and even in remembering the past mistakes can occur.

Psychology provides insight into the processing of memories. An example is the term 'weapon focus', which explains why eyewitnesses tend to have poor memory of a crime event, because their attention is focused on the weapon that the perpetrator is holding and not on their surroundings.[9] In other words, due to the stressful situation that people are in, their focus is drawn to the immediate threat and not on things that happen around them. In the case of soldiers under fire, their focus is on what's happening to them and not on what transpires around them. Regarding the men of the 614th Tank Destroyer Battalion, there is an interesting example in the sources where Lieutenant Charles Thomas describes this process clearly. When talking about the engagement at Climbach, he remarks about the different accounts of the battle:

> In just a few minutes they were returning the fire. They were functioning to a lesser degree, as I was, automatically. I knew what had to be done. […] They say men under stress can do unusual things. I imagine this was true in my case. I wonder how many men who earned medals can give you a detailed account of what happened? I know I hung onto one thought, deploy the guns and start firing or we're dead […] I learned afterwards that my men thought I had bought it. I'm pretty sure I was no longer on my feet, but I was not stretched out on the ground either. I just kept giving orders and made sure my line of vision was not blocked. No doubt a medic or someone was supporting me. They told me later I was a mess to behold,

a bloody mess that kept giving orders and urging them to do their best. I cannot tell you about the actions that won the men in my company their medals. It's strange but my vision was limited to the gun crews and the enemy guns.[10]

The human brain can also function less due to stress, injuries, or the natural decline of the human body. The extent to which these factors might have influenced the writings of the men is unknown, however, some of these things might explain minor inconsistencies in the material, such as wrong dates. When writing about events some men place different emphasis on, or narrate the events in another way. The conversations mentioned could be verbatim, but it could be that they capture the essence of the sentence rather than the actual phrasing.

This is perhaps most clear in the various accounts that were given about the engagement at Climbach. Every man was focused on their part in the struggle and thus paid attention to different details. Sometimes these accounts conflict with each other. However, all stressed the fierceness of the struggle and all accounts admit the bravery of the soldiers of third platoon that day when they engaged the enemy.

The sources suggest that the infantry attack took place before the other two guns were called to the line, because Dillard Booker, sergeant of one of the guns, recalls the fact that Thomas McDaniel, who had previously been returning fire with a .30 cal. machine gun, had passed on the orders from Lieutenant Mitchell to bring the two remaining 3-inch guns forward. Lieutenant Colonel Blackshear, the commander of the task force, also testified that infantry attempted to overrun the positions before the other two guns deployed. While it's impossible to say for certain, Booker summarized it best when he wrote: 'All can't be recorded of the heroic actions of each individual man, but we will never forget those who will not be able to tell us personally of his actions, Corporal Peter Simmons, Corporal Shelton Murph, gunners, Private First Class William Phipps, jeep driver.'

The Sources, History, and Criticism   7

In a project of this size, it's impossible to do it alone and I would like to thank several people, whose help, time, and patience have made this possible. There are too many to name everyone individually, but I would like to mention some specifically. I'd like to thank my friends and family for their encouragement, support, and distractions. Thanks to the people at Pen and Sword, specifically Heather Williams and my editor Karyn Burnham, for the opportunity to bring this project to life.

There are several descendants of the men who served, and they've shared with me material from their brothers, fathers, uncles, grandfathers. There are the children of Lawrence Johnson, Larry Johnson and Arie Del Gray. There is Robert Coleman, the nephew of Walter Coleman, Carol Neyland, the daughter of Cyrus Awkard, and Karl Arrington, the son of Lun Arrington.

There is the daughter and the brother of James Kirk, who served with the 679th, Gabrielle Kirk-McDonald, Gordon W. Kirk, as well as the son of Reuben Yelding, who served with the 679th, John Yelding. I would also like to thank Cherri Branson, the granddaughter of Charles Branson, who served with the 827th Tank Destroyer Battalion.

Then there are historians and archivists that have helped me with the process of writing, gathering sources or answering my questions. I would like to thank the following people specifically: Bob Scherer and Joe Wilson Jr., for their explanations and suggestions related to the research. Kevin Bailey, from the Eisenhower Presidential Library and Museum, Carla Carlson, from the University of Southern Mississippi, Jennifer Loredo, from the United States Army Heritage and Education Center, Dr Robert Cameron, the Armor Branch Historian, Peter Pirker, for his research towards the 103d Infantry Division in Austria, Talgin Cannon, who conducted research towards black battalions during the Second World War, Gretchen de Witt, in locating descendants of men that served in the 614th, Jacqueline Wright, from the Directorate of Family and Morale, Welfare & Recreation (DFMWR) – Casey Memorial Library, Steve Dike and Rob Haldeman, from Tank Destroyer Net, whose website is a treasure trove for any historian interested in the history of the Tank Destroyers.

There's one final person I'd like to mention: Jim Lankford, who served as a mentor, counselor, and confessor during the research. Throughout the project he helped with providing information, assistance in any way possible and doing everything within his reach to help out with discovering more of the 614th. He shared in the hardships and the triumphs of this project and without him it wouldn't have been possible.

Lastly, I would like to thank you as the reader. Your interest in the 614th Tank Destroyer Battalion keeps their legacy and what they fought for alive. Thank you.

Chapter 2

Activating the 614th Tank Destroyer Battalion

The first Tank Destroyers

The first tanks had entered the battlefield during the Battle of the Somme during the First World War. These British Mark Is were called 'water tanks' or mobile water carriers to obscure the true purpose of these combat vehicles. While the tanks initially appeared fearsome, their use in battle was a disappointment. Only nine out of the committed forty-nine vehicles would support the attacking infantry. Nine others would be involved with mopping-up operations. The remainder got stuck, developed mechanical problems or didn't even reach the starting line.[1]

Although these so-called 'mobile water carriers' might not have worked as intended, they sparked an arms race that continued well after the First World War. The tanks had several benefits compared to the common soldier. Their armor protected them against injuries that would have incapacitated a person, while their engines enabled them to carry fearsome weaponry across the battlefield. Lastly, their tracks made it possible to cross terrain that would have hampered or stopped a person on foot.

This arms race led to various developments. There were improvements related to the tanks themselves, allowing them to carry different weapons or increase their armor, while also progress was made in anti-tank defenses. This led to an alternating cycle of improvements and countermeasures in tank technology. It contributed to the development of the German panzer division. Unique was the German emphasis on movement, which was intended to bring back maneuverability and speed to the battlefield.

After Adolf Hitler came to power in Germany in 1933, he started rearming the German military, in violation of the Treaty of Versailles. He envisioned a new greater Germany, in which there would be no place for inferior races. To achieve this, new vehicles, a new oath, new firearms, and a new doctrine were needed for his soldiers.

Based upon the tactics of German stormtroopers during the First World War, which bypassed the strongest defensive positions to proceed toward the rear, a doctrine was developed. Revolutionary in this doctrine was that it centered on the mobility of the tank rather than the common soldier. The strategy stressed that a breakthrough on the enemy front had to be achieved with tanks and other vehicles to dislocate the enemy. The mechanized forces would then advance to another position, while infantry and artillery would engage any bypassed points of resistance. To force a gap in hostile lines as well as provide any assistance that the tanks might need, close cooperation was necessary with the Luftwaffe, the German air force. Due to the mission-type tactics employed by the German army, commanders were encouraged to show initiative and flexibility. With this strategy a war of movement was created, where smaller units with proper leadership could destroy larger units. To achieve this, good communication was vital, and German tanks were equipped with radios from the start of the hostilities.[2]

Twice the new offensive doctrine was successfully employed, and the resulting tactics were quickly dubbed Blitzkrieg, German for 'lightening war', by the Allied press, although it wasn't a term the Germans used. The world first learned the power of the panzer divisions when the Third Reich invaded Poland on 1 September 1939, and again later in May 1940 when France was attacked. The German successes on the first occasion, however, were incorrectly attributed to the inadequacy of the Polish army. The second time the Germans achieved victory, it wasn't due to their significant numerical superiority, but because they had concentrated their tanks in panzer divisions, instead of spread-out along the front as the French had done.

The Germans hadn't achieved victory due to the tanks themselves, as the Americans thought, but due to their integrated arms employment on the battlefield. The American interpretation was that Germany would launch mass tank attacks to disrupt the defensive line on a small section of the front.[3] This misconception, together with other problems such as inadequate equipment, would fester through in the development of the Tank Destroyer arm and the initial plan for so many tank destroyer battalions.

Essential to the blitzkrieg success was the close cooperation between different branches of the German army. The artillery, infantry, and cavalry all performed specific tasks on the battlefield and close cooperation enabled them to maximize their different strengths. With this strategy the Third Reich managed to conquer vast areas of Europe, which consequently came under Hitler's sway. Furthermore, the German anti-tank defenses kept pace with their own panzer divisions, thus equipping them with what was necessary as if they needed to defeat their own armored formations.

After the First World War the U.S. Army devoted few resources to anti-tank developments. The War Department itself also gave little guidance and offered advice that befitted the tanks of the First World War, but not the coming conflict. Soldiers were recommended to engage with small arms fire, because the bullets striking the hull would interfere with the crew's actions, while snipers needed to target specific spots. If all else failed, the rifle barrel could still be plunged into the track mechanism.[4]

As the war raged across the European continent, the American government watched the German advances into Poland, and later France, while searching for an appropriate response. Among others, the American army started to develop armored divisions, which were intended to be like the German panzer units. However, since the threat wasn't properly identified, the response in the form of Tank Destroyer Battalions would also be inadequate. The assumption was that Germans would launch massive attacks with their tanks, but didn't address the mission-type tactics employed by the German military or the combined arms approach of a panzer division.

On 13 May 1941 General George C. Marshall, Chief of Staff of the American army, noted that within the War Department there was much resistance against the adoption of new ideas. To remedy this, on 14 May he instructed the War Department to take immediate action on anti-tank measures and to create a Planning Branch, whose only function was to devise new methods of warfare. The next day a Planning Branch was established under Lieutenant Colonel Andrew D. Bruce.[5] Although Bruce was tasked with implementing a proper anti-tank defense for the army, he was subordinate to McNair, who held the responsibility for tank destroyer training, organization, and doctrine.

General Lesley McNair, the Chief of Staff of the Army General Headquarters in 1940, also believed that the American anti-tank weaponry was outdated. The common American anti-tank gun, the 37 mm gun M3, was inadequate, and he was impressed by the German 88 mm anti-aircraft gun, that could also be employed in an anti-tank role. During the Spanish Civil War and early in the Second World War these anti-aircraft guns could be employed as anti-tank weapons and in early 1941 they were fielded in increasing quantities in other roles, where they were mounted on halftracks or other chassis.[6] It started to replace the PaK 36, which until that time was the common German anti-tank gun. The 88 mm gun could be used in a variety of purposes. In a static version it could be used as coastal artillery or to engage Allied bombers, while a mobile version of this weapon could serve as an assault gun.

As McNair himself said:

> The tank was introduced to protect against automatic small arms fire, which was developed so greatly during and since the [First] World War. Its answer is fire against which the tank does not protect-the anti-tank gun. That this answer failed [against the Germans in 1940] was due primarily to the

pitifully inadequate number and power of French and British anti-tank guns, as well as their incorrect organization.[7]

As the commander of the American Ground Forces and in favor of towed guns, McNair held a different view than Bruce, who was chosen to provide the American army with a reply against the German panzer divisions. Their different responsibilities clashed at times.

Bruce stated that the Tank Destroyers had one goal: 'There is but one battle objective of the tank destroyer units, this being plainly inferred by their designation. It is the destruction of hostile tanks.'[8] For his Tank Destroyers Bruce had ambitious plans, whose task he described as follows:

> The autocrat of the ground battle in this war, has been the tank. With the tank destroyer we think we have its number. The destroyer's gun and mount don't have the tank's armor, but its crew commands greater speed, visibility. And maneuverability, and at least equal fire power. It can pick the time and place to deliver its punch and then hightail it to a new position to strike again. One good tank destroyer can be produced for materially less than the cost of a tank, and in far less time and with less critical materials. And by using tank destroyers to stop enemy tanks, you leave your own tanks free to dash through and spread hell among the enemy.[9]

To solidify the offensive spirit, it was featured in the insignia, a black panther crushing a tank between its jaws, and motto, 'Seek, strike, destroy', of the Tank Destroyers.[10]

While Bruce was enthusiastic about the destroyers of tanks, others had their doubts. Certainly, there were good aspects to the tank destroyers, but there were also flaws in the organization. Major General George Patton acknowledged the superior speed and maneuverability of the vehicle, but predicted that given time, it would become another tank.[11]

For the destruction of enemy tanks, Bruce had envisioned a vehicle that could quickly deploy, shoot, and disappear again. In this way, the tank destroyer prevented hostile retaliation. To maintain their high speed, the armor needed to be light, which also enabled the tank destroyers to reach places tanks couldn't due to their weight. For example, the tank destroyers could cross bridges, which would collapse under the weight of the tanks, and swamps, where the tanks would be bogged down.[12]

Other differences between the tanks and tank destroyers were more obvious, such as the lack of a forward-facing machine gun on the early tank destroyers. They weren't designed to fight hostile infantry, but tanks only, derived from the misconception of the massed tank attack. The tank destroyers were supposed to fight them off from a distance, so the open-topped turret and lack of infantry defense were less of an issue.

During the Louisiana Maneuvers of 1941, a series of large army exercises, defensive doctrines against possible German blitzkrieg attacks were tested. During these exercises Provisional Anti-Tank Groups were tested, which consisted of specialized anti-tank battalions. Furthermore, tests with warning systems to locate and track hostile armor had proven favorable. This contributed to the development of independent anti-tank battalions, which would ultimately become the Tank Destroyers.

On 18 August 1941 Bruce proposed to raise 220 anti-tank battalions. One would be given to each of the fifty-five divisions, fifty-five would be held at corps level and 110 would be held as general headquarters troops. To train these battalions a camp was established in Texas, where the Tank Destroyer Tactical and Firing Command would be located. The camp was named after Confederate General John Bell Hood. Later the Command would be demoted to the Tank Destroyer Tactical and Firing Center. This Command served three purposes: officers and enlisted men were taught how to perform their specializations; there were tactical exercises for the tank destroyer units; and finally, the training, tactics and weapons of the tank destroyers were improved.[13]

The expected training program estimated that all tank destroyer units would train at Camp Hood for two or three months, depending on their progress. Later a three-month training program would be standardized and it included five weeks of gunnery exercises, a week of battle conditioning, and six weeks of maneuver and instruction.[14]

However, Bruce and McNair disagreed about the equipment of the tank destroyers. McNair favored towed guns, which were cheaper to produce and the loss of one formed a more acceptable risk, considering that the Tank Destroyers were intended as a stopgap to blunt or counter a possible German tank attack. Given the defensive way in which they would be used, it wasn't a problem that the guns weren't as agile as their self-propelled counterparts. These self-propelled tank destroyers, which Bruce favored, were more mobile, but also more expensive. To make matters worse, Bruce didn't want expedient weapons, like the M3 and the M10, which would delay the development of dedicated weapons.

The two expedient weapons were the M3 Gun Motor Carriage and the 3-inch Gun Motor Carriage M10. The M3 was a halftrack equipped with a 75 mm field gun, while the M10 was a modified open turret placed on a Sherman tank chassis. It allowed the crew to survey their surroundings, but also put them at a greater risk from incoming fire. Bruce disliked both weapons. The M3 offered little protection and the M10 lacked the speed that he envisioned, but the Ordnance Department 'considered the existing design satisfactory and implemented its mass production without Bruce's consent.'[15] Although these vehicles were temporary, they did allow the men to get started with their training.

The vehicle that Bruce envisioned for the tank destroyers had to meet several qualifications: the vehicle needed to be ready for mass production, cheap, simple, light, fast, and be equipped with a 76mm gun that could be crewed by five soldiers.[16] The resulting tank destroyer would be the M18 Hellcat, officially known as the 76 mm Gun Motor Carriage M18. The first vehicles would be produced in July 1943. The M18 was lighter and faster than the M10, but like the M10 it was open topped.

However, the biggest flaw of the tank destroyer arm was that its doctrine was developed in solitude. Unlike the German anti-tank developments, which kept pace with their tank developments, the tank destroyers cooperated little with the other services. Thus, despite all their training, the tank destroyers would go into combat with unrealistic expectations and without proper armament. The exercises and preparations were not an actual representation of the strategies that the enemy would employ, and these tank destroyer tactics were also unknown to many senior officers of other branches. They employed them as they saw fit and if the results were lacking, the Tank Destroyer doctrine was criticized.[17]

Other problems arose in the deployment of the tank destroyers when the tank destroyer companies were assigned to units. The tank destroyer companies included only two officers, one of whom was administrative, and three platoon leaders. When liaisons needed to be made, the company commander was either kept away from his active duties or from the command post, where he was needed to coordinate things. To assign the administrative officer as liaison was not practical either, as this kept him from his administrative tasks.[18]

Senior officers would split up the combat companies and use them for other purposes than their intended tasks. The tank destroyer guns were used to bolster the anti-tank defenses of local units, or improve the anti-tank capabilities of certain task forces. The reconnaissance units, which would be two platoons in a towed outfit or a company in the self-propelled battalions, weren't used to track enemy armor, but were employed for other objectives. This meant that in a possible attack, the threat wasn't properly identified beforehand and that the guns could be dispersed over a broad area. This rendered them incapable of organizing a concerted defense. Towed battalions especially suffered from this problem, as they were less mobile than the self-propelled units. While the local guns might offer resistance, they lacked the overwhelming firepower necessary, thus denying them the tools they needed to succeed in their task.

Likewise in the field, when their lettered companies were assigned to various task forces or other units, tank destroyer commanders were left with few forces over which they had operational control. The troops that remained, often of a supporting nature, had less work to do. The commanders could become the anti-tank advisor of the unit to whom they were attached.

However, the changing circumstances of war also affected the Tank Destroyers. The Tank Destroyer Center, whose status was changed from Command in August 1942, closed several services on their own initiative in October 1943 when there seemed to be less demand for new tank destroyer battalions. Similar streamlining and changes were happening in other branches of the American army.

While in 1941 Bruce had proposed 220 Tank Destroyer Battalions, the war of 1943 needed even less than the 144 which were created. Only 106 Tank Destroyer Battalions would be active by the end of 1943. Sixty-one battalions, including three segregated battalions, would take part in the conflict in Europe. Ten would join the fight in the Pacific. Thirty-five became surplus and never left the United States. Out of those thirty-five, eleven would be converted to artillery, tank, or amphibious units. The rest were broken up or deactivated.[19]

The war and segregation

In December 1940, when large parts of Europe were under control of the Axis, President Roosevelt made a speech, renouncing American isolationism. In this speech he made it clear that although America wouldn't be involved in the fighting, it did need to provide weapons to the free countries to let them continue the fight. The United States would be 'the arsenal of democracy'.[20]

However, what was democracy like in the United States in 1940? The country had a segregated society, limiting the opportunities for black and Asian people within the nation. The idea of segregation had been that the black population would be treated as equals to, yet separate from, the white Americans. The legal basis for this 'separate but equal' mindset dated back to a US Supreme Court decision in the case of Plessy v. Ferguson in 1896. Briefly, following the Civil War in 1865, the Thirteenth, Fourteenth, and Fifteenth Amendments, were accepted to the American constitution. This meant that slavery became illegal throughout the nation, everyone born or naturalized in the United States received equal protection from the law, and finally, that all people regardless of race, would be allowed to vote. They were all intended to abolish slavery, giving equal rights to people regardless of race.

This was challenged when the state of Louisiana passed the Louisiana Separate Car Act in 1890; this law claimed 'to provide equal but separate accommodations for the white and colored races'.[21]

In 1892 Homer Plessy, who was of mixed descent, refused to leave a whites' only car and was arrested. The case was eventually brought before the Supreme Court, where it was decided in 1896 that his rights hadn't been violated and the court ruled in favor of the Louisiana Separate Car Act, 1890.

In practical terms, segregation in the early twentieth century meant that the black American community, which formed around 10 per cent of the U.S. population, would be separated from their white countrymen. While predominant in the southern states, it could be enforced across the country to a greater or lesser degree. Along racial lines, schools, neighborhoods, and factories were separated and inadequate or poor facilities were often assigned to blacks compared to whites.

White supremacy, the belief that white people were inherently superior to other races, was present throughout society and could manifest itself in many ways. If a situation escalated, it could result in one of the most deplorable practices in American history: lynching. Although the act of lynching was on the decline in the second half of the 1930s, eight black Americans lost their lives due to lynching in 1937. Six more would die a year later and in 1939 there would be three killings. There was even a lynching on an American army base in 1941, when Felix Hall was lynched by white soldiers at Fort Benning. His corpse was found six weeks later.

After the attack on Pearl Harbor, on 7 December 1941, America declared war on the Axis. This led to an unusual situation, because their enemies were openly racist, while America was a segregated society.

Yet black Americans did contribute to the war from the beginning. One of the first Americans to distinguish himself was Doris Miller, a black messman who manned a machine gun during the Pearl Harbor attack and aided wounded sailors. After a struggle for recognition, he was finally awarded the Navy Cross for his heroic actions. He perished when his ship sank on 24 November 1943.

A black American was also among the first casualties of the war. On 8 December 1941, the day after Pearl Harbor, the Japanese air force attacked Fort Stotsenburg, Philippines. Robert Brooks of the 192nd Tank Battalion died when he was running towards the machine gun on his halftrack, being struck by a bomb that exploded next to him. He became the first Armored Force casualty of the war. It was only when his parents were invited for the memorial ceremony at Fort Knox, Kentucky, that it was discovered that Brooks had been misidentified as white due to his light skin tone.

Other African Americans also distinguished themselves with heroic feats at, or behind, the front line. Many others were recognized for saving lives, although racism sometimes prevented this from being publicly acknowledged.

However, a few segregated American combat units existed and, in the navy, army, and air force, special units were created. At the front and behind the frontline, African American soldiers, sailors and pilots contributed to the struggle against the Axis. In the infantry, the 92nd and the 93rd division were made up of black soldiers. The 332nd Expeditionary Operations Group and the 477th Bombardment Group of the United States Army Air Forces consisted of black personnel. The 452nd and 870th Anti-Aircraft Artillery Battalion guarded the skies against hostile aircraft. There was even an all-black parachute outfit, the 555th Parachute Infantry Battalion, which was used to fight forest fires. When Technical Sergeant Alonzo Douglas of the 24th Infantry

Regiment killed a Japanese soldier in March 1944, he was the first black infantryman to kill a Japanese soldier in ground combat and it was celebrated by the African American community. They weren't just sweating for America, but also spilling their guts.

In doing their duty, the black American soldiers helped the advance of the Allies on all fronts. They served in labor units, in logistics, in service battalions or other outfits. They helped pave the way for tanks. They helped loading and unloading ships in the docks, or by driving these supplies to the front with the *Red Ball Express*. Black women served in the Women's Army Corps, and the 6888th Central Postal Directory Battalion handled 65,000 pieces of mail each shift. The less desirable task of burying the dead also often fell to the black soldiers.

However, not all black Americans were equally eager to go after the Italians, Germans and Japanese and make the world safe for democracy. Was it necessary to contribute to this fight? Why would they have to fight for something that they didn't have at home? Wasn't it better to first establish democracy at home, before going abroad and continuing there? Within the African American community there was a division and not all of them were certain that their full support of the war was necessary. Some stated that it was 'the white man's war'.[22] James G. Thompson, who had been recently drafted, wrote,

> would it be too much to demand full citizenships rights in exchange for the sacrificing of my life? The V for Victory sign is being displayed prominently in all so-called democratic countries fighting for victory over aggression, slavery, and tyranny. If this V sign means [all] that to those now engaged in this great conflict, then let we colored Americans adopt the double VV for a double victory over our enemies within. For surely those who perpetuate these ugly prejudices here are seeking to destroy our democratic form of government just as surely as the axis forces.[23]

Others were more pessimistic and argued that black Americans first had to fight for their right to fight. Few segregated combat units existed, and the majority of the black soldiers served in service units. William H. Hastie summed up the sentiments of many black people when he said:

> We will be American ditchdiggers. We will be American aviators. We will be American laborers. We will be anything that any other American should be in this whole program of national defense. But we won't be black auxiliaries.[24]

The right to fight as equals of white soldiers had to be earned. Some black Americans took an even more pessimistic standpoint, arguing that regardless of who won the war, black Americans would still be discriminated against. After the First World War not much had changed, although black Americans had volunteered and fought against the German enemies.

While some rejected this war as something that didn't concern them, others embraced it as an opportunity to prove their worthiness of being equal citizens. They considered it a chance for the betterment of their race and themselves. To their white countrymen they could prove that they deserved equal rights. The form in which this might be achieved was uncertain; there were those, such as Walter White, Executive Secretary of the National Association for the Advancement of Colored People, who argued for total integration in the armed forces. Others, such as *Pittsburgh Courier* editor Robert L. Vann, preferred segregated units staffed with only black personnel.[25] For different reasons, people might have supported or rejected certain plans. The boundaries of these groups were often drawn along regional or class lines.

Racial friction and justice
Segregation on army bases, or in army units, manifested itself in many ways. It could be that there were a restricted number of spaces in the cinema for black soldiers or separate recreational areas for white and

black soldiers. Despite this, clashes between black and white soldiers or black soldiers and white civilians occurred from time to time. This was amplified by the rapid expansion of the army leading up to, and continuing during, the war.

At Camp Patrick Henry, Virginia, violence erupted on 6 October 1944, when the men of the segregated 758th Tank Battalion clashed with white paratroopers. Sergeant Jefferson Hightower, of A Company, recollected how,

> the paratroopers wanted to know where did those niggers get all those stripes. We had pulled our 758 patches off, but all the NCOs still had stripes and just about everybody had some kind of rank. We answered that we received them from their mothers. I was CQ [Charge of Quarters] the night before the trouble, so I did not know that some of our men had been in arguments with the whites at the PX .... [Later] I was in the telephone building right across from our area when the MP came in and called for the guard. I ran back to the area some way and got back in the barracks even as shots were being fired across the road at the paratroopers who had tried to rush our area.[26]

One paratrooper died and a black soldier was wounded when he shot himself in the foot. No charges were filed against the unit and they departed a few days afterwards.

At Camp Hood, another well-known segregated unit served as school troops: The 761st Tank Battalion. This unit would become one of the most famous African American units in the Second World War. Their task at Camp Hood was to serve as adversaries for the white tank destroyer units. The black soldiers were the aggressive enemies that the Tank Destroyer Battalions in training had to engage, before they would go into combat, either in Europe, the Mediterranean, or the Pacific.

On 6 July 1944, while stationed at Camp Hood, Jackie Robinson, a Lieutenant of the 761st Tank Battalion, was sitting in a bus, when he was ordered to the back. He refused to follow orders and eventually the Military Police were called. Legal action would have been taken, but Lieutenant Colonel Bates, the commander of the 761st, refused to agree with this. In the end Lieutenant Robinson was transferred to the 758th Tank Battalion, where he was acquitted of all charges and transferred to a unit at Camp Breckinridge, Kentucky. Later he received an honorable discharge from the army.

The army reflected the society that created it, and in equal proportions black Americans were drafted. As Lieutenant Claude Ramsey, of the 614th Tank Destroyer Battalion, described, 'Civilian life is one thing, but to be drafted to fight to save the world for democracy only to find that you have entered the most undemocratic and racist organization in the whole country is quite another thing.'[27] Within the army there was racial friction and among the black population there were people who refused to adhere to the existing conditions. Transgressions of the status quo were not accepted and more than once violence flared up, including police brutality.

At the stockade in Camp Hood, where several men were locked up, violence threatened to erupt on 23 August 1943. On that day, there were around seventy to seventy-five black prisoners in the stockade, as well as several white inmates. These groups were housed in separate buildings. On that day a minor incident occurred:

> During noon roll call that day Private Clifton T. Glover failed to step up in line. Sergeant Robert O. Murphy, who was Sergeant of the guard at the stockade 'jerked him back in line'. That afternoon Sergeant Murphy put Glover 'on the rock pile' until about 4:45 p.m.[28]

After supper, there would be drill, extended by an extra hour. The bugle was sounded at 18:00 to assemble the men. The white prisoners came out of their barracks as well as some black prisoners, but not all of them. Twice more the men were summoned by Sergeant Murphy, but rather than falling out, they were talking among themselves and taking the bed connecting rods out of their bunkbeds. These were around 70 centimeters long and weighted around 1.5 kilograms. Murphy retreated and called in reinforcements, which arrived fifteen minutes later.

Armed with nightsticks, these additional military policemen waited outside until the arrival of the Provost Marshal of Camp Hood, Lester King. He ordered that the assembled prisoners be taken away. Together with a few military policemen, armed with tear-gas grenades, he went towards the building. Twice more the black prisoners were summoned out, but refused. On King's orders the gas grenades were hurled into the building; through the back door forty-five prisoners rapidly came out, clutching their crude clubs.

Once more they were ordered to fall in, but didn't do so. King 'then raised his pistol and stated "Fall in. This is the last time I am going to do it."'[29] The prisoners fell in and were told to throw down the bed connecting rods. Afterwards they were made to lie down with their faces to the ground. The crude weapons were gathered and thrown over the fence. A total of thirty-seven were found there, while nine were discovered near the door of the barracks and one elsewhere in the building. Within the building two more prisoners were located.

Out of the group, the following people, alongside Clifton T. Glover and Westley Golds, were sentenced to confinement for life: Private George Davis, of A Company, 614th Tank Destroyer Battalion; Joseph Washington, Headquarters Company, 758th Tank Battalion; Robert Jeffcoat, Truck Battalion, Tank Destroyer Center, Camp Hood. Private Henry Washington, C Company, 827th Tank Destroyer Battalion, and Private Clarence Burke, B Company, 758th Tank Battalion, were sentenced to thirty years of confinement. All were sentenced to dishonorable discharge and total forfeiture of all pay and allowances.

On the other hand, as with any conscription, people from all parts of society came into service, including those less fit for duty or with questionable morals. Among the segregated tank destroyers, an example is Technician Fifth Grade Dan Boswell, of the 827th Tank Destroyer Battalion.

Shortly after midnight on 1 September 1944, Staff Sergeant Otis Wilson, of Company A, 827th Tank Destroyer Battalion, was found dead in his company's mess hall at North Camp Hood. A scream had alerted people and his gruesomely mutilated body was found in a pool of blood. Among other injuries, there was a deep cut at the back of his neck, which 'extended from ear to ear', a deep laceration on the back of his head, and another cut that exposed part of his skull. Nearby a bloody stove grate shaker was found, while elsewhere Dan Boswell's bloody clothes were located and an eyewitness had seen a person leaving. When searching Boswell $1,622 was discovered in his sock, which he admitted had been taken from Wilson.

In his statement Boswell claimed that he had committed the murder together with Privates Amos Thomas, of B Company, and George Gill Jr., from the Reconnaissance Company. It had been Gill's idea to rob Wilson, and Gill had struck him several times with a meat cleaver after Boswell had knocked him down with a grate shaker, while Amos had cut his throat. By showing that the others had come up with the plan and committed the violent actions, he hoped to clear his own name.

Despite these attempts, there were a few flaws in this version of the story. Thomas and Boswell had never met before the crime, and neither Thomas nor Gill could know how much money would be gained after the murder, so it's unlikely that they would entrust this to Boswell. Both men also had a plausible alibi, as they had being doing what was expected of them.

After a review of the evidence, it was decided that Thomas and Gill were cleared of any charges. The only statements that tied them to the crime came from Boswell, while there were several witnesses that could provide an alibi for the men. Boswell himself was sentenced to death and he was hanged on 16 April 1945 at Camp Bowie, Texas.

The segregated Tank Destroyer Battalions in the American Army

Along with the 'separate but equal' mindset, a proportionate number of black Tank Destroyer Battalions were created. These were crewed by black enlisted men only. Sometimes the officers were black, although often, especially in the senior echelons, they were white. A few exceptions occurred, such as Lieutenant Colonel Theophilus Mann, the commander of the 795th Tank Destroyer Battalion. In fact, at the outset of war there were limited opportunities for black Americans to become an officer. In 1940 there were five black officers, of whom three were chaplains, compared to the 13,637 white officers in the American regular army at that time.[30] This was expanded throughout the war to provide officers for the segregated outfits.

It could be difficult for white officers assigned to segregated battalions; not all of them appreciated their position of authority and many held on to their prejudiced worldview, although others managed to overcome their biases. This varied per battalion and per officer. Often white men with experience with black people were selected as the officers in these units, and because the majority of the black population lived in the Southern States, it meant that many of their commanders were also southerners.[31] If white officers resented their position, it had a negative effect on the morale and performance of the black soldiers.

Out of the total 106 Tank Destroyer Battalions that were created during the Second World War, there were eleven segregated battalions. This is an accurate representation of the black American population at that time. However, when examining the thirty-five battalions that were deactivated, of which eight were crewed by black personnel, it is a disproportionate number. Out of the seventy-one battalions that were sent overseas, there were just three black units, the 614th, the 679th, and the 827th. Both the 614th and the 679th were towed units, while the 827th was a self-propelled battalion. In official communications the Tank Destroyer Battalions were marked with an * in front of their name. Elsewhere it explained that these battalions contained 'Negro enlisted personnel'.³² The reasons for deactivating the units are varied, such as the changed war circumstances and the diminishing need for tank destroyers, although prevalent prejudices might have influenced the decision.

The first dedicated black Tank Destroyer Battalions that were established consisted of retitled anti-tank units in December 1941. On 15 December the 846th Tank Destroyer Battalion was created from the 349th Field Artillery regiment, while the next day the 795th Tank Destroyer Battalion was activated from the 184th Field Artillery regiment.³³ More segregated units followed and, with time, a large number of the units became disbanded again.

Black Tank Destroyer Battalions during the Second World War

Tank Destroyer Battalion	Activation	Place	Deactivation	Place
846th	15-Dec-41	Camp Livingston, LA	13-Dec-43	Camp Swift, TX
795th	16-Dec-41	Fort Custer, MI	24-Apr-44	Hampton Roads, Port of Embarkation, VA
828th	30-May-42	Fort Knox, KY	7-Dec-43	Fort Huachuca, AZ
827th	20-Apr-42	Camp Forrest, TN	1-Dec-45	In America
614th	25-Jul-42	Camp Carson, CO	31-Jan-46	Camp Kilmer, NJ
829th	25-Jul-42	Camp Gruber, OK	27-Mar-44	Camp Hood, TX
646th	15-Dec-42	Fort Huachuca, AZ	1-May-44	Indiantown Gap Military Reservation [Fort Indiantown Gap], PA
649th	31-Mar-43	Camp Bowie, TX	?-Aug-43	unknown
659th	15-May-43	Camp Hood, TX	1-Dec-44	unknown
669th	19-Jun-43	Camp Hood, TX	15-Nov-44	Fort Huachuca, AZ
679th	26-Jun-43	Camp Hood, TX	27-Oct-45	New York, America

It is remarkable that some established battalions were disbanded, while others that had recently started their training were kept intact. Indeed, it seems to bear out the allegation that appeared in newspapers with a black readership that there was never any intention of sending these units into combat. In the *Jackson Advocate* it was bitterly commented upon:

> The army breaks these groups up but never abolishes them. They leave small segments, cadres. These, rumor says, serve the purpose of permitting the army to still boast that it has Negroes in every branch of the service.[34]

The feeling among the black community was that rather than using these units for what they were trained to do, they were kept as tokens. The army could claim that there were black Americans being trained, although they were never intended to be sent into battle.

The racism encountered by the segregated tank destroyers also extended to their officers. The officers of the 614th sought combat engagements for their men, arguing that they were well-trained and capable of fighting. However, one of their white officers was ridiculed in his hometown newspaper, where they called him a 'nigger-lover'.[35]

The 795th Tank Destroyer Battalion was activated in December 1941 and boasted as their title 'Res Mortis Delemus', Latin for 'Tanks, we destroy'. The rhinoceros was chosen as their mascot, because this armored beast resembled the tank destroyers themselves. It was deactivated in April 1944.

The 846th Tank Destroyer Battalion was activated in December 1941 and deactivated in December 1942.

The 828th Tank Destroyer Battalion was activated on 30 May 1942 and disbanded in December 1943.

The 649th Tank Destroyer Battalion was activated in March 1943 as a self-propelled unit. In July the unit was converted to a towed battalion, but it was deactivated a few months later in August 1943.

The 659th Tank Destroyer Battalion was activated in May 1943 and deactivated in December 1944. This unit was commanded by Frank S. Pritchard until 16 October 1943, when he was reassigned to the 614th Tank Destroyer Battalion.

The 829th Tank Destroyer Battalion was activated in July 1942. A regular weekday of the 829th Tank Destroyer Battalion in December 1942 gives insight into the training of the Tank Destroyer Battalions, which would have similar schedules, although these would be influenced by local circumstances. Sundays were different, as there would be time to go to church and no drill.[36]

Timetable 829th Tank Destroyer Battalion, Camp Gruber, Oklahoma, dated 28 December 1942.

	Reveille
06:30	First call
06:45	Assembly
07:00	Breakfast
08:00	Sick call
	Drill
07:55	First call
08:00	Assembly
12:00	Recall
12:10	Dinner
	Drill
12:50	First call
13:00	Assembly
17:00	Recall
	Guard mount
17:15	First call
17:25	Assembly
17:30	Guard mounting
	Retreat
17:40	First call
17:45	Assembly
17:50	Retreat

	Reveille
18:00	Supper
21:30	Tattoo
22:45	Call to quarters
23:00	Taps

In April 1943 the schedule was changed, allowing the men more free time in the evening, and the time was spent in the following way. Of course, on Sundays there would be time to go to church.[37]

Timetable 829th Tank Destroyer Battalion, Camp Hood, Texas, 21 April 1943.

06:15	Reveille, first call
06:20	March
06:30	Reveille and Assembly
07:00	Mess call
07:50	First call for Drill
08:00	Assembly
08:00	Fatigue call
11:00	Sick call
	Inspections if announced.
11:45	Recall from drill
12:15	Mess call
13:00	First call for Drill
13:15	Assembly
13:15	Fatigue call
17:00	Recall from Drill and fatigue
17:10	First call for retreat
17:15	Assembly
17:30	Mess call
18:00	Guard Mount
18:15	Assembly
21:00	Tattoo
22:45	Call to Quarters
23:00	Taps

Like many other Tank Destroyer Battalions, it was converted to a towed unit, and the outfit was disbanded in March 1944.

The 646th Tank Destroyer Battalion was activated on 15 December 1942 in Fort Huachuca, AZ. The unit started as a light towed formation but was changed into a self-propelled unit. The original cadre came from the 846th Tank Destroyer Battalion. In September the coat of arms was approved. It consisted of a Naosaurus, while the battalion motto was 'Prepared for anything', an expression of the possibilities turned into their war cry. In November more enlisted men arrived. In January 1943 Walt Disney presented a combat insignia, which was 'a mad bucking Bronco crushing with all four feet, a tank which is crumbling to pieces as he jumps on it'. The unit was deactivated in May 1944.

The 669th Tank Destroyer Battalion was formed in June 1943 and it received men from the 828th Tank Destroyer Battalion, which had been established earlier. In July the unit was reorganized from a self-propelled unit into a towed battalion. The men of the reconnaissance company were assigned to the other companies. In January Major Turner, the commanding officer, was assigned to the 679th Tank Destroyer Battalion, while twenty-six men were transferred to the 827th Tank Destroyer Battalion. Major King would take over, and in February three officers were transferred to other commands, while sixty-eight men and one officer were assigned to the 649th Tank Destroyer Battalion.

In March 1944 the men watched the documentary series *Why We Fight*. This documentary series, which consisted of seven films, was intended to explain why America became involved in the Second World War. It was revolutionary in that sound and vision were being used to motivate the soldiers for the first time, rather than speeches or printed matter.

However, the fate of the 669th was sealed in the fall of that year. Despite being rated 'satisfactory or better' by the Inspector General in May 1944 and being given a 'superior' rating in the Army Ground Forces test in October 1944, as well as having several men presented with the Good Conduct Medal, the 669th would soon be deactivated. Some of the better radio operators were transferred to the 679th Tank Destroyer. On 9 November the battalion commander Asa C. Black, gave a speech before the battalion.

> The CO made it quite clear that the battalion was not being broken up because we failed in our mission. The men served well under the leadership of Lieutenant Colonel Asa C. Black and anticipated serving under him in combat. If the TDs are no longer needed in this war, we can and will make good 'dough boys'.[38]

The disbandment followed shortly afterwards.

Curiously enough, the last Tank Destroyer Battalion to be activated, the 679th Tank Destroyer Battalion on 26 June 1943, using towed guns, continued to exist and served on the Mediterranean front. It would serve in combat, together with the 827th Tank Destroyer Battalion, which was activated in April 1942 and the 614th Tank Destroyer Battalion, which was activated in July 1942.

The fact that so many Tank Destroyer Battalions were being disbanded, which included several segregated units, did have an impact on morale throughout the branch. The primary reasons for deactivating several battalions were that in 1943 massed armored force attacks hadn't been made against the American army, and the fact that units at and behind the front needed new replacements.[39] Similar changes were happening throughout the army; instead of the 213 Divisions initially projected in 1941, only around ninety were expected in 1943.[40] Uncertainty about the future crept into the minds of the Tank Destroyer officers and troops alike, and this had a negative effect on training. After all, training served no purpose if they would never go to war.

Despite performing only continental service, casualties could occur. Accidents, mistakes or misfires all formed a threat. In the case of the

795th Tank Destroyer Battalion, Private Andrew McCloud died at Fort Custer on 19 September 1942. As he was relieving Private William Boynton and took a seat in a truck, the shotgun, which Boynton was holding, discharged and killed McCloud.[41] The only casualties that the 669th suffered during its brief existence were two wrecked cars and no loss of lives.

Several newspapers with a black readership lamented the disbandment of the segregated tank destroyer units. Indignant articles made their grief clear:

> The 846th Tank Destroyer Battalion, the oldest of the tank groups in point of service, broken up with all new men to train over. The 828th Tank Destroyer Battalion also at Camp Hood, Texas, broken up after it had gotten so far as California and had desert training. Sent to Vancouver barracks were more than 400 men as quartermasters. The balance went in the same category to Camp Swift, Texas. Those boys were crack soldiers. Even their white officers hated to see the change and privately expressed themselves as disgusted, according to some of the men. The 795th Tank Destroyer Battalion, Camp Hood, Colonel Theo Mann [Theophilus M. Mann], a tough officer whom even white fellow officers respected, commanded this outfit, which was activated at Ft. Custer. The 795th was busted. Colonel Mann is out in the woods in Texas with a small group of men marking time according to reports. His men, who had been trained, went to quartermaster and engineer corps.[42]

The article continued that in the artillery similar processes happened, where the army changed combat units into service outfits. It pointed out that the men's training was for nothing, as the skills they had acquired would not be used in combat, but rather in paving the way for others to go into combat. Not only was the disbandment a waste of time, but also money, as all the shells fired, were for naught.

Chapter 3

The 614th Tank Destroyer Battalion

Activating the 614th

On 25 July 1942 four Tank Destroyer Battalions were activated at Camp Carson, Colorado. Three of them, the 821st, the 822nd, the 823rd, were staffed with white soldiers. The fourth, the 614th Tank Destroyer Battalion, was made up of black troops. The initial cadre for this battalion came primarily from the 366th Infantry Regiment, which was stationed at Fort Devens, Massachusetts. At its inception, the battalion consisted of thirty-five officers and 140 enlisted men, to which were added sixteen enlisted men from the Infantry Replacement Training Center at Camp Wolters, Texas. Their commander was Lieutenant Colonel Blaisdell Kennon.

Shortly afterwards more troops arrived, bringing the total to 420 enlisted soldiers, as well as their first tank destroyers: the 75 mm Gun Motor Carriage M3, which were halftracks equipped with 75 mm cannons. These and other tank destroyer vehicles were the American answer to the German blitzkrieg.

However, the men of the 614th also continued their training. They were an odd mix. Some had followed an education at a college, while others were illiterate. Some came from the northern states, while others were raised in the south. A large number of them came from poor sharecropper families. While some were enlisted, others had volunteered to serve, like Lawrence Johnson. Born in 1920, he was the fifth of six children and after the death of his mother, had been raised by his oldest sister and father. With his enlistment he hoped that his younger brother wouldn't be called on to serve.

Their training at Camp Carson continued until December 1942, when the 614th was transferred to Camp Bowie, Texas, where they arrived on the 18th. More training and replacements followed, until the battalion went to another destination. On 23 March 1943, the men arrived at Camp Hood, Texas. An ironic twist was that these men were being trained to bring liberty and democracy to other people, while the camp where they trained at was named after someone that wished to deny them this liberty – Confederate General John Hood.[1]

At Camp Hood the men were taught to be Tank Destroyers. A group of fifty-eight enlisted men left the unit to augment the 659th Tank Destroyer Battalion, which was at that time under the command of Lieutenant Colonel Frank Pritchard. In July, the 614th was stationed at Camp Hood for educational purposes and were put at the disposal of the nearby officer candidate school. They were used to demonstrate movements and to try out specific scenarios or tactics regarding the performance, training, and improvements of the tank destroyers as a branch. On 17 July 1943 the 614th, like many others, was converted to a towed battalion.

The first combat experiences had, in the eyes of senior commanders, revealed several problems in the tank destroyer concept, which they considered unfit for the battlefield. Thus, in January 1943 tests had been conducted with towed cannons. The fighting in North Africa had suggested that towed tank destroyers were better suited for the task than their self-propelled counterparts. Defensively, the towed tank destroyers could be better hidden and camouflaged. They were also cheaper than hostile tanks, so General McNair ordered that half of the Tank Destroyer Battalions would be towed battalions. Although the halftracks stayed, they now pulled the cannons behind them instead of carrying them on their decks. While the Soviet Union and the Axis began creating self-propelled tank destroyer units, the Americans decided that half of all U.S. Tank Destroyer Battalions would be towed units.[2]

The 614th Tank Destroyer Battalion had at its disposal four companies: Headquarters and three lettered companies: A, B, & C. These companies in turn were made up of three platoons. Each platoon contained four squads, where each squad generally makes up a single gun and crew. The Headquarters Company consisted of headquarters, the maintenance and communications platoon, the transportation platoon and two reconnaissance platoons. At its disposal, the 614th Tank Destroyer Battalion had a total of 36 3-inch guns.

Ready for combat

Although the 614th was equipped with weapons of war, they still needed to train men to wield these arms and officers to lead those men. A few men out of the unit were selected and one of these men, Christopher Sturkey, was supposed to go, but was prevented by acute appendicitis. The surgery and recovery delayed his entry into Officer Candidate School (OCS) and once he was well again, the others were too far ahead for him to catch up so he continued to serve in the ranks. One of his friends, Charles Thomas, did go and the battalion took pride in their black officers. As Sturkey described his experiences:

> When our black officers-to-be finally graduated from [Officer Candidate School] and came to [Camp] Hood we were all mighty proud of them. My best friend, Charles Thomas, who I was to attend OCS with, was now my superior, but he was a helluva nice guy and a top officer so all I could feel was pride in spite of my disappointment.[3]

Among the first officers to arrive was Dr Thomas Campbell, who was appointed head of the medical section. His brother, William A. Campbell, served with the 99th Pursuit Squadron, also known as the Tuskegee Airmen, and was the first black American pilot to fly a combat mission against the enemy. He returned to the United States to train replacement pilots after his service in North Africa and later served in Italy.

While learning to wield their weapons, the men were also educated on another front: literacy. In the battalion served men who could neither read nor write and they needed to be taught these skills in order to perform their tasks as soldiers. Many black recruits from the South had never received a proper education. Classes were given to remedy this problem, and one of the teachers was Christopher Sturkey:

> I had not been idle after arriving at Camp Hood. I attended the enlisted men's school and the weapons school. I made Sergeant and was assigned to teaching the use of heavy weapons. Eight hours every day I taught, weaponry half of the time, the remaining hours were spent teaching men who were totally illiterate to read and write. These men, to a great extent, had come from the backwoods of the south: Louisiana, Mississippi, and Alabama. They had earned from seven to thirty dollars a month in civilian life. There were many sharecroppers among them. They became very good at their jobs, showing a tremendous adaptability at things demonstrated to them. Their coordination and ability in teamwork was outstanding.[4]

On 14 August 1943 several men left the unit to join the 133rd Tank Destroyer Training Battalion, where they would form the core of the new unit. The purpose of these training battalions was to provide recruits for the Tank Destroyer Battalions and the 133rd was the only segregated training battalion.

On 16 October 1943, the 614th greeted its new commander: Lieutenant Colonel Frank S. Pritchard, who had previously served as the commanding officer of the 659th Tank Destroyer Battalion, another segregated unit. Lieutenant Colonel Kennon had been transferred to the 364th Infantry Regiment.

In the First World War, Pritchard had served as a sergeant with an ammunition unit on the European Front. In 1924 he joined the *Lansing State Journal* (then still called *The State Journal*). In December 1940 Pritchard received orders to report for duty again and eventually took charge of the 614th Tank Destroyer Battalion.[5]

While still at Camp Hood, the battalion continued to serve as school troops. They needed to perform the scenarios that senior officers came up with. Frustration about their station or about their lack of progress became noticeable in the men, because they wanted to get into battle. They wanted to train towards that goal, instead of performing maneuvers for the senior officers. They were ready and eager for combat, as Christopher Sturkey recalled:

> There were seven hundred men in my outfit and when retreat was sounded those with passes would line up at the bus stop, as would the white soldiers from their camp some distance from us. The Negroes had to wait until the whites filled up the bus with the exception of the back seat. When this was done those number of Negroes the one back seat would accommodate were allowed to board. Waiting to get a seat to town could be a pretty hopeless task. A lot of guys like myself gave up trying. Besides when you got there, entertainment for black soldiers was two hole-in-the-wall dives. [...] Time kept passing, and according to the papers we weren't exactly winning the war and could use all of the help we could get, but for want of anything else to do with this battle-ready outfit they made us school troops. We did the problems for the OCS nearby; they would set up tactical problems and we would then perform like trained seals. We did this so long I figured the war was over for us. I had been in the army three years and hadn't moved from Texas and yet they were fighting and fighting over somewhere. Our battalion commander, Colonel Frank S. Pritchard, was doing everything possible to get us overseas. We were sent on maneuvers in Louisiana and then back to Camp Hood. Again we played school troops to the OCS. The Pittsburgh Courier was screaming its head off about no black combat troops in action but by now I was kind of indifferent about it all; I figured I would grow into an old man right there in Texas playing war.[6]

To raise morale, Pritchard once asked his men for two black gamecocks. He wanted to use them as mascots for the battalion. Eagerly the men did what was asked – and more; before long there were thirteen gamecocks. They kept the men awake at night, but according to Pritchard, 'those game cocks saved us a lot of grief, because General Orlando Ward never inspected our camp. He just visited my gamecock pen.'[7]

It isn't clear how accurate this anecdote is because Pritchard had only assumed command of the 614th on 16 October 1943, while Orlando Ward was transferred on 23 October 1943. More likely it was General John H. Hester, who took over from Ward. As for the birds themselves, Pritchard suspected that they ended up as fried chicken.[8]

Training intensified on 20 December 1943, when the battalion was made ready for overseas service. On 24 February 1944 the battalion received orders to move to Louisiana for maneuver training. Preparation began the following day, and on 29 February the battalion moved by rail and road to their new station. The motor column spent the night at Huntsville, Texas, and reached their new camp the following afternoon, where many movements and tests were conducted to prepare the battalion for combat. While the unit suffered – and inflicted – many simulated injuries, the real casualties were among the pigs that roamed the area. Many of them ended up on a spit over a campfire.

On 21 March 1944, after the battalion had received a satisfactory rating on the maneuvers, it went back to Camp Hood, Texas. In a single day the motor column made the trip, while the men that came by rail arrived two days later. More training was conducted to prepare the members of the battalion for what was to come.

On 11 April the battalion field exercise was completed satisfactorily. Two days later the battalion combat firing test was passed, and on 23 April the physical fitness test was finished. The men would go into combat soon and to prepare for this, an advance detachment of Lieutenant Robert Williams, Lieutenant Claude Ramsey and Technician Fifth Grade McGee were sent to the United Kingdom.

Their task was to arrange everything for the arrival of the 614th Tank Destroyer Battalion. On 1 June 1944 everything had been finished and at last the men were ready to go across the ocean!

However, it turned out not to be. The battalion was ready to board the trains at Killeen, Texas, and go to the port of embarkation, when the orders were suddenly cancelled. The 614th and other units wouldn't need to go across the sea yet. This was a blow to the morale of the unit, which had been both physically and mentally ready for combat. Spirits dropped and attempts to lift them again were made with leaves and furloughs, but the best remedy came when the battalion was given another assignment: to train in indirect fire, the secondary mission of tank destroyers.

Experiments in Africa had shown that the 3-inch guns could augment local artillery outfits. A Tank Destroyer Battalion had thirty-six tubes at its disposal and the shells were an addition to the common 105 mm cannons. Experiments in indirect fire, where a target was engaged that wasn't within line of sight, had proven so successful that indirect fire training became mandatory for new Tank Destroyer Battalions. The benefit of indirect fire was that the guns weren't exposed to direct fire in return and could engage targets that were further away. However, the trajectory would be influenced by wind and other circumstantial factors. Of course, the weight of shells could differ and needed to be calculated differently.

Spirits soared again once the men understood the nuances of artillery and they discussed these skills until well past sundown. For three weeks the battalion trained, until they received a 'very satisfactory' mark. The most impressive feat was when Staff Sergeant John O. Weir blew up a Texas outhouse with two rounds at 8,300 meters [9,000 yards].[9]

However, during that time, the battalion received queries from other units, asking why 'as only brass can ask'[10] the unit was not in England yet. Captain Charles Ogelsby, the officer in charge of intelligence and security, was supposed to pick up his maps for the D-Day landing, but he never collected them. The Third Army was expecting the 614th and knew nothing of the cancellation either. As

Pritchard wrote: 'We hope there was no hole in the line where we were supposed to be on D-Day.'[11] The cancellation had been so sudden that the advance detachment, hadn't been informed either, and as Pritchard wrote: 'They too did not know of the cancellation of orders and that instead of making ready to cross the channel we were studying mil relation [a method for calculating the range to the target] and shooting at Texas outhouses.'[12]

While the remark about D-Day is interesting, the 614th had been scheduled to depart Texas on 1 June, so wouldn't have arrived in time for the Allied invasion of 6 June 1944. Neither did the Third Army take part in D-Day, so it's probably that the units or armies were mixed up by the logistics of the war.

However, on 10 August the unit really did leave Camp Hood, and three days later they arrived at Camp Shanks, New York. Just two weeks were left before the battalion would board the *Esperance Bay* and the men used their last days on American soil to spend their wages accordingly. Finally, on 27 August, the engines started churning and the American coast was left behind them. Another continent lay ahead of them: Europe!

Across the ocean and to the front

The ship that would carry the battalion across the Atlantic Ocean, the *Esperance Bay*, had been a passenger ship (the *Hobson Bay*) before the war and had been converted by the British navy into an armed merchantman, before being changed into a troopship. As many soldiers as possible were ferried across on each trip and consequently, conditions on board were cramped.

Segregation continued and the African American soldiers were put at the bottom of the ship, where most of them remained for the duration of the journey. The enlisted men were put in racks stacked four or five high, where they slept in twelve-hour shifts. The men had to keep their duffel bags with them at all times, as there were not enough beds and it wasn't always possible to return to the same bunk later.

For most of the men it would have been the first time on a ship, and this is reflected in their experiences. As Pritchard remarked about the journey: 'The 614th Tank Destroyers were to prove themselves mighty fine soldiers, good men to have around when there was a bit of fighting going on, but as sailors the members were dismal failures.'[13] On the same ship was a familiar outfit: the 761st Tank Battalion, a segregated battalion known as the Black Panthers with whom they had served at Camp Hood. The journey was fairly uneventful and the men arrived at Avonmouth, near Bristol, on 7 September 1944.

Once the ship landed, Red Cross girls were waiting to hand out doughnuts and coffee, which raised everyone's spirits immediately after the dismal voyage across the ocean. The train was nearby and it took the men to Burley, where a trio of men were eagerly awaiting their arrival. Lieutenant Williams, Lieutenant Ramsey and Technician Fifth Grade McGee of the advance detachment that had been sent ahead months before, greeted them heartily.

It was the first time the men of the 614th had seen another continent and it was a real wonder to behold. England proved to be an exciting experience. The people drove on the 'wrong' side of the road and the trains were smaller than those that ran on the American lines. The British accents might have been hard to understand, but the men were received in a friendly manner and many pints were drunk in the local pubs in the company of friends. The men swiftly became accustomed to the customs of the British 'tuppence thruppence' monetary system, instead of the dollars and dimes at home.[14]

The tent camp in Burley, near Southhampton, was where the materiel was received by the battalion, but it would be packed again soon. On 2 October everything was prepared and stowed away, so that the battalion could continue its journey to the front. A night was spent in a staging area tent camp and the next day the men boarded a Landing Ship, Tank (LST).

LSTs were ships especially designed to carry tanks or other vehicles directly onto a beach. This type of ship had been created due to the need to deploy armored vehicles on hostile shores. These boats wouldn't need to use a pier but could sail directly onto the surf, where their flat bottoms allowed the ships to stay in position when grounded, although it did make them more susceptible to the elements while crossing the Channel, as Pritchard noted:

> No one who ever walked into the 'head' on the LST that brought battalion headquarters across the channel could ever forget the sight of the ceremony by which Captain Charles J. Richard became assistant battalion chaplain. Chaplain Johnson, seasick all the way, was on his knees, his head over a bowl. Cheerful Captain Richard walked in, but at the sight of the chaplain he too went to his knees in the next cubbyhole. 'Oh, Lord', shouted the chaplain as he heaved. 'Oh, Lord', came from Captain Richard, as he too heaved. The battle of 'Lords' went on, and when the two left neither had strength to say 'oh', much less 'Lord'.[15]

While the human cargo would recover quickly, the damage to the materiel cargo was harder to overcome. The rough sea caused the vehicles and trucks to shift, despite being tied down with ropes and chains. Two self-propelled tank destroyers from another unit got loose and, subjected to the rolling waves, proceeded to wreak havoc on board. The rampaging machines caused some casualties: a few motorcycles were crushed, and several armored cars dented, while also creating a new porthole in the hull of the ship.

The men landed in Normandy, France, after five days at sea, and between 8 and 10 October the battalion was unloaded. The men were in for another cultural experience, after experiencing England, they became familiar with the French countryside. They became especially familiar with two things: calvados (a local brandy made from apples) and mud. While the men took a liking to the calvados, they were less enthusiastic about the mud. This mud would stay with them for the days to come, as the battalion waited in a field near Surtainville, about 25 km south of Cherbourg. They resided in small two-man tents trying to stay dry, but it helped little. As Pritchard summed up: 'Thirty days here and only four without rain.'[16]

While in France, the men saw the destructiveness of war. Cities where the fighting had raged were in ruins, leaving a trail of silent witnesses in the shape of wrecked vehicles and abandoned buildings. There was also the ever-present danger of abandoned weapons and traps, which still claimed their victims. For the 614th this became obvious when two soldiers accidentally walked into a minefield on a beach. They were wounded and needed to be dragged out of it, which Lieutenant Ormond Forte and Captain Thomas Campbell finally managed to do.

The men learned about the tides in Normandy and while an educating experience, not everyone was happy with the lesson. According to Pritchard:

> It came about this way: An A Company soldier had taken his jeep to the beach where, he said, he could scrape the mud off it and grease it. But he left it (probably for calvados) and when he came back the tide had started in and his jeep was stuck. The soldier ran to the main road and halted a weapons carrier. The driver of the weapons carrier (also a 614th vehicle) tried to pull the jeep out but also mired down. Then the driver ran to the main road and stopped a halftrack. The halftrack driver, with his vehicle, succeeded in pulling the weapons carrier out but as he went back for the jeep his vehicle, too, settled into the sand. When Captain King, who had been called, arrived on the scene, the tide was in. The sun was setting in the west, a beautiful sunset marred only by two radio antennae sticking above the waves. And as the sun passed beneath the horizon a foot race started, according to interested spectators. The driver of the jeep and Captain King. The driver barely held

his own until the pair hit the muddy fields and then, being a lighter man than Captain King, he did not sink so deep. The soldier was not AWOL but absent from sight for two days until the rage of [Captain King] simmered down.[17]

Being one of the few black combat units, the men also began to realize the unique situation they were in. Lieutenant Walter Smith remembered being approached by black soldiers from service units in Cherbourg. They wanted to be transferred to a fighting unit and were even prepared to be reduced in rank if necessary. Unfortunately, little could be done for them.[18]

After a month of remaining stationary, the 614th Tank Destroyer Battalion received new orders and were on the move again. Their journey to the front continued and more witnesses to the war were passed. Columns of destroyed German vehicles, destroyed and repaired bridges, and shot up roads. They went by impressive churches and stalwart castles. They went all the way to Metz, where General Patton had halted after pursuing the retreating German forces across France. The men were stationed in Mars-la-Tour, where they could hear the rumbling of artillery.

The panzerwaffe on the Western front in 1944–1945

As the men of the 614th Tank Destroyer Battalion moved closer to the front, they would soon meet their enemy. The German forces, however, had changed a lot in the previous few years, both in armaments and strategy. Likewise, the panzers and the divisions in which they were deployed had adapted to the circumstances of the war. Although still a challenging foe, the German forces on the Western front in 1944 and 1945 were different to the units that had invaded Poland or France. Extensive fighting on various fronts had cost the Wehrmacht dearly, both in manpower and materiel. These losses had been replaced, but quality of training suffered as more and more reinforcements were rushed to the front. Their uniforms, which were baggy and of poor quality, seemed to reflect the quality of the soldiers who wore them.

While in the first years of the war the panzers, and the German army, held the initiative, the situation on the Western front was reversed in 1944 and 1945. The Allies dictated the battlefield and enjoyed numerical superiority. The sky was dominated by Allied planes, making travelling by day dangerous for the Axis forces. The feared German breakthroughs with armored units were a lesser threat now. Shortages of ammunition and fuel made the Germans much more hesitant about employing large formations of mechanized forces.

As the war was moving closer to Germany, the threat to the Third Reich increased and thus more sacrifices could be asked of the civilian population. The propaganda machine kept churning out horrible stories about what would happen if the Nazis lost the war, motivating their people to strive for victory above all else. However, despite shouting Sieg Heil (Hail Victory) louder and louder, victory seemed less likely with each passing day.

Although German tanks improved throughout the war, their tank formations became weaker. For example, in 1941 the Mark I and II tanks were being replaced by the Mark III and IV tanks, which were largely the fighting tanks of the panzer divisions. However, in the panzer divisions there were fewer tanks in total, as seen in their tables of organization. The worsening war situation forced the Third Reich to alter their panzer divisions. A panzer division in 1944 had a reduced strength of 15 to 30 per cent compared to their organization in 1943.[19] The most obvious reduction was in 1945, when a panzer division was made up of a single panzer regiment, which consisted of a single panzer battalion and a panzergrenadier battalion. This regiment was supported by two panzergrenadier regiments. Thus, the formation might have still been called a panzer division, however, these divisions contained fewer tanks than at the outset of the war.

According to American estimates, the Germans possessed between twenty to twenty-seven panzer divisions in 1941 and could add one more per month. In reality Germany had only twenty-one panzer divisions and one light division which had a reduced complement of tanks.[20] In 1942, only three more panzer divisions and one light division were established. In 1943 and 1944, new panzer divisions were still established, but these consisted of motorized infantry divisions that were turned into panzer units. They lacked the strength of their earlier counterparts.

Despite the ongoing combat and the decay in strength in the divisions, the years of fighting did lead to improved weapons, tactics, and other enhancements. The armor and weapons on the tanks were upgraded. The Mark III [Panzerkampfwagen III] that participated in the invasion of Poland, France and the war in Africa, had dwindled to just thirty-nine tanks in June 1944 in Western Europe. In the same month, there were 748 Mark IV [Panzerkampfwagen IV] and 663 Mark V [Panzerkampfwagen V Panther] tanks in the same area.[21] Moreover, newer tanks, such as the Tiger I and Tiger II entered the battlefield, becoming more common as the war progressed. In December 1944, when the 614th Tank Destroyer first entered the line, the Mark V was the prevalent German tank, of which 1,966 were ready for action on the Eastern and Western front.[22] American anti-tank guns that could have penetrated the armor of earlier German tanks were inadequate in later stages of the Second World War.

Tactical changes included Germany fielding their own dedicated tank destroyers, a response to the Allied tank threat. A variety of tanks and self-propelled guns appeared, built on different chassis for different tasks. Some were designed as anti-aircraft vehicles, while others served as assault guns. They had their own strength and weaknesses. For example, dedicated Jagdpanzer ('hunting tank' or tank destroyer) were designed to strike from ambushes and so lacked a rotating turret. Besides these vehicles, the towed German anti-tank guns, the Pak 40, and its successor, the Pak 41, remained a formidable threat. So not only did the American tank destroyers need to engage hostile tanks, but they encountered other mechanized guns, anti-tank guns, or transportation vehicles, as well.

Yet, defeat seemed to be inevitable. In 1945 only thirty-five understrength panzer divisions could be fielded. Seven of these belonged to the SS and one was a Luftwaffe formation. In spring 1945 the panzer divisions were reduced even further; their tank regiments were cut back to merely fifty tanks.[23] The once feared panzers, that had forced the American army to set up a special branch just to counter them, ceased to be threat to the Allied armies towards the end of the war.

Adaptions made by German forces likewise caused changes in the American armies. The initial fear was that after the Allied landings in Normandy, as the war moved closer to German soil, the Third Reich would start to deploy massive numbers of tanks. Although these numbers never materialized, the tank destroyer guns had to be improved, because their intended targets had changed. To achieve a penetrating hit on the latest panzers, specific areas, such as the rear, needed to be struck. The difference between towed and self-propelled tank destroyers was plainly made clear. Data from the Normandy landings indicated that on average the towed units destroyed 5.8 hostile tanks and 4.0 pillboxes, while the self-propelled battalions destroyed 22.5 panzers and 23.2 pillboxes.[24]

More problems with the tank destroyers were also revealed. Tank Destroyer Battalions were still broken up and used as smaller units to support the unit to which they were assigned, often in unintended ways. To defeat panzers, the tank destroyers needed overwhelming firepower, which was impossible if the units were dispersed over a broad area. The Tank Destroyer Battalions could be assigned as infantry support guns or security elements. Also, more casualties were sustained as the open-topped vehicles and gun shields offered less protection than the reinforced armor that other tanks carried. Snipers, mortars, grenades, and other hazards would take their toll on the crews.[25]

Chapter 4

Three-inch Fury

The first casualties

On 20 November 1944, the 614th Tank Destroyer Battalion was attached to the 95th Infantry Division. This division also had the 607th Tank Destroyer Battalion at its disposal. The 614th would be held in reserve and only the reconnaissance platoons were used. They protected the right flank of the division from a wood which was suspected of harboring German troops. Pritchard described this period as 'jumping from manure pile to manure pile, from ruined village to ruined village'. On the 22nd the battalion would suffer its first casualty in Europe. Private First Class Clarence Clark, from the second reconnaissance platoon, died in an accident.

The battalion stayed with the 95th Infantry Division until 23 November when it was moved to Perl, Germany, on the Moselle. The town was just beyond the German border on the corner where the borders with France and Luxembourg met. The battalion would serve on the left flank of the XX Corps and the Third Army, as a unit of Task Force Polk, which consisted largely of the Third Cavalry Group and attached Tank Destroyer Battalions. The battalion command post was set up in Oberperl and the gun companies were put in German villages nearby.

The fortifications of the infamous Siegfried line were close. This defensive line, also known as Westwall, had been created in the late 1930s as a defense system opposite of the French Maginot line. The line consisted of bunkers, pillboxes, and dragon's teeth, which suddenly gained new importance after the Allies had landed in Normandy. Improvements were made, but the Allies managed to break through in several places.

It was here that the tank destroyers engaged their new targets, consisting of bunkers, observation posts and pillboxes. These could be cleverly camouflaged, so that the Americans only knew they were there when they were almost upon them. Other pillboxes might look like barns or cottages. Sometimes smaller pillboxes were in front of larger ones.[1] As the men of the 103d Infantry Division described them:

> A big baby would have several embrasures covering various aspects of the terrain. The entrance would be two steel doors, opening inward. The steel 12.7 centimeters [five inches] thick. Inside would be a sleeping room with folding bunks on the walls, a couple of storage rooms for ammunition and rations, and two or three compartments with embrasures for defense. It would probably have running water, a telephone and kerosene or carbide lamps. Cramped, but pretty livable. […] A model attack on a Siegfried pillbox would call for tanks and TDs to force the occupants to button up. Then when the small arms fire is silenced the infantry can move in and take care of the fort with flamethrowers or satchel charges.[2]

The enemy also fired back, injuring one man. During the fighting in the area, the lines were stretched thin and only the towns were occupied by troops. The tank soldiers and their attached destroyers of tanks lacked the infantry to control all these areas, which left holes through which foot patrols could pass. However, their enemy seemed to lack likewise.[3]

During that time the men of the first platoon of C Company, under command of Walter Smith, were moving into position near Buschdorf, relieving the 705th Tank Destroyer Battalion, which was equipped with M18s. He was leading the way to find a suitable spot for setting up their cannons. Suddenly, hostile shells started raining down on the men.

Then Staff Sergeant Christopher Sturkey recounted these experiences:

> We started moving up again and soon I could hear the sound of guns. I recall my platoon leader coming back to me and saying, 'This is it, Sturkey.' [...] [Walter Smith] took us into action to relieve a white tank [destroyer] outfit that had been holding the flank of the German 6th Corps.[4] As they pulled out—you know tanks make noise and they did! All hell broke loose! Jerry threw everything he had in our direction. The men were scared and felt like running. Some did, but not away; they were seeking better protection. You really can't blame their reaction. This was their first time under fire and they were getting a real baptism. As we hit the dirt, the platoon leader called for me to form up the men and come up front. I couldn't even find them at first. Some were still crouched in the halftrack, others had dispersed in the area, and shells were falling like a heavy downpour.[5]

The platoon came under fire and was shot at with mortars and artillery. A man from B Company was wounded by a mortar blast. So many small pebbles puckered his skin that it took Dr Campbell two days to take them all out.[6]

Sergeant Chesterfield Jones, of the first platoon of C Company, recounted these experiences:

> We were to work in conjunction with the 95th Division & the 45th Cavalry. So from Buschdorf down the road to seek positions we went. So it began as we were traveling this road we came to a roadblock there it began, we received almost every kind of fire possible. Our platoon leader at that time First Lieutenant Walter Smith moved forward on a ¼ ton to locate

our positions. While he was gone, we waited on this road receiving fire from 88 [mm guns] & mortars. Well this was our first experience of being fired at. So we all remained on our vehicle under fire until our platoon leader returned. At that time we had traveled so fast we had only three of our halftracks in the column. So the platoon leader with those three [half] tracks heads down for our positions. Leaving the second Sergeant and his ¼ ton to wait there at that roadblock for the other vehicles. So as we moved along this sorry wooded trail, the tank destroyer platoon that we were relieving started moving out. The Germans must have seen them. Because at that time they fired at us and the other tank destroyer unit with everything they had. So that lasts for about 45 minutes. But in the meantime we tried to make it to the position. We received so much fire until we had to dismount from our halftracks. So we did and everybody tried to get some place where they could be protected from the fire. So the firing went on and we lay on the ground afraid. But after all there comes a time in every man's life that he may come in contact with fear. And so there it was for us. We had one man killed. A mortar got him and several more were wounded and two of our [Sergeants] were shell shocked. So all of these men had to be taken to an aid station or hospital. We had no means of taking them except by jeep. So we used the platoon leader's jeep to carry them to the aid station. And from the aid stations they were transferred to hospitals. This means that our platoon is short of men now. So what do we do. So now at time the firing has passed, every[one] is silent. At this time dark is coming fast. So we the few that was left remained there with the platoon leader and platoon sergeant, Staff Sergeant Sturkey so as night falls we remain there on this little wooded trail. Well it happened at this time First Lieutenant Charles Thomas gets the news which had happened. He comes down to find out if everything was right. Lieutenant Thomas was our company commander at that time, a swell man too. So after he and our platoon leader had a talk he went back to Buschdorf where our company command post was being set up. In the meantime, we the rest of the platoon don't know what the score is. So that night he sent some members of the 3rd platoon up to help us on our guard duty & security for that night. So now it is night the platoon leader told us to uncouple our guns and put them in position on the trail and so we did. We had machine guns .50 cal. & .30 cal. plus our 3-inch for security and every man had his own weapon. So here is where it is hard on us. We had never been used to this kind of stuff. We didn't sleep at all that night. The next morning we were sent some food. Well I should say 10-in-1 rations. [The 10-in-1 food parcels were intended to provide one meal to ten soldiers.] Now we realize this is war. We weren't hungry at all that morning. And everybody was muddy & dirty it was a sight. So our company commander comes back that morning and tell us we would move in our positions that morning. Now we weren't so afraid this time as before. So we move in our positions with the help of the fog within 500 yards [457 meters] of the dragon teeth. So we get our foxholes dug. And get set for a big day. So about noon time it began again. The German shell us with those 88 & mortars for at least three hours. And the hard part about it was that we couldn't see where it came from. They even fired burp guns and machine guns of all types. So all we could do was lay there in our holes and take it. We couldn't fire back at them because we couldn't see them. They were well dug in. So after a while the 95th Division laid down a heavy barrage so when that was over it became silent again. So we remain there that afternoon very quiet. So at six o'clock we received hot food so we come back to eat two or three at a time until we all had etc. So right after we had eaten, they began shelling again. We had taken it all without fighting back and then night came again.

There it was hard again we had to be very watchful at night for German patrols. And to do it was only a few of us. We really didn't know where the Germans were or how many it was. So after that night it came day again. And we felt much better. This is the 3rd day of combat for us now. So early that morning we received a lot of machine gun fire. Out to the left of Sgt Chesterfield Jones' gun we had security out there with a .30 cal. machine gun. With two men on it. Private David Campbell and Private First Class [Henry] B. Griffin were the men on it. The Germans fired so close to them until they were really excited. Griffin says to Campbell look there are those Jerry out there behind that haystack. Griffin says bump off one or two. So Campbell fires his machine gun. Which was the first weapon fired by the first platoon. And as soon as he fired it the Germans really gave it to us. They began with those 88 & mortars & machine guns. A German mortar came so close to Campbell's foxhole until it knocked him out of his hole so Campbell says. So now he and Griffin runs across the field to the woods for cover. About an hour later Lieutenant Thomas came up and asked how we was [and] everything. So the platoon leader told him. So when he finds out that Campbell & Griffin had left that machine gun, he says Campbell what happened. Campbell told him. He laughed and said are you afraid. Campbell told him 'Sir, I believe I have as much guts as the next man, but when a German mortar knocks you out of your hole it's time to go.' The Lieutenant smiled and said do you think you have as much guts as me Campbell says 'yes sir.' The Lieutenant said then well let's go get that machine [gun]. Campbell says yes sir. And so they did. So well it went on that afternoon we received a lot more fire. Sergeant Chesterfield Jones and his gun crew was pinned down in their fox holes. A German machine gun almost made a slit trench out of Sergeant Jones foxhole. So when he got a chance to get out he made it through the woods to the jeep where Lieutenant Smith had for his command post. There Jones told the Lieutenant of the way his gun crew was pinned down. So the Lieutenant tells Jones to go back and withdraw his crew back to the Jeep where his command post was. So Jones did. He withdrew all of his men except one. And that was Private First Class Fred Clements. Clements was pinned down by mortars. So in about ten or twenty minutes after that there was a cry. Fred Clements had been hit by a mortar. Jones and his Corporal Otis Pettigrew went for Clements. And brought him back to the Jeep where the command post was set up. Clements was hit in several places by shrapnel. So the company commander & platoon leader helped to give him first aid. And then Corporal Pettigrew took him on his back and tried to make it to the road where he could get someone to get him to the hospital. Pettigrew had to stop and drag Clements in the woods, the Germans saw him with Clements and fired a machine gun at them. So when that was over they tried it again. And they finally made it. So the company commander told us that night we would move out. So we waited for night to come. And so it did. The Germans seem to have known we were going to move out that night. They began shelling us and they shelled us until the 95th Division field artillery laid down another barrage. So we moved out while they were laying down that barrage. So we went back to a little town 7 miles from Buschdorf near Oberperl there we stayed for that night and the next day there were a lot of men with trench feet that went to the hospital. Roy Griffin, Roosvelt Ruffin, Luther J. Hall. All of these men were from Sergeant Jones' squad. So now the platoon is very thin. About 23 men left. So we leave Oberperl, Germany, and go to Luneville, France.[7]

The 30th, when the battalion was relieving the 705th Tank Destroyer Battalion, was a severe day for C company. Private Guilford Cutler was killed, while Corporal Lincoln Sterling, Private First Class Frederick Tucker, and Private Arlis Tarkington were wounded and taken away.

Meanwhile B Company had brought their twelve guns to bear against a German troop concentration, and the guns of A Company engaged a German pillbox. As the latter were doing so, they were filmed by the Signal Corps. Other filmed scenes included a soldier digging a foxhole and soldiers relaxing.[8] Captain Beauregard King had neutralized a German machine gunner by driving between the dragon's teeth with his M20. Once the gunner opened fire, Captain King engaged him. A firefight erupted in which 'hundreds of machine gun bullets glanced off his armored car, but Captain King got his man.'[9]

On 1 December, A Company was fired at by hostile artillery. Twice they were targeted. Around 12:00, seven shells landed on the first platoon. There was one direct hit, but little else; there were no casualties. The second platoon was fired at for fifteen minutes from 16:00 to 16:15. The reconnaissance platoon brought in two suspect Germans, which were turned over to the Counterintelligence Corps. Company A later fired on enemy pillboxes and expended 6 HE [High Explosive, intended for softer targets, like infantry] shells, 4 APC [Armor Piercing Capped, intended for harder targets, like tanks] shells and fifty .50 cal. bullets. They were under the impression that they had even hit an enemy command post. In the area of company B they saw enemy activity in the vicinity of Eft, Germany. Thirty-four mortar rounds struck around their positions and one person was injured. A total of sixty-four high-explosive grenades were fired indirectly at the enemy during three firing missions at Buren, Germany.

When supporting the 3rd Cavalry Reconnaissance Squadron, the tank destroyers engaged enemy held pillboxes north of Borg. The hostile soldiers raised a white flag, but when a patrol went out to capture them, the enemy went back into their hide-outs and fired on the men. The tank destroyers opened fire again until the enemy fled.[10]

Later that day the battalion was relieved from its attachment to the 3rd Mechanized Cavalry Group and a few days the 614th later went to Luneville, France. It arrived on 4 December and spent the night on a ruined racetrack. The next day better quarters were located, and time was spent on maintaining the vehicles. While servicing their equipment, on 6 December the men received their first recognition for participating in combat; the Battle Participation Award: Northern France Campaign. This was added to all the individual files from the personnel of the unit as proof of their first encounter with the enemy. For the men it was a real morale boost. They had encountered the Germans and lived to tell the tale. Technician Fifth Grade Willie Magby, Pritchard's driver, claimed that he was a veteran, as he was the first man to hear a shell explode nearby and every night he had driven to each position to check on them.

On 7 December the battalion left for Kuttolsheim, where it would be attached to the 103d Infantry Division. This division consisted of three infantry regiments: 409th Infantry Regiment, 410th Infantry Regiment, and 411th Infantry Regiment. To these were allotted additional supporting elements, such as artillery, reconnaissance and signal units. The division was known as the 'Cactus Division', due to their insignia.

The 103d had officially been activated on 15 November 1942 in Camp Claiborne, Louisiana. Their commander was Brigadier General Haffner.[11] On 20 October 1944, after fifteen days at sea, the division disembarked at Marseille and moved north, going into battle a little less than a month later. In early December the division had been involved in a bitter struggle for the walled town of Selestat and was given a few days respite when a new battalion was put under their command – the 614th Tank Destroyer Battalion. The infantry soldiers seemed to be displeased when they saw the black soldiers: 'As the 614th arrived and began to assemble in the division area, eyeballs of Cactus men rolled and a few remarks dropped; a few chuckles were exchanged.'[12]

The 103d Infantry Division did as many other divisions had done to their assigned tank destroyer battalions, splitting up the combat companies and using them for a variety of tasks. For example, the two Reconnaissance Platoons would be assigned objectives other than tracking enemy armor. A Company was attached to Task Force Forest, which consisted of the 103d Reconnaissance Troop, a company of the 409th Infantry Regiment, and D Company of the 756th Tank Battalion. Their purpose was to protect the division's flank and keep contact with the 79th Infantry Division. Reconnaissance had shown that the 256th Volksgrenadier Division was in the area, which had an estimated strength of 3,000 soldiers.

One platoon of B Company was assigned to guard the senior officers at the division's command post. This activity was given the moniker of being 'Palace Guard'.[13] There they provided security for senior officers, which wasn't a task for which the Tank Destroyers were intended. After a few days, they were relieved and returned to the battalion.

C Company was attached to the 411th Infantry Regiment, which went on the attack. Together with the 410th, the 411th pushed towards the northeast. Several towns were captured and they pushed towards the German border. Charles McGowan, second platoon, C Company, was there when they clashed with the Germans:

> [… W]e got a mission it was to move up to the town of Mietesheim and take up a position and shell the little village of Eschbach which was the next little town occupied by the Germans. We were attached to the 103d Division at the time. Most of us were excited at the time we moved up the majority was, but on the way there our [tank] destroyers had engine trouble and we were forced to drop out. But the others continued on. They went in position that night just on the edge of a little tree line. We guys talked that night and wondered how they were making it. We could hear and see the flash from our & the German artillery. We wonder what would be the outcome of this mission. Well the next morning around 09:00 First Sergeant Robert Cannon came and got us. He only could take so much and that was our gun and the crew. At that 9 was the gunners of the third gun squad, my

gun. Commander was Sergeant Henry T. Rhone. He ordered that no 1 & 2 cannoneers stay with the half truck. So just as we arrive on the outer edge of Mietesheim we ran in to sniper fire. It was pretty hot at times but we made it through without a single casualty. We never found out just which direction the fire was coming from. At least we had to stay on the move anyway, so we got there we had to go in position on a stay line the other had set up the past night. Most of the guys was afraid our gun was to fire on two church steeples, which was German observation posts the boys use to kid me about that especially firing on church steeples and so the time had about come to open fire. Our range was given at 3,200 and 5,400 to each gunner. Since our truck was out we had very little ammo not more than 30 rounds. We had been carrying a hundred rounds of ammo at all times but our truck was out. The very darn time we needed it the most. The boys spoke about it being a hell of a lot of trouble so they had to carry it up a little muddy road our platoon leader gave the fire order and we open up. Sergeant [Benjamin] W. Bryant was the first gun to shoot. His target was a little house down the hill was a machine gun position. It wasn't very long before we could see the blaze my second round was a direct hit in dead center. I could hear them yell hit hit. We had a perfect field day on the Krauts that day. Finally, my ammo ran out and I was forced to stop. About that time a cloud of dust rose up at our right front it was the Germans trying to knock us out we saw that they needed some more. I called for more ammo they only had a few rounds of smoke left and we all yelled hell lets fire this. We did there was a German tank over about 6,000 yards [5,500 meters] to our front but they soon withdrew. We got several more rounds from the Germans (88s) one of them was a direct hit on one of our (105s) we pulled out of position but we came back that night we didn't have to shell anymore and we didn't get any more fire. The next day they tried to get us by air. They strafed us also one of our boys soon put an end to the Jerry plane with a .50 cal. machine gun, Private James J. Albright was the one he fired it until the barrel was white as a cigarette. The 103d was to take the town that day. In fact they did they reported it was very daft going after what we gave it that was the 11th of Dec. Our next town was Woerth, France. It was very dark and dreary the infantry had moved up but not in the town. We were the first to occupy it the Germans were firing down the streets. They were our next door neighbor so we really prayed that night. We said if we could only get out of this alive we would all be good boys. You could hear those hard leather cob nails. Technicians Fifth Grade Rufus Sims and Private First Class John A. Burnell [were] at a road junction [when] there were 2 Krauts coming down the street. They yelled halt but they did not so they opened fire they didn't come back any more and after all the next morning we came to find out that they was almost a company of Krauts in the same building we took. [...]

The next morning hell broke loose, [when] the 410th Regiment [clashed] with the Krauts in what looked to be a 2-hour battle. We never lost any men that battle but it wasn't the Germans' fault. There was high ground just outside of Woerth and the Germans did not want to give it up. After a good battle they did. I was called to place my gun at a road block in case of armor attack. They didn't come. They knew we had it set up there.[14]

Meanwhile the battalion headquarters was stationed in Bitschhoffen, where the 614th had their first encounters with hostile aircraft on 10 December. An ME-109, a German fighter plane, was reported as shot down, but there was uncertainty about the claim as various units were firing at it. Unfortunately, Lewis Gregory got killed when he refused to abandon his .50 cal machinegun at the halftrack. Lawrence Johnson, of A Company, remembers being strafed by the Luftwaffe:

> In basic training, we were taught never to stop when you get out of sight of the enemy, so I ran 15 yards further into the bushes. The pilot thought I had stopped and I could see the fire jumping up from the ground. That was scary and I was lucky. We dug some foxholes then. That was my initiation of being under fire.[15]

During that period the remaining platoons of Company B participated in the attack on Soultz that was undertaken by the 2nd battalion of the 409th Infantry Regiment.[16] A few days later the Haguenau forest ceased to be a threat and Company A was relieved from Task Force Forest and attached to the 410th Infantry Regiment. The American troops advanced again, pushing towards the north. A counterattack was attempted by the Germans, but beaten back, and the Americans moved forwards again. In their path was a little village called Climbach.

The battle of Climbach

On 14 December 1944 a task force was assembled, under the command of Lieutenant Colonel John Blackshear. The task force consisted of F Company, from the 411th Infantry Regiment, under command of Lieutenant Willie Barrios, supplemented with a platoon of infantry with heavy weapons, artillery liaisons, 1st platoon of C Company, 47th Tank Battalion, with infantry riding on them, and a medical detachment of six persons. To provide additional anti-tank firepower to this taskforce, the third platoon of C Company of the 614th Tank Destroyer Battalion, commanded by company commander Lieutenant Charles Thomas, was attached to them.[17]

The goal of this taskforce was to take the town of Climbach, which was of strategic importance. Despite being a small town, with a population of only 520 in 1936, the roads allowed the enemy to supply the surrounding towns of Lembach and Wingen. The German commanders also realized this and dug-in their forces in and around Climbach. Yet the expectation was that the task force would be able to seize the village because, based upon prisoner interrogations, only sporadic resistance was anticipated and could be easily overcome by tanks.[18] Since such light opposition was expected, provisions for only a single day were taken along.

Being a new unit attached to the 103d, the men of the 614th felt the additional weight on their shoulders, and Dillard Booker remarks about this:

> It was said that a new unit was not respected until it proves itself in battle. We were considered as such with the 103d Infantry Division, until the morning of Dec 14, 1944. Captain Charles Thomas, then first Lieutenant, and company commander of 'C' Company, received an assignment to take the town of Climbach, France, then held by the enemy whose orders were to hold the town at all cost. [...] First Lieutenant George Mitchell, briefing his gun commanders on the situation, pointed out the importance of the mission in that it led to the entrance of Germany.[19]

After assembling and loading up, the column moved out. Before too long, they were stopped by a simple blockade of felled trees on the road. These were left behind by the retreating Germans to delay the Allied advances, as they had done many times in the days before. Luckily there weren't any traps left behind and the tanks dragged the trunks out of the road, allowing the column to proceed again after a thirty minute delay.

While on the road, the column was suddenly fired upon by enemy artillery. The men had little warning before the shells started exploding around them, inflicting several casualties, including Captain James Barda.[20] The jeep in which Willie Barrios was driving was disabled by a direct hit and he joined the task force commander, Lieutenant Colonel Blackshear, in his jeep. To prevent more losses, the vehicles sped up and enlarged the gaps between them.

Near a forest in the vicinity of Climbach, the task force came to a halt and the column realigned. Taking point would be Charles Thomas with his M20, who had volunteered for this task. Behind him came two towed tank destroyers from the 614th Tank Destroyer Battalion, commanded by Sergeant William Tabron and Corporal Al Hockaday respectively, and then the two tanks with their infantry. After that came Lieutenant Colonel Blackshear, the remaining two tank destroyers, commanded by Sergeant Dillard Booker and Sergeant Roosevelt Robertson, and the rest of the infantry in eight M35 trucks. John Blackshear was under the impression that the hostile fire was meant to delay the Americans as he thought there were few troops in the village, so he ordered to proceed again.

The M20 of Charles Thomas went ahead and was within 915 meters [1,000 yards] of Climbach when he topped a small rise. As soon as he appeared, a mine under the vehicle exploded and his vehicle was hit by anti-tank fire. All the occupants of the vehicle were wounded, and the wreck blocked the two-way lane to Climbach. It turned out that Climbach was defended, not just by infantry, but also by hostile armor and anti-tank guns. They held the high ground and were intent on keeping it.

Immediately, Lieutenant Charles Thomas tried to get out of his vehicle. In doing so, he was hit again by machine-gun bullets. Nevertheless, he ordered his men to get the guns into position. Sergeant Tabron and Corporal Hockaday immediately went into position in the open field with their crews. The 3-inch guns were driven forward as far as possible, uncoupled, and manhandled into position, while mud squelched around the men's boots. In the meantime, the Germans had opened fire on the anti-tank cannons that were deployed to the right of the road. All that they had in the vicinity was brought to bear on the two tank destroyers and losses rapidly started mounting.

Meanwhile Lieutenant Colonel Blackhear assessed the situation and wanted to move the tanks across the ridge, which the tank officer refused. The Shermans would become stuck in the mud and easy targets for the German anti-tank gunners; using the road wasn't possible either, since it was obviously mined. Thus the tank destroyers engaged the Germans on their own.[21]

Lieutenant Thomas refused to be evacuated until another officer was present to take over his platoon, refusing to leave his men without adequate leaders. All the while, he acted with 'one thought: deploy the guns and start firing or we're dead'.[22] Within minutes the cannons were returning fire. An infantry platoon was deployed in the woods to the right to protect the guns. It was around 13:30. The enemy continued to fire at the exposed cannons. As Charles Thomas described:

> My men were getting their guns into position with the whole world erupting around them. They were doing it swiftly and in good fashion in spite of the casualties we were beginning to sustain. In just a few minutes they were returning the fire. They were functioning to a lesser degree, as I was, automatically. I knew what had to be done. That is why I would not leave, or should I say allow myself to be evacuated, until the officer to replace me was on hand and all of our guns were firing.[23]

Under enemy fire, the numbers of wounded and dead started to mount. The men who were able, stayed with the 3-inch gun to help, while others aided by keeping the Germans at a distance. The cannon of Sergeant William Tabron was especially targeted. A halftrack driver, Technician Fourth Grade Arthur Perry, manned the machine gun in his vehicle, despite being wounded by shrapnel. Two other men, Shelton Murph and Leon Tobin, kept operating the cannons until they became wounded and couldn't fight anymore. Shelton Murph's leg was eventually shot off and he was evacuated. Peter Simmons continued to fight until he was mortally wounded. At the same time, sharpshooter Corporal Burnie Swindell fired at every target he saw. Earlier in the fight Private First Class William H. Phipps had been wounded when he drove with his jeep through an artillery barrage; ignoring his injuries he drove Lieutenant Mitchell to a position near a cannon. He decided to stay there and fight until his wounds felled him. Corporal Hockaday was the last man standing and operated both guns for a while, running between them to aim and fire.[24]

A German infantry assault attempted to dislodge the tank destroyers and overrun their positions. The guns were inadequate for dealing with such a threat and this put the remaining crews and infantry at risk. The men that could be spared were used to man the machine guns and other weapons at their disposal, while a few continued to pour fire on the town. Private Thomas McDaniel fired with his .30 machinegun, while Sergeant Tabron manned a .50 cal machinegun, and Whit Knight even left the 3-inch gun he was operating to drive back the enemy with a machine gun. The concentrated efforts of these men beat off the assault, but at the same time, one of the cannons had ceased firing.

Private Thomas McDaniel was sent back with orders from Lieutenant Mitchell to fetch the remaining two tank destroyers. Sergeant Roosevelt Robertson and Sergeant Dillard Booker brought their guns forward and went into position, respectively right and left of the road. The Germans saw this too and fired intensively at Robertson's 3-inch gun. Booker's gun was in luck, because his halftrack had become 'bogged down in the open field yet he had advantage of being in a slight draw.'[25] It offered a little more protection than the other positions. To provide covering fire for the guns, Lucius Riley shot from the halftrack with his .50 cal machinegun, until the vehicle was destroyed and he was killed.

The infantry, which had previously ridden on the American tanks, supported the tank destroyers from their positions; they also fought fiercely against the German troops. Sergeant Charles Henrikson, a member of F Company, was there with them:

> A few yards ahead was a German machine gun nest, but they weren't expecting us from this direction and we surprised them. They were going to open up when [Private First Class Richard] Myers [BAR man] gave a burst. There were two on the gun. One of them dropped and the other took off with a light bipod machine gun. Well, this was just the beginning. The German went for reinforcements. Meanwhile, Myers and I jumped in the hole left by the Krauts. This was located just outside the woods. I saw action in the woods and a couple of Krauts came out and surrendered. I sent Myers to the rear with the prisoners. I was now left alone and some Germans noticed this and saw their chance, so they thought. They started to set up another gun in the woods and each time I saw them setting it up I let them have it. It was getting twilight and no one around except two negroes with their legs off at the knees. The anti-tank gun was knocked out. One German I shot in the arm came out of the woods with 'Kamerad'. Well, I kept taking my ammunition out of my bandoliers and putting it in front of me because I thought this was my last moment. Each time the Krauts let up I shot the machine gunner. A couple of them came running at me from the left [corner] and I killed one and got the other in the head. I guess he died later. Anyhow, I kept firing as fast as I dared without using up all of my ammunition. By this time elements of the company were entering the town.[26]

The infantry suffered from the wet ground, as they could hardly dig foxholes. Any hole deeper than 15 to 20 cm [6–8 inches] was impossible, as water started to emerge. Besides there was the biting cold with temperatures around 2° Celsius [35 F].[27]

Eventually the enemy observation posts were destroyed and they started firing indiscriminately at the cannons. Tanks and other weapons were used to try to put the tank destroyers out of action. Around 15:30 a new problem presented itself for Booker, who commanded the only gun left firing, because he started to run out of ammunition. 'We felt stark, stripped naked,' Booker said, 'we figured this was it.'[28]

As soon as Technician Fifth Grade Robert Harris heard of this, he decided to bring up new shells with his halftrack. While underway, he was stopped by Colonel Blackshear, who said: 'soldier, you can't go up there. The enemy fire is too intense.' Harris replied: 'Get out of my way, my boys are up there.'[29] He drove his halftrack to within 45 meters [50 yards] of the gun and started unloading the ammunition and bringing it to the remaining gun. Booker's gun continued to fire throughout the rest of the day; all the others had been put out of action.

Charles Thomas, who has been injured at the beginning of the struggle, was eventually evacuated. He was aided by Lieutenant Floyd Stallings, who ran across the open field to help him. Technician Fourth Grade Paul Warner had also seen this and drove his vehicle forward. Once there, it took fifteen minutes, during which they were under fire, to get Charles Thomas on the vehicle and bring him to safety.

While the tank destroyers were in a deadly struggle with the dug-in Germans, the American tanks refused to go forward, due to the mines and the positioning of the hostile weapons. After artillery support had been coordinated, an outflanking attack was launched on Climbach by the remaining platoons of F Company. The harassing fire was meant to keep the Germans in hiding, until they could be overrun by the American infantry. The outlying districts of Climbach were reached at around 15:40, and at 19:00 Blackshear himself arrived in Climbach, after he had sent the remaining tank destroyers and tanks back to the regiment. An hour later it was determined that the enemy could no longer bring up supplies through Climbach. The fight had lasted for around five hours.

After the battle Lieutenant Willie Barrios, in command of F Company, identified a few crucial factors. First there had been more enemy soldiers than anticipated, and the information derived from prisoners was wrong. Overall, there were around twenty-five to thirty enemy killed, while twenty-five more were taken prisoner – how many more had fled was unknown.[30] Two tanks appeared to have been silenced.[31] Despite the inappropriate employment of the tank destroyers – three of the four guns were lost within an hour of the Germans opening fire – they were nevertheless instrumental in the success. There were problems with communications, and the tanks refused to go to Climbach. The infantry platoon, which had been deployed for the defense of the tank destroyers, couldn't be used in the attack on the town.[32]

The battle was won at a heavy price. Only the gun of Sergeant Booker survived the retaliating fire, although he was injured. During the battle three soldiers were killed immediately, while another died in the hospital. Charles L. Thomas, the company commander, was seriously injured and fourteen soldiers were taken away wounded. Tabron is considered one of the lucky ones; he was reported as a casualty but had sustained just a minor injury on his foot, which he discovered the next day. The officer in charge of Sturkey's platoon, Walter Smith, was moved up to be in command of C Company and Sturkey was put in charge of the platoon. Furthermore, two halftracks, an M20 armored car, and two Willy jeeps were destroyed by hostile actions.

Despite these setbacks, mistakes and faults, all the officers and soldiers of the 3rd platoon, C Company, 614th Tank Destroyer Battalion had distinguished themselves; Lieutenant Colonel Blackshear wrote proudly about the battle and would laugh when he told the story of how Harris brought up the ammunition. The platoon was recommended for the Distinguished Unit Citation and Lieutenant Charles Thomas was recommended for the Distinguished Service Cross, which he would receive shortly afterwards.

Charles Thomas was the second black American in the army to receive this award.[33] Private George Watson, of the 29th Quartermaster

Regiment, had received this award posthumously for helping soldiers into life rafts after the transport ship he was on was sunk on 8 March 1943. He died from exhaustion after saving many lives, unable to escape the suction of the ship as it went down. Four more silver stars were given out for the battle of Climbach, as well as nine Bronze Star Medals.

The pride of the unit surged. The soldiers and their officers were proud of what had been accomplished. Pritchard said in *Yank*: 'If you only knew how goddamn proud I am of my boys.' The bloody struggle not only impressed the men of the 614th Tank Destroyer Battalion, but also the 103d Infantry Division, which took pride in 'their' anti-tank battalion.[34]

However, the struggle wasn't over yet. As Sergeant Weldon Freeman wrote about his experiences:

> It was one real dark night in December when the second platoon entered into Climbach with two guns from the second section. The first section was in position guarding a roadblock before you enter Climbach. The city hadn't completely been taken. We had only a few patrols in the city. We moved two guns into Climbach. They were Sergeant Weldon D. Freeman and Sergeant Henry T. Rhone with their cannoneers. These two guns were moved in with the infantry. When we came into town there were guns barking all over the streets. Our platoon leader and platoon Sergeant, who was First Lieutenant Shaw and Staff Sergeant Benjamin Bryant moved in and picked gun positions for us. Sergeant Freeman's gun was placed on the northern end of town covering a crossroad. Sergeant Rhone's gun was placed on the southern end of town covering another roadblock. We put our guns into position and put our guards out, then we found billets for our men.
>
> The next morning our infantry open up around 7 o'clock. The town was full of patrols and snipers from the German army. They had street fights for about an hour. A mortar squad

had seen the two guns that we had set up in town and opened up on them. Finally, our infantry had them on the run. They were driven into the hills. On the afternoon the first section join us and we were given orders march order and get ready to move forward. When dark came we pulled our guns to the outskirts of town and waited for the engineers to put in a bridge.

Around nine o'clock we got orders to move our guns back into town and set them up at one side of the road. Sergeant Freeman pulled his gun to the outskirts of the village about three hundred yards from the last house in the village with his gun crew who consisted of Sergeant Weldon D. Freeman, Corporal James E. Fenner, Private First Class John H. Evans, Private First Class Jonathan Cureton, Private First Class Moses H. Wesley, Private First Class Rema Giles, Private Joseph Michel, Private First Class John William, and Technician Fifth Grade Alphonso Norfleet. Nine men.

The crew later found a German soldier standing nearby. The man was taken prisoner, but in the ensuing confusion, he tried to run away and was shot down. As Weldon Freeman tells of the experience: 'The rest of the night the guards were alert for more patrols to slip in. That taught me and the rest of the men a lesson to always be on the alert.'[35]

Soldiers, prisoners, and veterans

Despite losing half of the soldiers in the third platoon of C Company, the other platoons had remained intact. They would be needed in the coming struggle because on 16 December, far to the north of the 614th Tank Destroyer Battalion, the Germans launched their assault on the Ardennes. Early in the morning their artillery opened fire and after a ninety-minute barrage, the Germans advanced. The goal had been to take the port of Antwerp and force a wedge between the Allied lines. If this succeeded, a sizeable portion of the Allied army would be cut off from their provisions. Aided by the fog, a lack of intelligence, and overstretched Allied supply lines, the Germans managed to surprise the Allied forces.

While American and German forces clashed to the north, not all soldiers in the German armed forces were equally enthusiastic about fighting for the Führer and the Fatherland. In the past weeks, Dutch, Hungarians, Russians and Poles had been taken prisoner by the 103d Infantry Division. They claimed to have been pressed into service of the German army.[36] On 16 December Captain Charles J. Richard and his driver stumbled into a similar incident:

> With his driver [Captain Richard] was going out to one of the gun companies when two half-starved Poles, wearing German uniforms, came out of a wood. Captain Richard fumbled with his machine gun, accidentally fired one shot, and the soldiers came running, shouting 'Kamerad'. The Captain loaded them on the hood of the jeep and started back towards the battalion command post, where a company commanders' meeting was being held.
>
> It was a mean trick, but when the Captain was seen driving in with the prisoners, all present were instructed to ignore him. 'I', said Captain Richard. 'Don't interrupt', he was told. 'But I have two prisoners,' he said. 'We are talking about important things now,' was the answer. So Captain Richard, very angry, left to display his prisoners elsewhere.[37]

Despite being denied his moment, Captain Richard was very proud of the two prisoners he had secured, although it had happened in a rather unusual fashion.

While to the north the Battle of the Bulge was happening, the 614th were occupied with their own affairs. New plans for breaching the Siegfried Line were made, one of them involved dragging the 3-inch guns up the mountains and letting them rain shells down on the German positions. Company A, under the command of Captain Beauregard

King, was selected for this task and the guns would be taken apart. To help in bringing them up the mountains sixty mules, 300 soldiers and a few men from the ordnance sections were ready. However, before this could be done orders were received that the battalion needed to move to new positions.

On 22 December 1944, General Anthony McAuliffe, acting as commander of the 101st Airborne Division in absence of Major General Maxwell Taylor, received an offer to surrender from the German commander during the Battle of the Bulge. His reply was simple: 'Nuts!' Refusing to give up, despite being surrounded by a larger German force, he and his forces held out until relief came. As a reward, McAuliffe would be promoted and made commander of his own division.

On that same day, 22 December, the 614th Tank Destroyer Battalion was ordered to Neufvillage, France, where the unit would be attached to the XV Corps. Pritchard was appointed as the Anti-Tank Officer of the division, putting him in charge of the anti-tank defenses. This allowed Pritchard to take on additional duties. From his experiences as tank destroyer commander, he could give technical advice and insight that other senior officers might have lacked.[38] Reconnaissance and recommendations based upon Pritchard's advice followed. With the Tank Destroyers and the organic anti-tank units of the division, the panzer threat could be withstood, if there might even be one. On 24 December, Christmas Eve, the battalion command post was moved to St Jean Rohrbach. The next day they moved again, this time to Farschviller.

On 26 December the reconnaissance platoons were sent out on an anti-tank warning mission. The first platoon checked the area of the 411th Infantry Regiment, while the second platoon was assigned the sector of the 410th Infantry Regiment. The combat companies also kept busy. Company A was attached to the 410th Infantry Regiment, dividing the platoons among the three battalions of the regiment. Company C was attached to the 411th Infantry Regiment. Company B, who had earlier guarded the division command post, received the task of palace guard again, at the division command post and at the battalion command post. In between they helped the 44th Division and the 106th Cavalry Group.

On 27 December, thirty-three enlisted men were received by the battalion to serve as replacements for earlier sustained casualties. These men arrived just in time to see their new comrades be decorated the next day by Brigadier General John T. Pierce, the assistant division commander of the 103d Infantry Division, who decorated eight men of C Company with Bronze Star Medals. Leon Tobin and George W. Mitchell received the Silver Star. Private Sam Patraeck, also of C Company, was awarded the Purple Heart. The entire battalion was incredibly proud of their comrades and morale improved as a result.

On 31 December 1944, the battalion's liaison officer and his driver were injured in a vehicle accident when traveling from the battalion command post to the division command post. They were taken to the aid station of the 103d infantry division. Later that day a phone call came from the division to warn the battalion. All personnel were to stand to, and the guns had to be manned by their full crews. All companies were immediately informed, and the reason would soon become obvious.

Chapter 5

Getting out of the Northern Wind

Losses of men and materiel
The last day of 1944 ended with an alert for the American forces: Germany had launched a new operation: Unternehmnen Nordwind. The attack in the Ardennes was not proceeding as planned and the German high command realized that the Allied troops in the Alsace had been weakened. Many troops were rushed towards the north to help in the Battle of the Bulge. Hitler and Gerd von Rundstedt, the German Oberbefehlshaber West (high commander in the west), noticed this shift in Allied forces and the subsequent establishing of new lines and gave the task of exploiting this to General Johannes Blaskowitz. To prevent Allied materiel superiority being brought to bear, the attacks needed to be made fast and continuously against a weakened enemy. Germany needed to act fast to make the most out of a deteriorating situation.[1] If they waited too long, the weakened units would have been reorganized and the gaps in the Allied lines fortified.[2] The goal of the attack was simple; as Hitler stressed to his subordinates, the goal was not to conquer terrain or prestige, but annihilating 'manpower... the destruction of enemy forces.'[3]

The Allied commanders received note of increasing German forces in the area, although they weren't aware of the exact strength of the hostile forces and intentions. They started to bolster their own defenses and ready the men for the coming fight. Despite the cold, and sometimes snow storms, defense works were established and obstacles erected. This went even further, when 'on New Year's Eve, a Sunday evening, [Alexander] Patch [commander of the U.S. Seventh Army] met with both his Corps commanders at Fenetrange [...] and warned them to expect a major enemy attack during the early morning hours of New Year's Day.[4] New Year's Day, like Christmas, would be spent in the foxholes. All celebrations would have to be postponed and the first attacks started a few hours before 1 January.

For the 614th the first day of the year 1945 started violently when an outpost of Company A was attacked by a thirteen-man German patrol. A firefight swiftly erupted, and the outpost was cut off from American lines for an hour. When the smoke settled, however, there were nine dead Germans and two prisoners, while the outpost suffered no casualties. Those weren't the only prisoners caught; on 7 January the second reconnaissance platoon caught two more after Lieutenant Joseph L. Keeby fired indirect with the 37 mm guns from his armored cars near Folkling.

On 2 January the second platoon of A Company fired at Lixing, France, in support of a raid of the 410th Infantry. Company B was attached to the 776th Tank Destroyer Battalion, where two guns would be deployed on 3 January in the vicinity of Folpersviller, relieving two self-propelled M36s of the B Company of the 776th.[5] That night C Company fired star shells into the sky to illuminate the enemy defensive installations for a patrol of the 411th Infantry Regiment, which was in the area. Red star shells illuminated the area.[6] The patrol got excellent results with the light from the star shells that had been fired. That day, Staff Sergeant Christopher J. Sturkey also received his promotion to 2nd Lieutenant. This resulted in a minor reshuffling in the Company, which Chesterfield Jones described:

> There we had a new commanding officer. Our platoon leader, Lieutenant Walter S. Smith, had been made commanding officer. Lieutenant Thomas had been wounded so Lieutenant Smith took over. Our platoon Sergeant, Staff Sergeant Sturkey had been made platoon leader. And Sergeant Summer one of the gun sergeants had been made platoon Sergeant.[7]

A change in leadership was also made within the 103d Division. On 8 January the ailing Major General Charles Haffner, who had been with the division since its training, had resigned on account of ill health and gone back to America. On 11 January, Brigadier General Anthony McAuliffe took command of the 103d Infantry Division.[8] The promotion to Major General came shortly afterwards and the soldiers liked their new commander, who made himself popular with orientation talks and with the efforts he made to meet the many men under his command. On 3 January 1945, Company A was released from the 410th Infantry Regiment again and returned to the battalion as a reserve. They moved to Puttenlange, France. Company B was relieved of its attachment of the 410th Infantry Regiment and attached to the 44th Infantry Division. Company C kept lighting up the sky, this time in support of an infantry patrol of the 410th. While these flares slowly drifted down to earth, they granted the Americans the light they needed to carry out their assignments.

On 4 January, Company A was attached to the 928th Field Artillery Battalion, an artillery unit organic to the 103d Infantry Division. The 3-inch cannons complemented the 105 mm howitzers of this battalion nicely and allowed the artillery observers to engage targets out of range of the howitzers, while alleviating the shortages of ammunition. Until being relieved on 11 January, they fired 1,080 shells in support of the artillery battalion.

On 11 January 1945, Company B was moved from the 44th Infantry Division to the 106th Cavalry Group. The company command post was set up in Lauterbach, Germany. The next day the first section of the first platoon of C Company went into position and fired directly at an enemy observation post in Forbach, France; 143 grenades were expended, where all but four hit their target. The hostile observation post was destroyed and 190 minutes after the section had gone into position, they moved out again.

On 13 January the third platoon of C Company, which had been involved in heavy fighting at Climbach, fired seventy-eight grenades when they were near Gaubiving, France. This was conducted to support a small attack from the 411th Infantry Regiment. One pillbox was destroyed. The 614th Tank Destroyer Battalion was also attached to the XXI Corps and relieved from the XV Corps. The frozen ground proved hard to dig in, so dynamite was used.[9]

On 14 January the different companies were attached to the infantry regiments again and they moved to the VI Corps sector. Company A was attached to the 409th Infantry Regiment. Company B was attached to the 411th Infantry Regiment and Company C was attached to the 410th. The next day the battalion, without their detached units, moved back to Reichshoffen. It had recently changed hands twice, being captured by the enemy and retaken again. The battalion command post was set up in a factory area, together with the Headquarters Company and the reconnaissance platoon.

General McAuliffe also took the time to visit the tank destroyers under his command. He came by the command post of the 614th Tank Destroyer Battalion on 16 January. He noted that the vehicles were parked too close together. If hostile artillery ever fired on them, they would suffer extensive damages. The vehicles were promptly dispersed and an encounter with the enemy's artillery would come sooner than expected.

A few hours later, on 17 January at 05:00 in the morning, a large artillery shell wrecked a factory that stood near the battalion command post. Major Robert Thorne, an air operations officer of the 358th Fighter Group who was in Reichshoffen at the moment, wrote about that day in his journal:

> A TD outfit has moved into this CP – colored unit. Artillery hit close by early this AM. It was all large caliber; one missed this CP by 300 yards – shell over 11' in diameter – probably railway gun. Looks as though by the number of shells in near vicinity that they were after this place. Sure did shake this house and rattle windows. Some plaster fell but no other damage.[10]

The unusually large shell even attracted specialists from the division, who examined the crater. Based upon the damage caused, it was believed to have been fired by a Krupp K5, the 280 mm German railroad gun. These Krupp K5s were capable of firing shells that weighed more than 250 kilograms, but luckily enough, this time they claimed no victims.

On 19 January the reconnaissance platoons were sent out to establish contact with two other Tank Destroyer Battalions. The first platoon was sent to the 827th Tank Destroyer Battalion, which was also a segregated unit, but self-propelled. The men drove M18s, the vehicles which Lieutenant Colonel Bruce had wanted for his dedicated destroyers of tank forces. The second platoon was sent to contact the 813th Tank Destroyer Battalion, outfitted with M10s. Furthermore, a warning was issued about enemy traffic, which was dispended among all the units. B Company returned after their trip with the 106th Cavalry group. A day later orders were issued that the units had to move back to the west of Haguenau.

Since the 614th had been attached to the 103d for some time, the men had become accustomed to one another. Christopher Sturkey recounted how mixed race patrols would venture out. Accompanying the infantry on some patrols would be a few soldiers of the 614th. Some men did it out of friendship, while others did it to stay busy.[11] Private First Class Leonard Diana, Company A, 410th, related another story of how he and a black soldier worked together:

> A few days later when we were in the same position, we learned by phone that we should send a man to company headquarters immediately. Again we had word that German patrols were out that night. Headquarters was in town some distance away and no one wanted to go. Finally, I volunteered. Key West, one of the 614th TD troops with us declared he would not let me take that trek alone. After a time Key West took his carbine off his right shoulder, transferred it to his left shoulder with the muzzle pointing behind us and fired. He explained that he heard a noise behind us and thought he had better fire, just in case.[12]

The trip by the two soldiers happened somewhere in January and it's possible that Key West had been one of the new reinforcements that suffered an accidental discharge. Firing backwards over his shoulder isn't effective, regardless of whether he intended to hit something. It would only alert the people around them. Probably it served as an excuse for West's accidental discharge. The name Key West might have been a nickname for a soldier. Regardless, as an African American soldier Key West volunteered to accompany a white soldier so that the latter wouldn't have to risk meeting the Germans alone. It's an example of the selflessness and dedication of the men that served in the 614th Tank Destroyer Battalion.

Retreat by night

The pressure of Operation Nordwind on the weakened American lines, where troops had been rushed to the north, forced the Allies to shorten the frontline. It left more soldiers available to man the newly established positions. Among others, it was decided that the VI Corps, to which the 103d Infantry Division belonged, would withdraw. Although hard-won ground was yielded, it was necessary to prevent a possible German breakthrough.

On the night of 20 January, the 103d Infantry Division withdrew from their positions towards the west of the Haguenau while a blizzard was raging. During this slow retreat, the men of the 614th moved back with the units to which they were attached and struggled through the cold night on the icy roads. Both A and C Company were attached to the 409th Infantry Regiment for the move, although C Company would later return to the 410th Infantry Regiment.

Shortly before the retreat, the Alsatians seemed to have caught wind of the impending retreat and feared the Germans would return. As the American vehicles drove by, children hurled snowballs at them.[13] The Germans hadn't expected this retreat and didn't immediately go after the Americans.[14] During the retreat any crossed bridges were blown up to hamper the enemy, and what couldn't be taken along was destroyed to prevent the Germans from ever using it.

Frank Rogers, who served in G Company of the 409th Infantry Regiment, described the retreat in detail:

> As soon as we came to the main road leading out of the bulge, we encountered long lines of tanks, halftracks, trucks, and other vehicles of the 14th Armored [Division] – slowed by the icy roads. With so much traffic over roads with a heavy coat of new snow, as cold as it was, the snow had packed until it was, for all practical purposes, ice. Consequently, many vehicles slipped and slid, causing the convoys to slow to a crawl. Often one or more of these vehicles slid off the road into the ditch. Then, if it was decided that there was no way to get the vehicle back on the road, it had to be disabled so it would be of no use to the enemy. Not only did we see tanks and trucks that had been disabled, but also big artillery pieces, 'Long Tom' artillery guns [the 155 mm M1] that had had their breeches blown. The withdrawal was surely a very costly one for the Allies.[15]

The retreat for B Company and the Headquarters Company began in the afternoon, while A and C would retreat under the cover of darkness. Shortly before the company headquarters closed down, a special guest arrived. Victor Jones, a correspondent from the Boston Globe, had stopped by the 614th Tank Destroyer Battalion to find out more about the battle at Climbach. He was given the information that he needed and left shortly afterwards. The new battalion headquarters would be set up in Printzheim, France.

A strange feeling was in the air, as Sergeant Dillard Booker of C Company, recounted:

> Rumors circulated rapidly on the night of the twentieth of January. We had learned the Jerries were pouring trucks across the Rhine river and it wouldn't be long before our guns

would be blazing at elements of Rommel's panzer divisions. The battalion had set up a perimeter defense in the vicinity of Niederbronn and Woerth, France. Every three inch gun was well camouflaged, every relief was constantly observing to the front. Without explanation, we were given orders to prepare to move. Halftracks and guns lined the road and slowly began moving back from the present line of resistance, as did all our units with the Seventh Army. This night was especially cold, snow laid a foot deep. Our men were uneasy, as was every man that made the withdrawal. Traveling to Zinswiller, France, we learned that we had gone too far beyond the Allied front, we would had faced a possible encirclement had we not withdrawn.[16]

Sergeant Booker wouldn't have known it, but the German General Erwin Rommel had been forced to commit suicide on 14 October 1944 for his involvement of the 20 July plot, a failed assassination attempt on Adolf Hitler. It's a testament to the General's reputation that the American soldiers feared him.

Two company commanders of the 614th tried with a few of their man to get as much materiel across the bridges, before they would be blown up. They even stayed behind the covering force. Captain King and eighteen of his men returned sixteen hours after the infantry that had been assigned as the rearguard. C Company had their own troubles of which an unnamed man wrote:

> During the withdrawal on or about 21 January 1945 the 2nd platoon, Co C, 614th TD Bn ran into quite a few difficulties and created a new record for the ¼-ton jeep which has probably never been done before. At Ebach [probably Eberbach], France, two halftracks with 3" guns ran off the road into a creek beside it due to the heavy snow and ice on the roads. After several hours of winching and attempting to receive a

wrecker from other units passing through, we were only able to get the guns out. It was near approximately 0200 hours and the covering force was withdrawing at 0300 hours. The platoon leader, First Lieutenant Thomas H. Shaw ordered the platoon Sergeant, Staff Sergeant Benjamin Bryant to take as many men as he could get on the vehicles running and to tow one of the guns with the ammunition vehicle leaving its trailer and to move out. After they had gone there were fourteen men left and the platoon leader with a jeep and 3" gun. Several men were sent out on foot to stop either a wrecker or one of the 14th Armored Division's tanks to free the halftracks. A tank couldn't be gotten because they had lost tanks all along the road due to slippery roads. At about 0500 hours the covering force reached Ebach and insisted that the gun be abandoned, and the men withdraw on foot. The platoon leader decided he would pull the gun as far possible with the jeep. It was coupled to the jeep and as many men as possible got on the jeep and the others mounted up on various parts of the gun. At times it was thought it couldn't be made, however, in spite of all difficulties, Zinswiller, France was reached at about 1000 hours with fourteen cold, wet and very tired soldiers, but valuable equipment had been saved, a 3" gun.[17]

Despite the actions of Lieutenant Shaw saving a cannon, there were other losses. Three guns had been abandoned. Like the rest of the retreating forces, they too demolished some of their own equipment to prevent its capture. Six halftracks became lost after they slid off the road and couldn't get back on it. While the nightly withdrawal was difficult, the men of the Seventh Army had done splendidly and were complimented by Lieutenant General Jacob L. Devers.

The battalion headquarters were set up in Printzheim, while Company A set up in Obermodern, and Companies B and C set up in Ingwiller, using a bulldozer from the Engineers to establish their positions.[18] On 21 January the battalion provided anti-tank defense within the division's assigned sector and the next day a meeting was held with the company commanders of A and B, after Pritchard had a meeting with the division's headquarters.

On 23 January the men in Printzheim, France, were alerted for hostile actions. A guard was placed at every entrance and machine guns were set up. All the roads were watched. The next day company B fired nineteen rounds at an enemy's observation post, knocking it out. The second reconnaissance platoon proceeded to Uhrwiller and while there drew enemy fire. They retaliated by killing two enemy soldiers and getting out again before suffering any casualties.

The losses of the third platoon

The third platoon of C Company had been set up in Schillersdorf, France, which lay in the area of the second battalion of the 410th Infantry Regiment. Battalion headquarters were established in this town also. While at Schillersdorf, an almost prophetic incident occurred. A sergeant of the tank destroyers was placed ahead of the supporting infantry; this concerned him enough for him to speak to an infantry officer:

> 'What shall I do if the Germans attack,' he asked the officer from the 103d Division. 'Run back to us,' the infantry officer replied. 'How will you tell me from the Germans?', the Sergeant asked. 'Just yell G.I.', the Captain said.
> 'Captain, you may hear me yell 'G.', but when I yell 'I.', I am going to be way past you,' the Sergeant said.[19]

Fighting in the previous days had been hard, and on 25 January, around 04:30, a battalion of around 450 SS soldiers from the 6. SS-Gebirgs-Division 'Nord' struck the village. The Waffen-SS mountain division had previously been fighting in Finland against the Soviet Union, but was transferred to the Western front after Finland signed an armistice with the Soviet Union in September 1944. Before the attack, alcohol had been handed out and the men went into combat dressed in white clothing and screaming English obscenities. For the Americans there was little indication of an attack until the hostile troops were already upon them.

In the disorganized retreat, most of the 103d Infantry Division units in town managed to get out, although the third platoon of C Company, 614th Tank Destroyer Battalion, wasn't so lucky according to Sergeant Dillard Booker:

> After the platoon had suffered fifty per cent casualties and a loss of over half of its equipment, the platoon almost suffered complete annihilation at Schillersdorf, France, on the morning of the 25th of January of 1945. The men who were not on guard were aroused from their different quarters by guards who exclaimed, 'the Jerries are attacking the town.' The men hastily gathered their arms and were placed in position to afford the best fields to fire. This particular morning was very dark. The snow was knee deep. The Jerries attacked in overwhelming numbers, forcing the infantry to withdraw leaving the TD's guns and halftracks. The TD's fought gallantly beside the doughboys. Later when the platoon was accounted for the enemy had captured fourteen of our men including the platoon leader and platoon Sergeant thus the platoon had been depleted from fifty-two to twenty men.[20]

That day the Germans took a total of forty-eight prisoners.[21] It was a frightening experience for the black soldiers as they were at the mercy of their captors – fanatical soldiers who viewed black people as subhuman. Luckily for them, they transported to the rear and returned safely to American control once the war was over.

In Schillersdorf one gun was destroyed by the crew, while two more 3-inch guns, three jeeps, two halftracks, and a 1½ ton [Chevrolet] truck were abandoned.[22] B Company then transferred a gun and a prime mover to the third platoon, in order to increase its strength.

The next day a counterattack was staged and two of the missing men were found again. They had managed to stay hidden in a barn and thus evaded capture. Once the village had been reconquered, it turned out that the Germans had taken two jeeps and many personal possessions. The rest could be recovered and new guns were requested. At Schillersdorf the following men were captured by the Germans: Lieutenant George Mitchell, Staff Sergeant William Tabron, Sergeants Wilbert Welch and Walter West, Corporals Whit Knight, Blease Spell, and Plato King, Technician Fifth Grade Thomas J. Hanebel, Private First Class Robert Bullock, and Privates Reed Jones Jr., George Punch and Charlie Rattler. Thomas Hanebel and Charlie Rattler stayed in Stalag 13C, although it's unknown in what camps the others were interred.

There were three more casualties on the 25th in Zutzendorf, which was occupied by 2nd platoon of C Company. An enemy shell killed Private First Class Scott Jarrett, while Sergeant Bonnie O. Harris and Private First Class Henry Eaton were wounded, the former more severely than the latter. Furthermore three vehicles were damaged by the enemy.

The remaining days of January were quiet. The enemy fired his artillery sparingly and the time was used to improve the current firing positions and scout for potential new ones. Lieutenant Colonel Pritchard inspected the positions.

A tragic incident took place at Lixhausen on 26 January 1945 – a guard of A Company shot a civilian at 21:00, leading the soldier to be placed under guard and investigated. The battalion commander of the 807th Tank Destroyer Battalion, another towed battalion, visited the command post the next day. At a later moment the liaison officer of that tank destroyer company visited and was given an overlay of the gun positions.

The last days of January 1945 were quiet, mainly because on 26 January, the German high command decided to cease further attacks in the local area. For two days prior to this they had tried but failed to achieve the hoped-for successes. Reserves had been exhausted. Several units were pulled out of the line and transferred to the Eastern front to fight against the Red Army.[23] The Seventh Army had suffered 14,000 casualties due to the German attacks, while the Germans had lost 23,000 men and officers.[24]

Chapter 6

Fighting and Resting

Raiding the old mill

The first days of February were easy. Reconnaissance was conducted and the current positions reinforced. There was a report that three tanks were in the area. Although the enemy seemed to be passive, that didn't mean the men could rest. On 2 February 1945 a friendly fire incident occurred, when the companies were fired at by their own artillery. While at the front things seemed to be at ease, behind the frontline there was a lot of activity. Men were moving about, measuring distances, discussing and instructing others. The 614th was planning and rehearsing a possible attack on a mill located between Bischholtz, and Mulhausen, France, where prisoners needed to be taken. Information about the enemy was necessary and prisoners would have to be brought in. Previous attempts by the infantry of the 103d Division had failed when they encountered minefields. Two officers and thirty men, from the first and second reconnaissance platoon, were tasked with carrying out this assignment on an old mill. For three days, the men had been preparing their 'minstrel show' as they called the raid.[1] To aid them, air reconnaissance had taken pictures and maps were created. The men were well prepared and knew what was expected of them. Even reconnaissance patrols were conducted, and Private Thomas Ingram remembered them well:

> The ground was covered with snow and it was very cold but our mission had to be accomplished. Four of us volunteered to go. (There was Sergeant Elijah Gibson, Technician Fifth Grade Austin Johnson, Private First Class Thomas Phillips, and myself, at that time a Private First Class, now Sergeant

> Thomas Ingram.) After we were orientated, we started down the hill to Bitschhoffen every bit of the way was open terrain. We had to advance in leaps and bound and be very cautious because we were in enemy territory. We must have been seen or heard because the Krauts shot several flares above our heads and as the flares lit up we lay very quiet because usually when the Krauts shot up flares they shot a burst of deadly machine gun fire, and which if they had, we had no cover, and would have been wiped out.[2]

After those days of extensive training, aided by their new-gained knowledge, the men left at 20:00 hours on 5 February and proceeded towards the enemy. Unseen, they managed to slip through the lines and as Private Thomas Ingram tells the story:

> There was thirty-two of us. And in each man's heart he felt that some of us were not coming back. Again we started the long journey down the hill to Bitschhoffen. This time the Krauts did not shoot flares, but on each man's lip there was a silent prayer that they didn't.[3]

During the advance, the raiding party brought with them a telephone cable that led back to an observation post. If the enemy tried to reinforce the outpost, by rushing in reinforcements, these would be fired upon by the Allied artillery. On both sides of the mill machine guns were set up, while two groups of raiders, both consisting of six men, stalked towards the buildings. One group would surround it, while the other group entered the mill. Private Ingram continued his narrative:

> As we advanced Sergeant Samuel Booker heard the clicking of a Kraut gun and he hollered hard, but received no reply. Sergeant Booker tried to fire his gun but his gun failed to fire. But Private First Class Leo D. Greer's gun didn't fail to

fire. He killed one Kraut and wounded another. By that time the Krauts broke loose with all hell. There was quite a lot of exchanging fire but suddenly the Krauts stop firing and six of them came towards us crying 'comrade'. Eight of their men were killed. One of them had his head blown off from a hand grenade thrown by one of our platoon leaders, First Lieutenant Joseph L. Keeby. There was a quick count of our men. All thirty-two of us were there. None wounded – none killed.[4]

As Ingram mentioned, six prisoners were taken, who provided valuable information. The unit hadn't suffered any casualties, and it resulted in five Bronze Star Medals for the men involved. Lieutenant Joseph Keeby, Private First Class Henry Weaver, Private First Class Thomas Ingram, Private George Bass, and Private Leo Greer were decorated for their actions.

Rearming, regrouping, and retaking

The following days the enemy continued to harass the men of the 614th Tank Destroyers, but attempted little else. Company A seemed to be their preferred target, being struck by the most shells. On 8 February a few mortar rounds were fired at their first and second platoon. Later one man from the third platoon of B Company was slightly injured by a rocket that came down near him. Two days later again, A Company was targeted. On 14 February six more shells were sent to A Company and Blanchard L. Parker died in an accident. A day later, Technician Fifth Grade, James Barbee, became wounded, followed the next day by Private Curtis Swinger, who was wounded when a mortar fell near him. On the 17th the Germans hurled yet more lethal metal at A Company, but inflicted no casualties. One man from B Company was wounded when a mortar shell fell within the vicinity of the company command post. The next day the enemy attempted again to harm A Company by aiming at their third platoon, but the fourteen shells caused no casualties. Fifteen mortar rounds followed the next day, but again to little effect.

During that time the men didn't do much. On 23 February, all company commanders were gathered for a meeting at the battalion command post. On the 25th the first reconnaissance platoon was selected to patrol the roads within the divisional sector in conjunction with other units, a violation of their intended task. The unit was supposed to track hostile armor and not be employed as highway patrolmen.

The next day one gun from the first platoon of C Company was appointed to the 411th Infantry Regiment to fire at a self-propelled gun, which was seen whenever American tanks were in the area. However, the enemy didn't appear this time, and later the 3-inch gun returned to its previous positions. Although during the next two days there was little enemy activity, Private First Class Riley Weeks of C Company got lightly wounded by enemy action.

From 1 to 9 March the 614th Tank Destroyer Battalion stayed in the same locations, securing their positions. On 1 March Lieutenant General Patch, the commander of the Seventh Army, visited the battalion command post and complimented the neatness of it and their canteen. From time to time the enemy fired a few shells, but they inflicted no casualties. On 3 March six shells came down in Ingwiller.

The men used their time to maintain their equipment, vehicles and to train themselves and the replacements, such as on the firing range. On 3 March all companies were ordered to send their platoon sergeants to Pritchard, who was at the command post of C Company, so they could exchange ideas and to inspect the gun positions. The reconnaissance platoons were kept busy patrolling their designated sectors, roving along the roads.

On 10 March McAuliffe, the commander of the 103d Division, and Pritchard, the commander of the 614th Tank Destroyer Battalion, inspected the gun positions, made suggestions and improvements, such as the need for adjustment to fields of fire and corrections to the camouflage. This was carried out until the 14th, because the next day the Seventh Army went on the attack again.

In the early morning of 15 March, the Seventh Army started to advance again into Germany. Preparations had been made in the past days and the 103d Infantry Division had been brought up to strength. Artillery sounded the start of the offensive and shortly afterwards the infantry regiments moved out and the combat companies of the 614th Tank Destroyer Battalion went along with their designated units.

B Company was attached to the 409th Infantry Regiment, while C Company was assigned to the 411th Infantry Regiment. A Company moved up with the 410th Infantry Regiment. The 614th battalion command post was moved to Menchhoffen, France, shuttling the men and materiel to the new location. Companies B and C helped their units by providing direct fire support. The towed cannons could be deployed rapidly and then moved to another position. Targets that hampered the advance of the infantry were swiftly neutralized and C Company would take fourteen prisoners that day.

Certain enemy strongpoints had been bypassed earlier, but still needed to be taken. C Company could only move up after a bridge had been completed across the river that the infantry had crossed. Together with the tanks they pursued the troops they were supposed to support.[5] Two towns were captured by the 614th that day.

A Company proceeded towards Schillersdorf, where in January Lieutenant Mitchell and eleven other men were taken prisoner. Kindwiller had been circumvented earlier and a task force was rapidly assembled from the company headquarters platoon. They moved towards the town and approached it from the rear. When in the vicinity of the town, the taskforce was suddenly fired upon and Captain Beauregard King became injured by a machinegun. Despite being wounded, King urged the others forward, 'Don't stop for me – finish the job!'[6] Thomas Kilgo, a member of the medical detachment, went across the open field in order to provide first aid. Sergeant Charles Parks took command and after the wounded officer had been evacuated, cleared the town with members of the first reconnaissance platoon. The second and third platoon provided support and fired forty HE shells and thirty APC

[Armor Piercing Capped] shells. Fourteen enemy soldiers were killed, while thirteen were captured. Four machinegun nests were destroyed, as well as an anti-aircraft gun. King, Kilgo, and Parks were decorated with the Bronze star Medal for their actions.

The other town was Bischholtz, which was stormed by the two reconnaissance platoons, led by Pritchard himself, and supported by the first platoon of B Company. The 3-inch guns poured direct fire on the German positions as the task force took the town without any casualties. In return they captured forty-one prisoners, which included one officer, despite going through heavily mined areas. The taskforce then proceeded to Rothbach and Offwiller, France, but they encountered no opposition.

On 16 March, Technician Fifth Grade Lester Latson was wounded by a mine near Rothbach. Enemy resistance was light, and the first platoon of A Company destroyed six machine gun nests and two anti-tank guns. Four prisoners were captured by the second reconnaissance platoon northeast of Offwiller. That evening the tank destroyers attached to the third platoon were deployed in the town of Gumbrechtshoffen to provide anti-tank security.[7] The next day A Company detached from the 410th Infantry Regiment, while B and C displaced forward with their respective units. B Company spent the night in Gundershoffen, while C Company set up quarters in Niederbronn, France.

During this period, according to Pritchard, another memorable incident occurred:

> In the town of Lampersloch, as Colonel Pritchard, Major Robert J. O'Leary, and Lieutenant Leonard I. Burch were making a reconnaissance preparatory to moving the command post to the town. The Krauts, disturbed by the sight of Magby running around looking for schnapps, opened fire with 88s. Magby ran into a house with two other drivers. Lieutenant Burch picked another house, the commanding officer picked a third, but Major O'Leary picked a pile of tile. The commanding

officer was where he could watch Major O'Leary, crouching behind the tile as the shells whistled in. The expression on the O'Leary face turned from doubt to anxiety, to wonder, to despair, to hope, and then, as the shelling ceased, to certainty. But there were shell fragments all around him. In the meantime, a shell had knocked the roof off the room where Magby and the other two drivers sat.[8]

On the 18th the enemy offered no resistance. C Company moved to Wingen, in the vicinity of Climbach, and A Company to Mitschdorf. The battalion command post, together with B Company moved to Reichshoffen. In Reichshoffen the men set up in the same building that they had occupied a few weeks earlier, before they were forced to retreat. However, they didn't stay long as the next day they moved forward again and went to Goersdorf, France. This time their quarters consisted of an old castle. The infantry regiments were supported by the gun companies, while the two reconnaissance platoons were tasked with clearing the roads between Wingen, France, and Nothweiler, just beyond the German border. Although the enemy offered strong resistance, the platoons completed their task.

On 19 March the reconnaissance platoons were sent to contact F Company of the 411th Infantry Regiment, who was supposed to be in Nothweiler, but they weren't there. Lieutenant Colonel Pritchard, Major Robert O'Leary and Lieutenant Keeby proceeded until they approached a destroyed bridge. The reconnaissance men dismounted and continued on foot, until they and the officers were stopped by machinegun fire from four bunkers. Sergeant Elijah Gibson was wounded. Private Mark Ray managed to get him out and back to a place where he could be properly aided. During these actions, the Germans disclosed their positions, which was useful later when overcoming the positions. He was awarded with the Bronze Star Medal for his heroic actions.

The 103d's artillery, under the impression that only Germans were in the area, then proceeded to fire on Nothweiler, adding to the chaos.

A group of engineers had been taking measurements of a blown-up bridge in order to replace it when they were caught in between. All escaped apart from one engineer, who was hiding behind rubble near the water. At last, the soldier managed to escape unharmed because Lieutenant Keeby laid down a smoke screen.

The next day, the 20th, the battalion headquarters moved up to Nothweiler, establishing themselves on German soil, and the reconnaissance platoons established roadblocks on the outskirts of the town. At the front, there was heavy fighting around Bobenthal. It was a little town, some five kilometers to the east of Nothweiler. However, according to Sergeant Booker, the fighting at Bobenthal was also the first combat experience for some of his men:

> It [had taken] several weeks to receive replacements, the gun commanders were disappointed to find very few of them with combat training, mostly all were from quartermasters and engineers. Each man was trained as to his particular job when time permitted. Sergeant Booker had one old man, the gunner, out of a squad of nine, and the gunner had never fired before. The big test came for his men at Bobenthal, Germany, the 20th of March 1945. This was a particular hot spot the enemy were fighting from pillboxes on the Siegfried line [and] our infantry suffered enormous losses. Sergeant Booker's gun was brought on the line during the night and placed on the side of the road facing several pillboxes. Shells fell continuously during the night. The next morning Captain Walter S. Smith gave Sergeant Booker orders to destroy two pillboxes. The test for the crew had come. The men quickly put the gun in position as the commander shouted his commands. Samuel Williams laid dead sight on the target missing not once. Robert Nunley pulled the lanyard like a veteran. Clarence Reese ran and passed ammunition to the loader Napoleon King like a track star. James B. Williams though short moved lively

uncasing the ammunition. From then on there wasn't no doubt in Booker's mind as to the performance of his men.[9]

When Booker and others fired at their target, the infantry soldiers around them danced as the buildings crumbled. Everyone was happy, despite the incoming fire of the enemy. Later that night, the men moved into town, as Booker continues:

> As usual we made our entrance into the town during the night, the jerries were firing the largest shells they had. First Sergeant Robert Cannon received orders personally from General McAuliffe to take his guns forward. Five tanks which tried to go up to the main line of resistance during the morning were knocked out on the road. The jerries guns were emplaced behind the mountains, their observation post had to be in one of two pillboxes, which were very visible. First Sergeant Cannon seeing no need for two of his guns sent them back leaving Sergeant Roosevelt Robertson and Sergeant Dillard Booker crews to stand the intense shelling and snipering. Booker's gun stood in the road surrounded by a rock emplacement his men built that night. The guns were to be moved further forward during early morning when a bridge that had been knocked out was put in, but it took longer than anticipated; also the Germans had too good of an artillery bracket around the bridge. During the morning First Sergeant Cannon gave Booker orders to fire on the two pillboxes facing his gun. It wasn't long before eighty rounds were emptied into the boxes. Later we learned the jerries had numerous machine guns trained on the road, for some reason they never did fire.[10]

That same day, when in the village, First Sergeant Cannon distinguished himself when he walked through the streets ignoring everything around him. All the while, every move caused machine guns to open fire. According to an officer who witnessed it, Sergeant Cannon was one of the bravest men he ever saw.[11]

That same day, various officers also had a close encounter with German machine guns. Captain Carn, Lieutenant Carey, the new commander of A Company after Captain King got wounded, Lieutenant Berry and Staff Sergeant Bryant went out to select gun positions to cover the road on the left flank of the division. When they had picked out several spots, the Germans suddenly fired a burst of small arms fire. Lucky for them, they all managed to escape unharmed. Later it was discovered that they were within 180 meters [200 yards] of a camouflaged bunker.

On the 21st the battalion continued to provide security on the left flank. C Company was shelled by enemy mortars and while no casualties were reported, two vehicles were damaged. The first section of third platoon shot up an enemy bunker, which forced thirty-three enemy soldiers to surrender. The battalion was kept in position to provide security, with C Company held ready in case support was needed.

On the 23rd the battalion took 111 prisoners. That same day, an accident occurred when one halftrack turned over and Henry Hart, of B Company, died in the accident. Several others were also injured, including Albert T. Dobey, who had been injured before. Later that evening the battalion moved to Lauterschwan, Germany.

Task Force Rhine

On 21 March 1945, while the gun companies were busy fighting their way forward, the second reconnaissance platoon under command of Lieutenant Serreo Nelson was given a special assignment; it was attached to Task Force Rhine. This task force consisted of three companies, A, B, D, of the 761st Tank Battalion, with whom the men of the 614th had sailed across the sea, a signal detachment, and the second battalion of the 409th Infantry Regiment of the 103d Division. As a commander of this mixed-race task force, Lieutenant Colonel Paul Bates, the commanding officer of the 761st, was chosen. In charge of the infantry, who rode upon the tanks, was Major Hennighausen, of the 409th battalion.[12]

The task force's goal was to rush through a gap in the Siegfried Line that had been created within the division's sector. Once through the defensive lines, the town of Klingenmünster had to be captured. This would allow a combat command of the 14th Armored Division to push their way deeper into the German countryside and circumvent the Siegfried Line. According to the 409th Regimental history, 'The combination might have been called Task Force Revenge instead of Task Force Rhine. Every unit had some old scores to settle with the Germans.'[13]

The 409th Infantry had been attacking the Siegfried Line with the remaining two battalions to force a gap in the fortified line. The German troops defended themselves well in their trenches, pillboxes, and behind roadblocks to halt the American advance. For several days the Allied troops battered the German lines to breach through. Once a gap had been created, Task Force Rhine would push through and proceed towards Klingenmünster.

On 22 March the task force set off and that afternoon they captured the town of Reisdorf. When they proceeded again, Task Force Rhine was split into two columns. One went to the east, towards Bollenborn, where a paved road lay ahead of them. The other went north, where it followed a dirt road which the Germans used to supply their units at the front, where they were hindered by an anti-tank ditch that needed to be filled.

The eastern column came across a 180 meter [200 yards] long roadblock. The engineers, aided by the first platoon of F Company, cleared the road, while the second platoon of F Company acted as a covering force. When the last tree of the roadblock was removed, a hidden anti-tank gun opened fire on the column. One Sherman tank went up in flames. The regimental commander, Colonel Lloyd, happened to be making a reconnaissance in the area, calmed the troops and began issuing orders. As the northern column had already captured the town of Birkenhordt, the eastern column was redirected towards them, followed by the rest of the regiment at a later moment.

An uneasy night followed, as the taskforce was behind German lines and few men could sleep easily. The advance continued in the night towards Silz and then eastwards towards Klingenmünster, which needed to be taken before sunrise. Shortly after midnight the tanks appeared on the edge of Silz and their attack was so swift that an anti-tank gun was destroyed before the crew even managed to man their weapon. In the darkness, the column had managed to surprise the enemy, and the town burned brightly from the fires.

The 761st soldiers were in an aggressive mood and during the mission they used reconnaissance by fire. All along the march, the ground was,

> systematically and mercilessly searched by fire from 75 mm, 76 mm and 37 mm cannons and .30 and .50 caliber machine guns. This was fire power with vengeance. As one of the colored gunners put it: 'Man, we learned this jive from General Patton.' Not to be outdone, the Cactus foot soldiers kept a steady stream of .30 caliber ammunition blazing off into the ditches and hills along the road. M1 rifles and Browning automatics were red hot.[14]

However, the town of Silz turned into a nightmare. The civilians were terrified and the wounded screamed for help as fires raged around them. One soldier of G Company helped a screaming woman to get her cow out of a barn that was on fire. They got the beast out before the roof collapsed. Shortly afterwards, the task force moved out again, going in the direction of Münchweiler, where they overtook a Wehrmacht column. Artillery, anti-tank guns, supplies, vehicles, horse-drawn wagons were lined up. As the 409th history continued:

> This was an opportunity that had never been encountered by the power-crazed tank pilots. They sent their steel monsters

bulling into the German column, strewing wreckage as they thundered forward. Tanks crushed men and horses. Cannon fire blasted trucks into twisted masses of flaming steel. Erstwhile Supermen ran screaming down the road attempting to surrender.[15]

In the end twenty-five trucks, ten automobiles, twelve kitchen vehicles, five 88 mm guns, two 50 mm anti-tank guns, twelve 37 mm guns, five 75 mm guns, one 170 mm guns, 116 horse-drawn vehicles, nine Nebelwerfers and twelve horse-drawn caissons were lost.[16] How many men and horses were killed or crushed beneath the tracks remains unknown, as these weren't counted.

Once the task force was in Münchweiler, the enemy used the reigning confusion to their advantage. When a German ammunition truck started to explode, the American tanks became separated from their supporting elements, leaving the lighter tanks and the supply vehicles cut off from the tanks. The tanks pushed on without them, leaving the supply vehicles to catch up later.

A patrol that was sent towards the rear from the advancing columns encountered Germans who had moved back into their previously occupied positions. They had come out of the hills and wanted to cut off the rearguard. The men in the jeeps fought their way back to the tanks and continued to serve as a rearguard.

On the night of 22 March, the reconnaissance platoon was ambushed by the Germans and Sergeant Matthew Spencer saved Serreo Nelson's life, when the lieutenant was threatened by a German officer with a submachine gun. The platoon had been stopped by fire and an officer aimed his gun at Lieutenant Nelson. Not in a position to shoot the German officer, Spencer struck the German with his own weapon. After the officer was dispatched and returning fire, the platoon could proceed on its way.

Lieutenant Nelson commanded the reconnaissance platoon as it raced through hostile territory. When part of the reconnaissance element was ambushed by the Germans, they were told to surrender. In reply, Lieutenant Nelson started firing his machine gun and the men withdrew without any losses. When going back, the platoon was stopped when a wagon had quickly been placed across the road and Lieutenant Nelson dismounted, returned fire and helped clear the road with his men. Like a one-man-army, Ronald Pollard first used his machine gun, and after it malfunctioned, a submachine gun, until that weapon ran out of bullets, then he continued firing with a submachine gun from another platoon member. When the enemy attempted to free their prisoners shortly after, Nelson organized the men and broke up the hostile attempt. Afterwards they formed the rearguard of the main body.

At sunrise on the 24th, the task force reached its objective: Klingenmünster. More fighting took place, as a soldier fired a panzerfaust at the rear of the column. The task force then took the town and consolidated their positions, waiting for their support to arrive.

The supply vehicles and the lighter tanks were assisted by the third battalion, riding on their decks, and they went after the task force to close any holes in the line. They arrived later, at noon on the 25th, partly because a few German soldiers seemed intent on defending their little corner of the Third Reich, but also because there was wreckage from the previous night which needed to be cleared up. 'To remove a two-mile-long column of German horses tangled in their harness, and wrecked vehicles. This enormous roadblock of living flesh and wrecked vehicles was probably the most difficult that the 409th Infantry Regiment had ever removed.'[17] Horses, vehicles, men were all ground into the dirt when the tanks advanced through them. During the attack three men of the 614th distinguished themselves: Lieutenant Serreo Nelson, Sergeant Matthew Spencer and Private First Class Ronald Pollard. Two Bronze Star Medals and a Silver Star were awarded for their actions.

The Task Force Rhine was in luck, because the same route they advanced had been used by the Germans to pull back, which left it clear of roadblocks, mines, or demolished bridges. The task force suffered few casualties and took over 100 prisoners. How many casualties they inflicted is unknown, as there could have been corpses all along the way, unknown victims of the reconnaissance by fire. Regardless, the task force had breached the Siegfried Line and the American forces proceeded to pour through it, spilling out across the German plains.

Chapter 7

Racing through the Alps

Getting ready for the last dash
Over the past couple of days the 614th Tank Destroyer Battalion, just like the 103d Infantry Division, had seen extensive combat. The Third Reich was crumbling and the Allies were advancing from all sides. The battalion was given a short rest before it would advance again on 20 April. In the meantime, the battalion aided the local military government. They helped keep order in the towns, helped rebuilding, and started the process of denazification. Roadblocks and guard posts were established in the assigned sectors and prisoners captured. Liberated prisoners of war or deported workers needed assistance along with misplaced persons. French persons were sent to the Bensheim French Government, while troublesome Soviets were sent to Aschaffenburg. On a personal level, training schedules were set up, the officers held meetings with officers to exchange information, while the men used the available time to maintain their clothing, equipment, and vehicles.

On 24 March the battalion, minus A Company, was assembled at Impflingen, Germany, and the building where the battalion command post was erected showed signs of looting. The second reconnaissance platoon had safely returned from Task Force Rhine. On the 28th the battalion moved to Waldsee, Germany, on the west side of the Rhine. The companies were assigned to the surrounding places. The battalion stayed there until 2 April and then moved to the west, where the command post was set up a forester's lodge near Elmstein.

While there, the battalion received special guests. Major General McAulliffe, Brigade General Pierce and Colonel Guy S. Meloy arrived for dinner, and along with them came another guest, the famous actress

Marlene Dietrich. She was making a tour of the front at that time to raise morale and one of her stops was the 614th Tank Destroyer Battalion.[1]

The 103d Infantry Division had been moved to Darmstadt, where it would serve as Supreme Headquarters Allied Expeditionary Force reserve, while the battalion set up quarters nearby. On 12 April President Franklin Roosevelt died in Warm Springs, Georgia; he had been suffering from a declining health for a long time. Harry Truman succeeded him as the 33rd President of the United States. The men of the 103d Infantry Division would hear the news the next day. Regardless of what the men personally thought of him, all mourned his passing.

On the 17th the battalion was alerted for movement to Oberhofen, Germany, which they did on 19 April. On the 18th orders had been given but canceled later. Soon the relative peace would change as the 103d Infantry Division would move out again. Germany was losing on all fronts, but the war wasn't over yet.

Austria and Italy

Everyone knew that the war would be over soon. The Seventh army was advancing eastwards, before turning towards the southeast, roughly holding a line between the city of Stuttgart to Nuremberg.[2] The 103d Infantry Division had been held back as a reserve of the Supreme Headquarters Allied Expeditionary Force, building up its strength and taking care of equipment while providing occupational duties. This changed on 20 April, when the 103d Infantry Division went on the attack again, attached to the VI Corps. Their task was to move south, towards the Swiss and Austrian border, splitting the German forces to the south.[3]

The gun companies were assigned to the regiments of the 103d Infantry Division again. A Company was assigned to the 410th Infantry Regiment, B Company was attached to the 409th Infantry Regiment, while C Company moved up with the 411th Infantry Regiment. In the case of A Company, the three platoons were attached to various battalions and also were supplied with food, gas, and other needs by the regiment. The two reconnaissance platoons were ordered to stand by and move out for any mission within fifteen minutes. The race towards Innsbruck and the Brenner Pass had started. The regiments moved out and their assigned destroyers of tanks went with them. The German resistance had largely broken in both the west and the east, and the Allied forces rushed to meet each other.

In Austria, the Seventh Army was rushing towards the south to meet up with the Fifth Army in Italy. Enemy resistance was feeble and many towns were rapidly captured, although the quartering party of the 411th Infantry Regiment was fired upon in Metzingen, when the town hadn't been fully cleared.[4]

On 21 April the two reconnaissance platoons reported to the 411th Infantry Regiment. They would scout ahead of the two battalions to see if the towns were clear. Meanwhile the battalion command post, which consisted of only the Headquarters Company, moved to Pluderhausen. The next day the battalion command post moved to Kircheim, and also received a notice that Staff Sergeant James McDougald, of B Company, had been killed. Seven others were captured, and one man was reported missing.

Private L.C. Walker, Private Frank Jackson, Private Hurley English, Corporal James Morrison, Private George W. Owens, Technician Fifth Grade George Donaldson, and Technician Fourth Grade Isiah Polk, told this story of their capture:

> On Sunday, 22 April 45, around 14:30, near Hegenlohe, Germany, we were in a one ton and a half truck, coming back from picking up rations and gas, when we were fired upon and about 100 yards [91 meters] up the road, the enemy felled a tree, blocking the road. At the first burst of fire upon us, Staff Sergeant James McDougald, was killed. The Germans continued to fire, and only three rounds were returned. The reason for not returning the fire is that we were completely surrounded by approximately 200 Germans, and they had us covered. The Germans motioned for us to come to where they

were off to both sides of the road, back in the woods. We had our hands above our heads and started towards them. One of the soldiers opened fire on us, only slightly creased Sergeant Polk above the eye. Sergeant Ernest Joynes stood up in the cab of the truck, but didn't have his hands above his head. A shot was fired and Sergeant Joynes fell out of the truck on the ground. We do not know what happened to him from then on, and haven't seen or heard of him since. [Sergeant Joynes was reported as lightly wounded in action.] We walked over to where the enemy were, were searched, and taken on into the woods. Later on that night, one of the German soldiers who spoke English, translated what the German officer asked us. They asked us how long we had been in Europe and we said about six months, how long we had been in England and we replied about a month; if we were married or single, how old we were, have any children; if we had killed any German soldiers and we said no; how much pay we received a day how many cigarettes issued a day; did we get good food and if the officers ate the same food that we did; what kind of an insignia we had on our jackets. and we replied a cat; asked us if we were from America or Africa; why did we fight and a few other questions which didn't mean much. Never once we're we asked what our unit was, where located, or anything else to do with the location or size of units. We only had a sandwich a day, and drank water from the creek. We then started through the woods, carrying equipment, mostly belonging to the officers. We were told that we were prisoners of war and if we tried to escape, we would be shot. At night we slept on the ground without any blankets, with four men guarding us. During the day, we had one guard with each of us, and always kept in the middle of the column. We were also asked that if before we were captured, if we saw them in the woods – replied no. About 05:00, 24 April 45, we were told to 'furth' – which we knew meant to go. However, with all the other German soldiers in the woods, we decided it would be best to stay behind them and follow them into the town toward which they were headed because we saw some American vehicles in the town. When we got near the town, we took off and reported in to the 216th [anti-aircraft artillery battalion]. Sergeant Polk, who had taken cover in a foxhole, was left behind, and after staying there for about two hours, finally made his way to the 4078th Service Company. We were not mistreated or punished in any way, except we were required to carry their equipment. Whatever we were told to do, we did.[5]

While the men were captured and marched away on 23 April, A Company, with their command post in Bohringen, was engaged with the resisting German soldiers. They expended sixty-eight rounds of high explosives, but captured twenty enemy soldiers and destroyed two anti-tank guns, one hostile observation post and neutralized other enemy strongpoints. Company B, their command post located in Owen, had fired sixty rounds of high explosives, neutralizing various resistance nests. C Company, with its command post in Metzingen, used up fifty-six rounds of high explosive and twenty APC [Armor Piercing Capped] shells, but they destroyed one enemy machine gun nest, one rocket launcher and ten buildings, while killing eighteen enemies. The company suffered no casualties. Dillard Booker was there when hostile forces were overcome:

> On the 24th of April a task force composed of one company of infantry men and one three-inch gun started for a town not far from Metzingen, Germany. We were told there would be little or no resistance. As the leading infantry jeep got within one hundred yards of the town it was hit by a bazooka shell killing the officer driving. The infantry quickly deployed, Sergeant Booker had his gun placed into action beside a house affording the best field of fire and protection from small arm

fire. We noticed German soldiers running from one house to another. Sergeant Cannon fired on them with his carbine to no avail. Sergeant Booker waited anxiously for Captain Smith to give First Sergeant Cannon permission for him to fire. When orders did come every suspicious house was fired upon. It was quite a show for the infantry for they liked to see our guns roar. It wasn't long before the mayor of the town came forward with a white flag to reveal the jerries had left. Thus the TDs added another town to their list.[6]

The Headquarters Company didn't remain idle either, as when a report was received that there were hostile troops in the vicinity of Schlierbach, Pritchard himself organized a small task force of twelve soldiers from the command post and the reconnaissance vehicles, two M20s, to seek them out. However, during the extensive search through the hills and woods, they found no hostile troops.

On 24 April, one prisoner was captured on the road. The battalion moved to Gerslingen and the captured men of B Company were reunited with their unit. On that same day further to the east the Germans who had captured the enlisted men clashed with Americans from the 45th Infantry Division. It resulted in several enemies captured or neutralized, while the captured enlisted men managed to get away.

The battalion command post moved to Bernstadt, Germany, on 25 April. Technician Fifth Grade Luell L. Love from B Company was wounded by hostile mortar fire, but luckily his injuries were slight. The command post in Bernstadt was in a filthy building located next to a jeweler's store which had been looted by American forces who had stolen all the watches. One of the possible perpetrators left a clue behind, because inside the shop; a letter was found addressed to 'Pvt Wm C. White Hq Co 2nd Bn 409th Inf'.[7]

The battalion command post left again on 26 April and moved to Burlafingen, where they captured fifty enemy soldiers before moving on to Aletshausen the following day. Five hundred prisoners were taken and transported to the rear. The command post moved again, this time to Schongau, before moving to arrive at Kirchberg on the 29th, where the 614th captured 125 prisoners.

One of those prisoners was a major in the German army and while many prisoners supplied valuable information to their American interrogators, this major gave information that saved a lot of lives. He told of a chemical dump in Strass where between 1,200 to 2,500 poison bombs remained, and asked the Americans not to shell the plant as it would result in disaster. The plant was subsequently investigated, and the story confirmed.[8]

The situation was growing more dire for the Third Reich with each passing day. On 30 April Adolf Hitler and his wife Eva Braun committed suicide in a bunker in Berlin. On that day, far from Berlin, the 614th Tank Destroyer Battalion took 181 German soldiers prisoner.

The month of May started with the battalion command post being erected in Oberau, while the various companies and reconnaissance platoons advanced with their respective units. The 103d Reconnaissance Troop, the scouts of the division, alternated with the reconnaissance platoons as spearhead for the division. The next day the battalion command post moved to Partenkirchen.

That same day, a task force was heading towards Scharnitz, Austria, when the leading armored car was taken under fire by anti-tank weapons and machine guns. According to Thomas Ingram, it went like this:

> We received orders from Captain Durant of the 103d Infantry Division Reconnaissance Troop that we were to cross the Austrian border and to proceed on to Italy. Suddenly we came to a halt and received orders to send two of our armored cars on a Task Force Reconnaissance across the Austrian Border. As our armored cars crossed the Austrian border, they ran upon a Kraut anti-tank gun + crew. Staff Sergeant Leroy Williams fired three rows from his 37 mm gun but was unable to knock out the Kraut gun. [He was struck by recoil of his own gun.]

But in the meantime, 1st Lieutenant Joseph L. Keeby who was in the other armored car ran upon a mine [in an attempt to get around the other car]. His armored car was knocked out when the mine exploded. Lieutenant Keeby was wounded in the right hip. He ran from his armored car to the one of Sergeant Williams and tried to call for help over his 608 short wave [radio] set. As he climbed up to the top of the car he was shot in the head by a sniper. Sniper fire also shot and killed Staff Sergeant Leroy Williams, Technician Fifth Grade Robert L. Smith, Technician Fifth Grade Austin Johnson, Privates First Class James Harper and Jerome Whitfield. Private First Class Thomas Phillips was shot in the leg and arm and Private First Class Clifton Moody was captured.[9]

Thomas Philips and Clifton Moody were both in Innsbruck when the Allied soldiers reached the city.

The Battalion Command post was moved to Hall, Austria, on 3 May and a platoon from C Company was assigned to a task force that headed for the Brenner pass to link up with the American troops in Italy. The other units were all gathered in and around Innsbruck, Austria.

Booker wrote about these final days:

When the Allies crossed the Rhine the German army became disorganized, the American army lost no time pushing ahead, in fact, we moved so fast from our rear elements equipment couldn't be replaced rapidly. Many of our halftracks needed to be replaced, but time did not permit. Sergeant Daniel James halftrack developed engine trouble which our mechanics couldn't remedy, thus he was left with his crew until ordnance towed him in. The few nights they spent on the road was none too pleasant. Small bands of Germans, who were bypassed during our hasty advance, roved the woods harassing American troops at night which Sergeant James vividly remembers. One night while his men huddled around a fire thirty jerries' fired on them, Sergeant James dispersed his men fighting them off with small arm and machine gun fire.

The last important mission we performed was our march with specially picked units to meet elements of General Clarks Fifth Army in Italy. The Task Force left Nittenwald, Germany, May 5, to travel one hundred miles through the snowcapped mountainous Alps of Austria. Though there was practically no resistance during our march there was constant fear that vehicles would slip on the icy road and fall down into any one of the canyons we frequently passed. Misfortunately several vehicles overturned, while descending an unusual steep hill several men were seriously injured. During our entire combat days the men got along swell with the men of the 103d Infantry Division as they did when fifteen to twenty rode our halftracks during the long trek that took us as far as the Brenner Pass.[10]

William Sproesser, from the 103d Infantry Division, who had once before been saved by the 614th from a perilous spot, remembered the dangers of linking up with the Fifth Army quite well, because the roads weren't designed for military traffic.

In those days, before the superhighways, the road south from Innsbruck was very dangerous. About 30 miles south of Innsbruck, two of the tank destroyer halftracks – towing 3" guns – lost their brakes. Both drivers decided to drive into the hill instead of going over the edge. The 3" guns caught up with the halftracks throwing the entire assembly high in the air. The halftracks were both filled to overflowing with black & white soldiers. This was the single biggest incident of carnage I ever witnessed. There were broken backs, fractured skulls – one driver had his arm amputated, but no one was killed. All we had was an aid man with bandages. The road was so narrow we had to bounce a jeep around to send it back to Innsbruck for help. AND THE WAR WAS OVER![11]

The next couple of days were uneventful apart from a halftrack overturning on 4 May which caused several casualties. As Chesterfield Jones narrated:

On the night entering Austria, going down a long steep hill Sergeant Jones halftrack turned over and one man was killed and four hurt. James O. Parker was the man killed. He was one of the replacements we had gotten.[12]

However, during these final days, tenacious resistance was still encountered from hardened Nazis that couldn't comprehend the collapse of the Third Reich, or were unable to believe that their prophetic Führer had been mistaken, perhaps guided by a misplaced belief that bloodshed at the last moment might achieve anything. As Thomas Ingram describes such an incident;

[It was] when the Reconnaissance Platoon were leading a task force to Worgel, Austria to make contact with the 36th Infantry division and the 21st Corps. As the leading armored car was coming around a curve. They met three SS men on a motorcycle [with a sidecar] armed with burp guns and pistols. Before the armored car crew could get their 37 mm gun in action the krauts swung around behind the car and began to shoot at the crew, but by that time the following armored car came around the curve and began to shoot at the krauts. In the medley of the battle Sergeant Samuel Booker was wounded and Technician Fifth Grade Wylon Davis was also wounded. But again, we won out because the three Krauts were killed by Staff Sergeant John O. Weir, Technician Fifth Grade George Ogletree and Private First Class John Strayhorne.[13]

Other Nazis attempted to get away and according to Pritchard this caused an unusual situation:

> It was on this last dash that Lieutenant Stubbs's platoon fired on a railroad train moving from Innsbruck to what the Germans and Austrians aboard believed was safety. Lieutenant Stubbs shells halted the train, but the two cars he had selected as targets contained, not people, but the only liquor aboard the train, choice items that the Germans were attempting to evacuate. And the shells from his platoon riddled all but two or three of the several hundred cases of the choicest beverages in all Austria.[14]

All units came under battalion control again on the 6th, and the next day they moved off to Leutasch, Austria, where they set up the usual occupational duties, such as setting up guard posts and establishing roadblocks, and established a patrol in order to enact control. That same day the battalion buried the men killed in combat near Scharnitz: Keeby, Johnson, Williams, Harper, and Smith.

While the unconditional surrender of the German forces was signed, the 614th Tank Destroyer Battalion was in Leutasch. VE day was celebrated the following day, 8 May; on the 9th one more casualty was buried, James Parker, who had died when the halftrack overturned.

On 11 May B Company moved from Seefeld to Mosern, and on the 12th a big ceremony was held where Major General Anthony McAuliffe personally presented the third platoon of C Company with the Presidential Unit Citation for their actions in Climbach on 14 December 1944. The third platoon had suffered many casualties since then.

Also decorated were Captain Walter S. Smith, First Lieutenant Serreo S. Nelson, and Second Lieutenant Christopher J. Sturkey, who were presented with the silver star by McAuliffe.

Operations continued as normal for the rest of May, with the maintenance of vehicles and equipment and daily training exercises.

At Leutasch the battalion could finally come to rest. As the conflict was over and the noises of war faded away, the men had time for more pleasurable affairs. Passes and furloughs were granted and men went to Paris, London, Brussels, and the Riviera to see the highlights of each city. Contact with the local population went well, which at first were hesitant and reserved with the black soldiers. However, the troops won them over with their polite behavior. Previously the battalion had been on the move so much, there had been little time to get to know the local population. When this had ended the men also became acquainted with local women, which in turn led to an unfortunate rise in cases of venereal disease.[15] In July the 4th French Moroccan Mountain Division took over and the local population was saddened to see their American soldiers leave.[16] Despite combat in Europe being over, there were two more casualties to mourn, although it's unclear how the soldiers perished. Private First Class Alfred W. Nichols died on 22 June 1945 and Eddie L. Bond died on 19 July 1945.

On 10 July the battalion command post moved to Stafferied, Bavaria and moved on to Marseille nine days later. In Marseille it turned out that the battalion would be broken up and the men sent to service battalions. This indignation was prevented by the intervention of General McAuliffe and Colonel Chester Sargent; instead, the battalion was supposed to be sent to the Pacific or continue occupation duties.

Before the battalion could ship, however, two atom bombs were dropped on Japan. With Nagasaki and Hiroshima destroyed, the Japanese surrendered and the battalion could go home. On 10 September 1945 the remaining 450 men and twenty-five officers went back to Germany to assist with the occupation. The battalion command post was set up in Hofheim and the company stayed in schoolhouses, castles and barracks in nearby towns. The battalion was attached to the 79th Division and later the 1st Division and finally the XV Corps. More decorations were handed out and among others, Pritchard, Major Leroy Sample, Major Robert O'Leary and lieutenant Ormond Forte as well as five soldiers received the Bronze Star Medal.

Chapter 8

The 827th and the 679th Tank Destroyer Battalion

Two other segregated Tank Destroyer Battalions served in combat during the Second World War. Both units had vastly different experiences. The 827th Tank Destroyer Battalion used the M18 Hellcat and served in France, arriving at around the same time at the front as the 614th. They were pulled from the line a while afterwards. The 679th Tank Destroyer Battalion served with towed guns in Italy during the last few weeks of the war, fighting until the German surrender.

The 827th Tank Destroyer Battalion

Few army units have such a turbulent history as the 827th Tank Destroyer Battalion. They were the only segregated battalion that served in combat with self-propelled tank destroyers. It entered the line in December 1944 and was pulled from it in February, being used for other assignments until the end of the war in Europe. The 827th Tank Destroyer Battalion was activated on 20 April 1942 at Camp Forrest, Tennessee. The original cadre consisted of men from the 4th Cavalry Brigade and additional soldiers from other camps in America. Originally the unit was intended as a self-propelled battalion equipped with M3s, but the battalion was changed to a towed unit on 4 June 1943, thus deactivating the reconnaissance company, and changed to a self-propelled Tank Destroyer Battalion on 13 July 1943, establishing the reconnaissance company once more. The men were equipped with M10s, but the unit was converted to the M18 Hellcat before going into battle.

Just as the equipment was changed, so too changed the commanding officers of the unit. Captain Francis McKaine Oliver was the commanding officer at the inception of the unit, but he was replaced by Lieutenant Colonel Frederick Ryder on 13 May 1942. After attending Command and General Staff School, Major Oliver returned in August 1942. He was soon replaced by Major John W. Darrah, who assumed command on 25 September 1942. He was eventually replaced by Lieutenant Colonel George Hudson on 29 July 1943.

Lieutenant Joseph Awkard, who served under Hudson, remembered him as ill-suited for the task. Hudson openly stated that he hated Jews and would order him and the other officers out of their beds in the middle of the night to play craps with him. The same commander would have falsified the ratings of the black officers to dismiss them from the service. Awkard took action to prevent this and instead the officer was dismissed. After serving with the 827th, Awkard was moved to the 372nd Infantry Regiment and later the 614th Tank Destroyer Battalion.[1]

Hudson was relieved a month later by Lieutenant Colonel Herschel D. Baker on 25 August 1943. Baker stayed in command for almost a year, when he was replaced on 5 August 1944 by Lieutenant Colonel Philip J. VanderZwiep, who would command the 827th throughout its short combat history.

Initial training consisted of weapon familiarization and toughening the men. Training consisted of firing the M1917 Enfield and running an obstacle course every day, except for Sundays. Besides that, there were marches and the usual garrison duties. The unit left for Camp Hood on 2 September 1942 and arrived there two days later. At Camp Hood the men trained for twelve weeks at the Advanced Unit Training Center, where they were prepared for tactical duties and administrative training. On the firing range, the 827th established a good record with the .30 machine gun and was commended by Brigadier General Richard Tindall.

After completing its training at the Advanced Unit Training Center the battalion was used for educational purposes at Camp Hood until 21 July 1943, performing scenarios and tactical problems that the senior officers came up with. Several men and officers left the unit to establish the 649th Tank Destroyer Battalion, while a few officers left for other assignments. More men left the unit for the 649th in March. In return, for the first time, black officers were given to the battalion. On 20 April 1943 the battalion celebrated its first anniversary.

It left for Desert Training Center, California, on 18 September 1943. The last day of September 1943 the unit was inspected and rated unsatisfactory. Training continued and the unit was prepared to move overseas at the end of 1943, but in February 1944 another unit was sent in its place. In September the unit was once more held up, when two courts martial took place. Men in the unit had been involved in a shooting in Las Vegas, where three soldiers were wounded and another one killed. While this happened, the accompanying officers had been asleep in a nearby carpark.[2] In a separate incident referred to earlier, Dan Boswell murdered Staff Sergeant Otis Wilson.

Charles Branson, born on 11 November 1921, served in the 827th. When asked to describe his duties, he explained:

> I served in the 4th platoon of the 827th Tank Destroyer Battalion, Company C. We had M-18 tank destroyer vehicles, which was a medium tank chassis with a 76-milimeter gun mounted, a 30-millimeter machine gun in the assistant driver's section. [...] On the turret was mounted a .50 caliber machine gun. In the turret were three persons, the tank [...] destroyer commander, gunner, and assistant gunner. I served as the assistant gunner, who was to load on command and depose of the spent shells. [...] [The tank destroyer commander] would spot the target, and would call for the type of ammunition to be used. For instance, see he'd say one round HE or one round AP, and I,

as the assistant gunner, would remove that shell from the rack, which is an ammunition rack inside the turret, and place it into the breach block of the heavy weapon to be fired by the gunner.[3]

Despite the training of the men, the unit was ill prepared for combat. As Lee, the author of *The Employment of Negro Troops*, concluded in his studies:

> By August 1944 the 827th had already failed five Army Ground Forces battalion tests. It never did complete its training. Training in indirect fire, one of the chief requirements for certain of the secondary missions of Tank Destroyer Battalions, was waived entirely. During a round of training tests and retests in August 1944, the new battalion commander and most of his officers became firmly convinced that the unit's enlisted men could not and would not learn to maintain communications, read maps, or perform first and second echelon maintenance on their vehicles. Officers generally were convinced that their noncommissioned officers were incompetent and that no better noncommissioned officer material existed within the unit.[4]

Although the 827th wasn't fully prepared, it was decided to send the battalion overseas. While moving up towards the front, problems demonstrated themselves. There were several accidents, due to carelessness and the icy roads. Once at its destination, the vehicles needed to get immediate repairs.

The weather affected the open-topped vehicles harshly and if the men opened the escape hatch, the snow prevented them from escaping.[5] According to Branson, there were more problems,

> We weren't as mobile as we would hoped to have been because some advantages of the M-18 destroyer were its speed and

maneuverability. But in the heavy snow and ice, there was, at that time, you weren't able to, you couldn't generate much speed and you weren't as mobile or as maneuverable as you might have been, and that was scary when you find that your destroyer is slipping and sliding all over the place. Of course, I know it must have been an awful experience for the driver and assistant driver.[6]

It was attached to the 12th Armored Division, operating under the Seventh Army, and on 20 December 1944 one company was attached to the 714th Tank Battalion. While in their positions, the men of the 614th Tank Destroyer Battalion tried to help the 827th. However, problems were soon revealed when the men of the 827th left their vehicles unattended and built fires, in violation of their instructions, as this could reveal their positions to the Germans.

On 6 January 1945 the battalion received orders to join Task Force Wahl of the 79th Division. However, before the battalion could move out, two shootings occurred. An officer was accidentally shot during a scuffle while trying to resolve a disturbance, and in a separate incident a sergeant attempted to defend himself against a soldier who attacked him; rather than hitting his assailant however, he hit an innocent bystander.

Once these issues had been resolved, the unit moved out together with Task Force Wahl. The villages of Rittershoffen and Hatten were hotly contested, with the Germans holding the eastern parts and the Americans holding the western sectors, and it's here that the battalion first entered combat. Fighting was fierce, as described by Clarke and Smith:

> The battle [...] boiled down to a desperate infantry fight within the towns, with dismounted panzer grenadiers and armored infantrymen fighting side by side with the more lowly foot infantry. Almost every structure was hotly contested, and

Above left: Walter Coleman, 1945. (*Courtesy of the Coleman family*)

Above right: Lawrence Johnson and Bertha Mae Robinson after the war. (*Courtesy of the Johnson family*)

Right: Staff Sergeant Lawrence Johnson, 1945. (*Courtesy of the Johnson family*)

Men of the 614th with a halftrack in France, February 1945. (*Courtesy of the US Army Heritage and Education Center*)

Private Charlie Rattler poses with a bazooka, February 1945. (*Courtesy of the US Army Heritage and Education Center*)

This photograph of Private Charlie Rattler was published in *Yank: The Army Weekly*, February 1945. (*Courtesy of the US Army Heritage and Education Center*)

Private Charlie Rattler and unidentified soldier posing with a bazooka, February 1945. (*Courtesy of the US Army Heritage and Education Center*)

A camouflaged 3-inch gun of the 614th in firing position. (*Courtesy of the US Army Heritage and Education Center*)

An uncamouflaged firing position of the 614th. (*Courtesy of the US Army Heritage and Education Center*)

A soldier of the 614th holding a round for the 3-inch gun. (*Courtesy of the US Army Heritage and Education Center*)

Two NCOs and an officer kneel next to a 3-inch gun. (*Courtesy of the US Army Heritage and Education Center*)

Above and below: Motorcycle riders of the 795th Tank Destroyer Battalion, August 1942. (*Courtesy of the US Army Heritage and Education Center*)

Using the motorcycle as cover, this soldier of the 795th Tank Destroyer Battalion is well-protected, August 1942. (*Courtesy of the US Army Heritage and Education Center*)

The same soldier of the 795th Tank Destroyer Battalion but from another angle, August 1942. (*Courtesy of Ike Skelton Combined Arms Research Library Digital Library*)

A convoy of M3 Tank Destroyers and halftracks from an unidentified black unit driving across a field, date unknown. (*Courtesy of Ike Skelton Combined Arms Research Library Digital Library*)

An M3 Tank Destroyer crewed by black American soldiers, date unknown. (*Courtesy of the Library of Congress*)

A gun crew of the 614th Tank Destroyer Battalion load their gun during a training exercise in England before leaving for the real thing on the continent. L to R: Pfc. Aurbery Morris (Hobbsville, NC), Pfc. J. C. Heatem (Detroit, MI), Pfc. Robert B. Russell (Ashville, NC), 1st Lt. U.V. Watkins (Huntsville, TX), Pfc. Cebe Young (Ashville, NC), Pfc. James H. Mason (Williamston, NC). (*Courtesy of the National Archives and Records Administration*)

Soldiers of the 827th Tank Destroyer Division celebrate the closing of the Colmar Pocket, February 1945. (*Courtesy of the National Archives and Records Administration*)

Soldiers and vehicles go ashore on Omaha Beach, June 1944. Various Landing Ship Tanks have been grounded to unload their cargo. Ships like this brought the 614th Tank Destroyer Battalion from England to France. The blimps in the picture were let up by the 320th Barrage Balloon Battalion; the only segregated unit that went ashore on D-Day. (*Courtesy of the National Archives and Records Administration*)

B Company of the 614th Tank Destroyer Battalion. Note the pendant of the unit, which shows the M3 Tank Destroyer. (*Courtesy of Henry Anderson and tankdestroyer.net*)

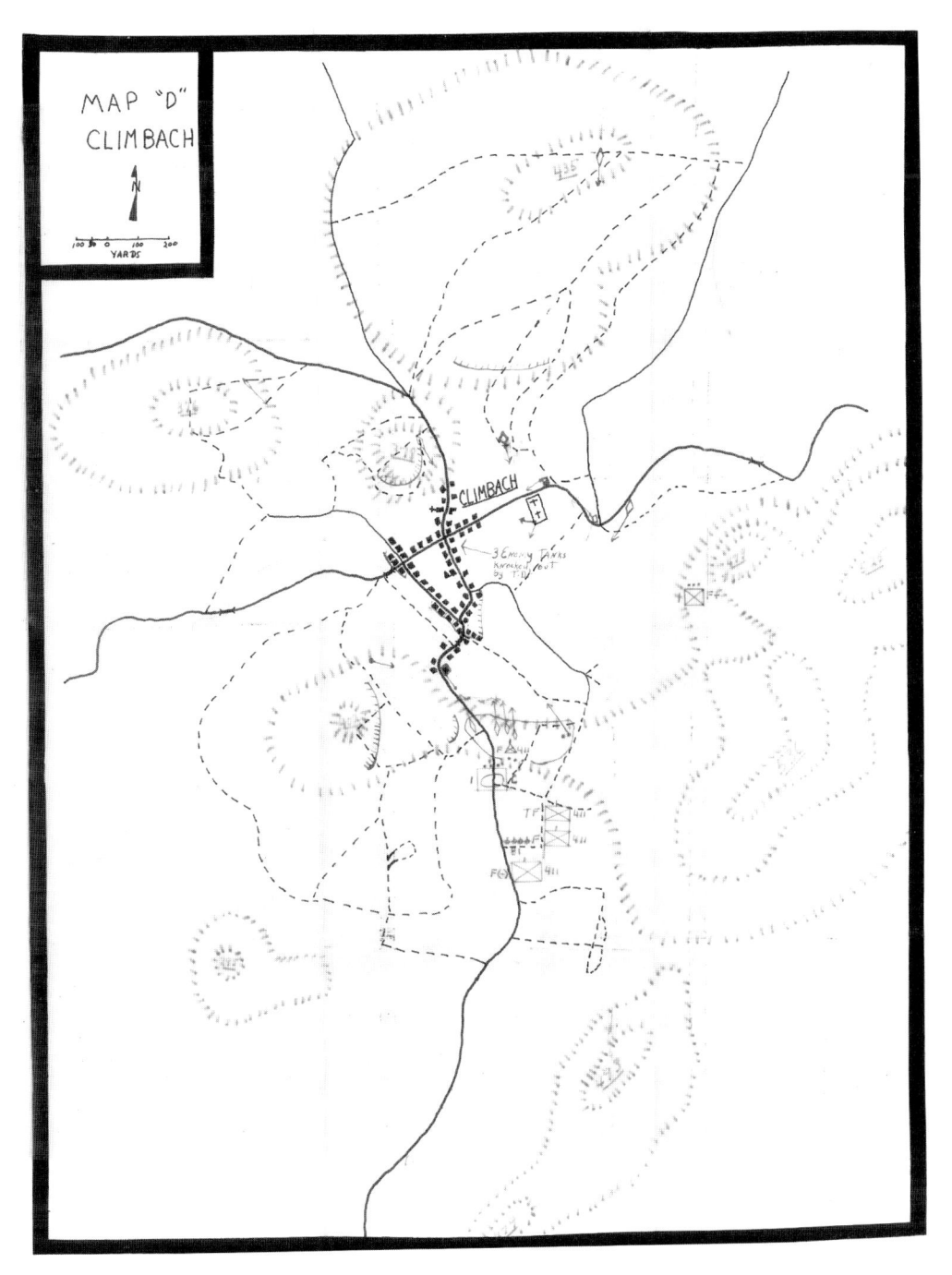

A situation sketch of the Battle of Climbach, 14 December 1944, by Willie Barrios. (*Map image courtesy of The Donovan Research Library, Fort Benning*)

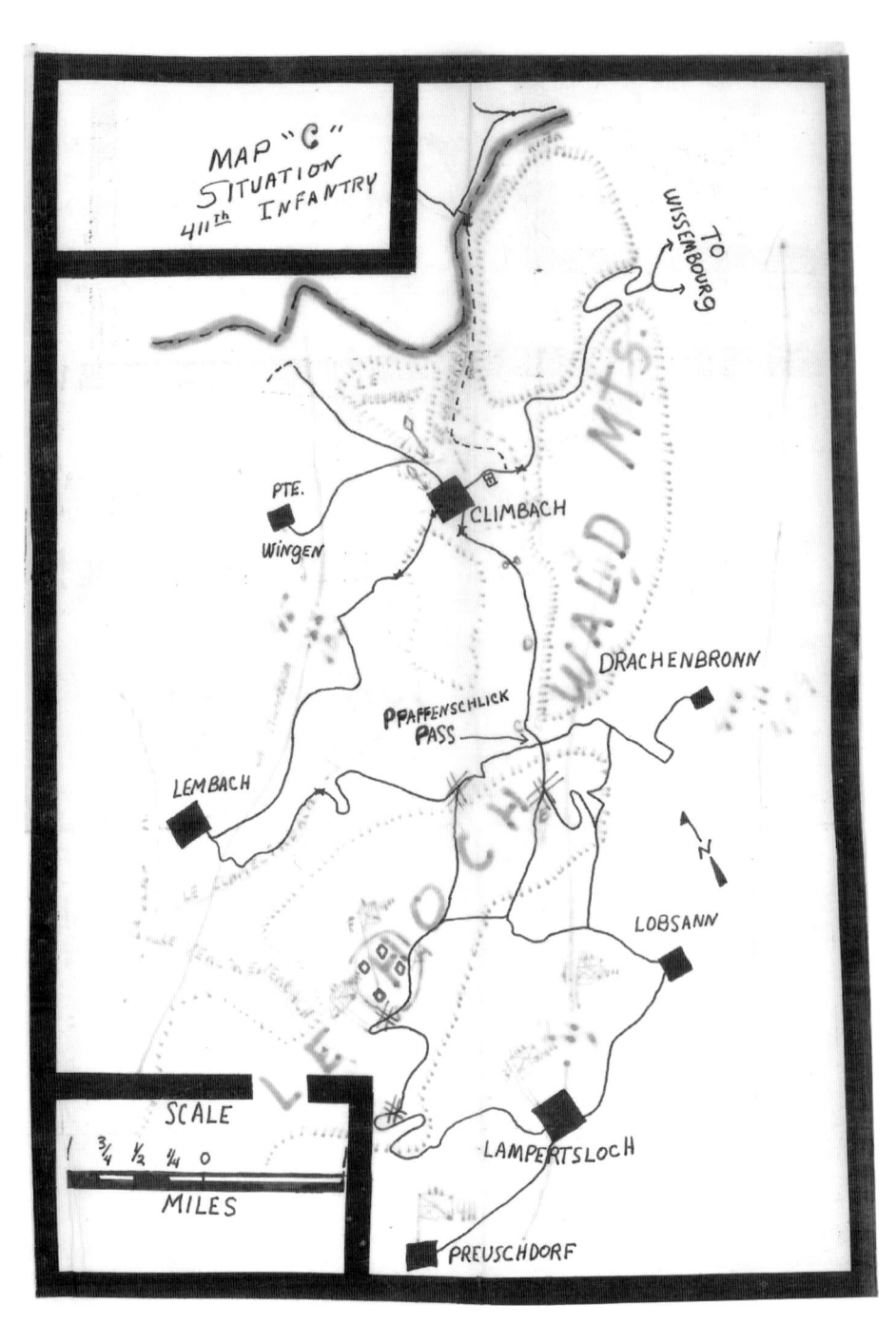

A sketch of the route of task force Blackshear on 14 December 1944, by Willie Barrios. (*Map image courtesy of The Donovan Research Library, Fort Benning*)

Above and below: An M18 Tank Destroyer of Company B, 827th Tank Destroyer Battalion, in France. (*Courtesy of World War Photos*)

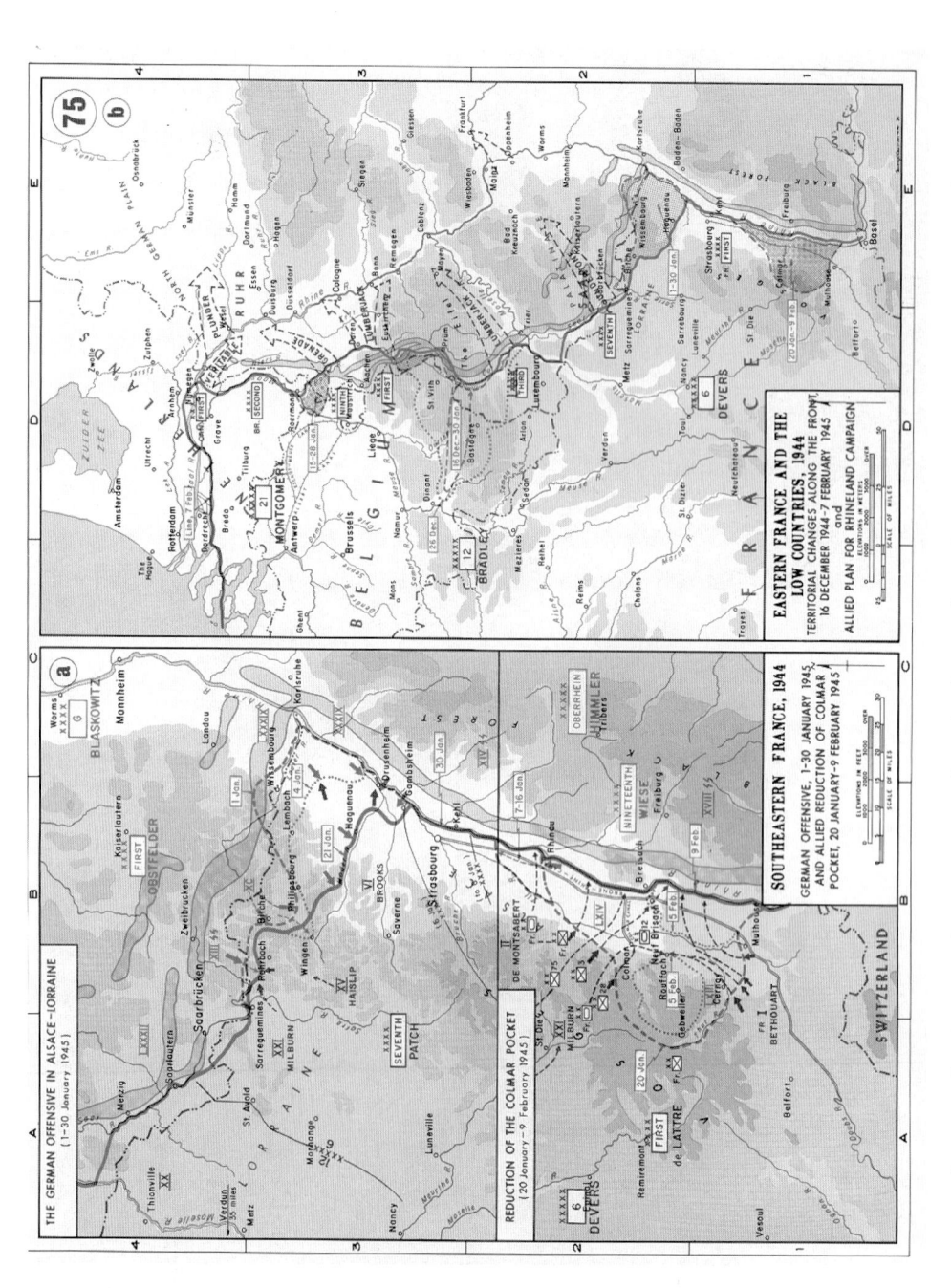

A map showing the German Operation Nordwind. The 614th Tank Destroyer Battalion served in the VI Corps. (*Courtesy of the United States Military Academy*)

Brigadier General Benjamin O. Davis (left) awarding the Distinguished Service Cross to Captain Charles Thomas, who is still recovering from his wounds received at Climbach. (*Courtesy of the Library of Congress*)

Lieutenant Charles Thomas. (*Courtesy of Joe Wilson Jr.*)

An M10 Tank Destroyer boarding an LST as several people look on. Ships like this transported the 614th Tank Destroyer Battalion to France. (*Courtesy of the National Archives and Records Administration*)

at the end of every day each side totaled up the number of houses and buildings it controlled in an attempt to measure the progress of the battle.

Often in the smoke, haze, and darkness, friendly troops found themselves firing at one another, and few ventured into the narrow but open streets, preferring to advance or withdraw through the blown-out interior walls of the gutted homes and businesses. Both sides employed armor inside the town, but the half-blind tank crews had to be protected by a moving perimeter of infantrymen and could only play a limited supporting role. In Hatten, even with strong infantry and artillery support, no German or American tanker dared push his vehicle around 'the bend'— a slight turn in the town's marginally wider main street that was covered by several anti-tank weapons from both sides.[7]

To make matters even more complicated, the town was strafed by Messerschmitt 262s, German jet-engine fighters. At that time, these fighters were faster than any plane the Allies had. Charles Branson saw one fly over, drop a bomb and disappear so fast, that he wondered where it had gone.[8]

In these circumstances, the 827th received its initiation into battle. Fighting was fierce and elements performed exceptionally, considering their training, but others performed rather poorly. The confusing combat hampered the 827th on all levels.

When in combat, it was unclear if the 827th was attached to the 813th or whether they were supposed to 'coordinate' together, or even be 'mixed in together'. The 813th Tank Destroyer Battalion assumed that the entire 827th was put under their control.[9] The tank destroyers were sometimes confused for tanks, although the open-topped vehicles weren't intended to be used as such. The men of the 827th expected to be given fire orders by their own officers, but these officers couldn't always be everywhere. Thus, the men didn't engage targets on their own, although an unexpected benefit of this was that the infantry officers assumed that the soldiers of the 827th engaged only good targets.

Other incidents contributed to the frustration about the 827th. An infantry officer threatened to shoot the entire crew of a M18 Hellcat if it didn't fire on a stuck German tank. Before they could fire, however, the Germans had recovered their vehicle and left. At another event an M18 was parked in a burning barn where mines were also stored. The crew, despite orders from their sergeant to drive out the vehicle, refused to do so. An infantry battalion commander ordered a lieutenant to fire upon the crew, although the lieutenant missed with his five shots. The issue was only resolved when infantry soldiers carried the mines out of the barn. The battalion commander then requested white crews for the tank destroyers. It is likely that such events intensified the racial problems that already existed.

During that time, there was heavy fighting going on in and around the villages of Hatten and Rittershoffen. Clashes were fierce between the German and American armor, as the two men of the 614th Tank Destroyer Battalion accidentally discovered. While attempting to locate a unit on their right flank, Lieutenant Burch and driver Magby got lost.

> 'Lieutenant, there ain't no GI's down this road,' [Magby told him. However Burch] insisted that he was right, while Magby kept insisting that he had never been on that road. As they arrived into a little town, all hell broke loose. They remained in the town only as long as was necessary, and when they left, exploding shells followed the Hell Kitten right down the road.[10]

However, while at Hatten, the platoon under command of second Lieutenant Robert F. Jones performed remarkably. On 10 January he and his four tank destroyers arrived in town. Engaging in combat,

> several of those colored boys really were wonderful, standing right there swapping punch for punch with Tiger tanks. Their

platoon leader, second Lieutenant [Jones] deserves the Silver Star. They found an abandoned M-10 tank destroyer there in good condition and decided to use it instead of one of their own. At our forward positions the main street bent so that they could not see German tanks coming – particularly at night. Jones took a machine-gun for signaling and laid it on the steps of the forward house, with a tank destroyer farther back and zeroed on the bend.

Jones was supposed to trip the machine-gun trigger with a string, but when the first Tiger poked its snout around the bend at night he just didn't have any sense. He got right out on the steps and held the trigger down, spraying the Tiger. The tank opened fire and blew the steps right out from under Jones, but he wasn't hurt. His gunner, Staff Sergeant Harry Johnson, of Philadelphia, opened fire and drove the Tiger back.[11]

Later in combat Johnson worked together with a white soldier of the 79th Infantry Division that had started a conversation with him. The soldier would call a target through the field telephone and Johnson would engage it.[12] This lasted well into the night and the platoon was praised by the 79th Infantry Division. Lieutenant Jones would receive the Silver Star in March, while in May Johnson was decorated with the Bronze Star Medal.

However, despite the praise, as Lee wrote: 'By 14 January, there existed a tangle of fact and opinion from which the unit was never to extricate itself.'[13] The resulting mess of opinion and fact stuck to the 827th. Crews of the 813th, trained in M10s, had taken over some of the M18s and an investigation into the 827th Tank Destroyer Battalion revealed several problems. The first investigation revealed errors and suggested that the unit be given additional training, that the men who refused to fight be tried, and that the noncommissioned officers be improved. However, another suggestion, made by the Commanding General of the VI Corps recommended that the unit be disbanded, except those who were worthy. During these investigations only the officers were interviewed, as well as officers from units that had fought alongside the 827th.

Another investigation was tried, where twelve enlisted men were questioned about their duties, revealing that they had sufficient knowledge of their tasks. When asked if they wanted to return to combat, only one man answered immediately that he wanted to do so. The others hesitated or answered that they would do as told.

A good example of Lee's fact and opinion is the trial of Beecher R. Nolan of second platoon, A Company. He was accused of desertion, because on 2 February 1945 he had intended to avoid combat with the Germans. On that day he had received orders from Sergeant Ray F. McAfee to be prepared to move out. The unit was to join elements of the 12th Armored Division in combat near Colmar. After hearing this, Nolan asked permission to play games in a barn and from there two different accounts started about what transpired.

According to McAfee, who had told them they would be moving out soon, Nolan had stood up when told of this, but didn't follow. When the others left, the accused's possessions in one of the vehicles left with them, but he remained behind. A while later, around 22:00, Nolan was still gambling in the barn and asked by First Sergeant Joe Oliver, also of A Company, if he had been left behind. Oliver's tank destroyer lacked a crew member, so Nolan could ride in it or he could hitch a ride in one of the other vehicles. When these tank destroyers left however, Nolan wasn't with them.[14]

At 01:30 Nolan was brought before Second Lieutenant James W. Detwiller, of the third platoon. Nolan explained that he had been asleep and no one had woken him up. On Detwiller's orders, Nolan was to join Technical Sergeant Jessie N. Simpson in a jeep that had been attached to A Company, but since it was late they decided to spend the night at the battalion command post.

The next day Nolan was ordered to join Private First Class Joe Flowers and again they set out for A Company. However, the two soldiers got lost on the way and returned to the battalion command post. The next day they set out for A Company once more, but again lost the way. When Flowers returned after asking for directions, Nolan was gone.[15]

According to Nolan, McAfee had participated in the gambling and during the game Nolan lost track of time. Afterwards he fell asleep and missed the ride, which he had been intended to catch. When he woke up after midnight, he reported to Lieutenant Detwiller on his own volition and he joined Joe Flowers in his jeep. However, since Flowers lost the way and was drunk, Nolan decided to leave him, declaring that it wasn't safe to drive with Flowers, as he had almost run into a roadblock.[16]

Afterwards he spent some time with the French Interior Forces and when he met up with black American soldiers from a construction company, they attempted to locate his unit, but were unable. He was turned over to the military police and eventually he was collected by soldiers from his unit.

McAfee denied the gambling and Flowers denied the drinking. Regardless of what exactly transpired, the moment Nolan decided to continue gambling when ordered to stand by, he failed to perform his duty. Nolan was sentenced to dishonorable discharge, forfeiting all payments and allowances and confinement to hard labor for life.[17]

Regardless of Nolan's intent, whether he wanted to gamble or wanted to get out of combat, it's an example of the problems that existed within the 827th. For the remainder of the war the unit served as a guard detail, but there were still issues. Private Willie R. Saxton, who deserted the unit in October 1945, was involved in selling possessions of the American army to French civilians, and was apprehended in January 1946 near Marseille. After his arrest, he claimed that he had been threatened and mistreated by the police. They forced him to make a statement, which was overturned in a later trial and his sentence reduced from eight to four years of confinement and dishonorable discharge.[18]

The battalion was designated as a surplus unit once the fighting in Europe was over, so it could return to the United States. However, a lot of the personnel had already been transferred to other units. On 1 December 1945 the battalion was deactivated.

The 679th Tank Destroyer Battalion

In the previous years there had been many ambitious plans for the tank destroyers. Originally the plan had been to establish 220 battalions as a counter against the Axis tanks. However, as the war progressed fewer Tank Destroyer Battalions were needed and on 26 June 1943, the last Tank Destroyer Battalion was activated at Camp Hood: the 679th. Like the 827th and 614th, it was a segregated unit, crewed only by black soldiers.

The men of the unit came from all parts of America. Reuben Yelding, born on 26 October 1922 and a former student at Tuskegee Institute of Agriculture and Technology, was one of them. His first semester was almost over when Pearl Harbor happened. He was taken into the service and completed basic training. His next destination was Camp Hood and, like many other soldiers throughout the American Armed Forces, he traveled there by train. However, he and other black soldiers were told to pull down the shades of their carriage windows to avoid offending the white people in the places through which they passed; the concern was that these white people might pelt the soldiers with rocks or fire rifles at them.

Another man to join the 679th was James Kirk, born 19 June 1920 in Portland, Oregon, although his family later moved St Paul, Minnesota. There he completed his high school and studied for two years at a college, before working for Northern Pacific Railroad dining cars from 1939 to 1942. He married in 1941, had two children and worked in various wartime industries before being drafted in April 1944.

After completing basic training at Camp Wheeler, Georgia, he was sent to Texas and assigned to the 679th Tank Destroyer Battalion, where he became a rifleman in the Headquarters Company, serving in one of the reconnaissance platoons. As a crewmember onboard of an M8 he explained his task and vehicle:

> The weapon was known as an M8. It was an armored [six]-wheel vehicle, a rubber tired vehicle which had a 37mm gun on it and a .50 caliber machine gun. […] We were in a reconnaissance platoon, which meant we spent most of our time ahead of the forces, directing shell fire. So many times, I could hear the German shells coming over our heads going back towards where the main company was stationed. […] There were three of us in there. The machine gunner, the driver and the rifleman. I was the rifleman; I carried a rifle. I knew how to fire the 37mm gun, but that wasn't my main job. The driver took care of the machine gun.[19]

While at Camp Hood, Kirk noticed how black soldiers from the southern states were often illiterate. He helped them with writing letters to their families. When he had any free time, he often stayed at the base. Other black soldiers did likewise, although some friends of James Kirk did go into town.

Reuben Yelding did go into town, but it presented a struggle, as they had to be back at a certain time. However, as they were ordered to the back of the bus, there wasn't always room to take all of them along. Once this issue rose to such a level that several of Yelding's squad members were arrested, although due to his rank Sergeant Yelding was exempted. He didn't accept this treatment and insisted that if his men were taken in, he had to be taken as well. Eventually the matter got so heated that senior officers became involved and due to this, according to Yelding, the places on the bus were assigned on a 'first come, first served' basis.[20]

The 679th Tank Destroyer Battalion started as a self-propelled unit, but in July 1943 they changed to a towed battalion. The reconnaissance company was deactivated and the battalion altered to fit the new table of organization. However, training started only in August, when enough men had been supplied for the battalion. The rest of 1943 was spent on training and there were a few minor transfers as men moved between the Tank Destroyer Battalions. Unlike other Tank Destroyer Battalions, the combat companies consisted of only two platoons with six guns each.[21]

Furthermore, the commanders themselves needed to be properly trained. On 7 February 1944, the battalion diary noted: 'Men improving daily,' and 'Biggest faults – lack of proper fire commands by gun commanders, improper citations by gun commanders.'[22] Training was soon started and along with it came inspections of the men and equipment. Things progressed well, although the battalion had suffered its first casualty on 16 December 1943, when Private Finger died of pneumonia.[23]

The disbandment of other tank destroyers affected the men and their morale, as they wondered why they should train if they too were going to be deactivated? In March 1944 the diary noted:

> Squad section + platoon tactics – men receptive. Officers showed they had knowledge, but were not enthusiastic in their presentation. Obstacles to training showed in report that officers + non-coms lacked aggressiveness and leadership. Apparent cause – low morale due to inactivation of colored units in the 24th Group. Feel that we probably will be next to get the axe.[24]

If it was any consolation, in the sideline was noted that the 'unit [was] judged satisfactory'. However, the fear was legitimate. In August 1943 the first segregated Tank Destroyer Battalion had been disbanded, the 649th, followed by the 828th and 846th, on 7 and 13 December 1943 respectively. On 27 March 1944 the 829th had been disbanded. The next month the 795th, the unit that had been the longest in training, was disbanded and on 1 May 1944 the 646th had been disbanded. Indeed, the rapid disbanding of the African American tank destroyer units, partially the result of the changing war circumstances, must have discouraged the men of the 679th from conducting their training and exercises. The 795th and 846th were the first segregated tank destroyer battalions to be created. However, they had both been deactivated, despite their progress. Other segregated tank destroyer battalions, which were further along in training, were now being deactivated. Since the 679th was the last tank destroyer battalion to be activated, and thus had progressed the least in their training, they feared that they would sooner or later 'get the axe' as well.

Out of the 106 Tank Destroyer Battalions activated, thirty-five were disbanded before the war. A disproportionate number of eight segregated tank destroyer battalions were among the outfits deactivated. The second to last unit to be activated, the white 672nd Tank Destroyer Battalion, had been converted to an Amphibian Tractor battalion on 15 April 1944 and set off for the Pacific in September 1944. There they carried troops to the beaches and fought until the end of the war. While they were transported across the ocean, the 679th continued their training.

Despite the feelings of the men, the training continued and in May 1944 another tragedy struck the battalion. On the 14th Eddie Knight, of C Company, drowned in the Leon river, Texas, and his body was recovered two days later. He was the second casualty of the battalion; it was a grim reminder of what was to come. On 18 May wounded men from a nearby hospital were brought over to share their battle experiences with the new troops. Hopefully the stories prevented the untested troops from suffering similar injuries.[25]

In July and August firing tests were conducted by the battalion and these were passed satisfactory. More tests were conducted and soon the battalion would be moved overseas. However, not all was well yet. On 15 and 16 November, the indirect fire test was rated unsatisfactory. On 25 November, a new commander arrived to take over the battalion: Lieutenant Colonel Donald McGrayne, who had previously overseen the 659th Tank Destroyer Battalion, which would be disbanded in December 1944.

On 9 December the advance detachment left for overseas. A small group of men was sent ahead of the main force in order to secure proper accommodation and supplies when the rest of the battalion and their equipment arrived. The rest of the unit went by train to Camp Shanks, New York, on 22 December and arrived there at Christmas. They were just in time to enjoy an excellent Christmas supper. New Year was celebrated there and on 7 January 1945 the battalion was notified of their imminent shipment. Three days later they would board the ship that would carry them across the sea, the USS *Monticello*.

The USS *Monticello* (AP-61) was a troopship that had been acquired by the American government on 16 April 1942, after the ship had been interned in Brazil. The ship had been previously named the *Conte Grande* and sailed under the Italian flag between South America and Italy. After being acquired, it was converted into a troop ship and began carrying passengers across once again; this time however, the people on board were armed to the teeth and ready for battle.

As the engines churned, they brought the men closer to the war. On 21 January 1945 the troops disembarked at Le Havre, France, and went by truck to camp Lucky Strike, arriving early the next day. Camp Lucky Strike, located near Saint-Sylvian, was the biggest of the several 'cigarette' camps established by the Americans near Le Havre, where the American troops were put ashore. The large tent camps were named after cigarette brands for the familiarization of the American troops, as well as keeping their exact locations secret from the Germans.

At the camp the battalion were reunited with the advance detachment, which had gone over to England before being sent to France. This wouldn't be the only incident where elements or belongings of the battalion were sent to the wrong destination.

On 22 February the battalion, without the vehicles, left Camp Lucky Strike and went through Le Havre towards Marseille. The vehicle convoy left on 24 February and went straight to Marseille, where they arrived two days later. On the 28th the first group of the battalion embarked a ship and was transported to Livorno, or Leghorn as the Americans knew it, in Italy. The harbor was located about twenty kilometers [around twelve miles] to the south of Pisa. On the same day that the first group arrived, 1 March, the second group embarked in Marseille and went after them, arriving the next day.

On 6 March the battalion was attached to IV Corps and the 92nd Infantry Division, one of the two segregated infantry divisions. The 92nd had been fighting in Italy since the summer of 1944. In early 1945 the division had attempted to seize the town of Massa, some forty kilometers [twenty-five miles] to the north of Pisa; they failed in part because of the hostile guns on the Punta Bianca. It was the principal defense point of La Spezia, where there was an important harbor. Tanks, self-propelled guns and AA guns were used by the Germans to hold the peninsula.

At Punta Bianca elaborate defenses were established, which included what appeared to be six captured Russian 152 mm guns, designated 15.2 cm KH.433/1(r). Due to materiel shortages and large quantities of captured weapons, such weapons were often pressed into service. The 152 mm guns were often used for coastal defense in Italy, France, or elsewhere. To these were added four 128 mm emplaced coastal guns and 90 mm dual purpose guns.[26] At Punta Bianca, the guns were put in entrenched positions, where concrete emplacements and closing doors enabled the defenders to open fire at their convenience and retreat before retaliatory fire could strike them. They were set up in batteries of three or four guns, obscured by a smoke generator, which were designated by the Americans: ASB, ALB, AMB, and could hold off the American forces, whose counterbattery fire was wasted on pounding against closed doors.

These powerful guns hampered the advance of the Americans in the area and a plan was created to neutralize them. During the February assault, the guns of Punta Bianca had wreaked havoc among the 92nd Infantry Division. According to Dennette Harrod, a Lieutenant of the 366th Infantry regiment: 'The sound of gunfire from Punta Bianca never ceased and the sound and sight of the heavy shells falling and exploding among us was terrifying.'[27] The attacks in February were halted, which included defenses of the Punta Bianca guns.

Serving in Italy was a pleasant surprise for the soldiers, and James Kirk remembered it fondly:

> Most beautiful [country] I've ever seen in my life. Everything over there is … most of these structures are made of marble. It's just beautiful. I remember once we were guarding a tunnel. It was right on the Aegean Sea, and every morning I would get up and go out swimming in the ocean. I know I was bitten by a jellyfish one day. My leg was swollen. But the place was so beautiful. All over Italy. [...] I had a chance to go to the Tower of Pisa, which was very interesting.[28]

He could communicate with the Italians because he picked up a quite a bit of the language. The Americans got along well with the Italians, and the fondness of the Italians towards Americans extended towards everything they brought, they were interested in everything and trade was common. As Kirk described it:

> Anything that you had, they would buy. Food, cigarettes. [...] We had one incident where one of [our soldiers] had buried a whole Jeep. He was going to sell it. I don't know if they ever sold it or not. But he buried it so he could sell it later.[29]

Reuben Yelding had similar pleasant experiences in Italy and France. He remembered how the black soldiers were regarded as heroes, just like the white soldiers, but this changed with the import of American segregation. The people became more distant when white Americans told the local civilians that the blacks weren't to be treated as equals.

It was into this situation that the 679th arrived, deploying their towed guns in the mountainous terrain, and on 18 March: '[we] fired our first round in anger at the enemy.'[30] However, despite being on the retreat on all fronts, the Germans hadn't surrendered yet and the war was bitterly fought. To support the Allied advance, the battalion conducted several fire missions.

For the advance, the 92nd had to take the town of Massa. This town could either be approached by an attack over the hills or along the coastal plain. In February, an attempt along the coastal plains against these strong defenses had been made. An Allied attack from the south on the mountains would bypass these heavily defended positions on the coast and force the enemy to abandon them.[31]

On 5 April, they fired in preparation for the start for the operation of the 370th Infantry Regiment. There was no return fire from the enemy and no rounds fell short. However, the 370th failed to reach its objectives for the first two days, although during these actions, First Lieutenant Vernon Baker would distinguish himself in combat; he killed nine enemy soldiers, and took out three machine gun positions, a dugout, and an observation post. The next day he volunteered to lead his battalion in their advance up the mountain. These actions would earn him the Distinguished Service Cross, which would later be upgraded to the Medal of Honor.

On 11 April the battalion received an unexpected – and very welcome gift. Twenty-four bags of mail arrived, which had been delayed in France. Just like the advance detachment, there had been a mistake and it took longer than usual before the men received their mail.

The 679th was given a special assignment on 14 April – they had to silence the guns at Punta Bianca. There had been several failed attempts since 2 April, but the damaging fire of the Punta Bianca bunkers continued. For four days the bunkers were bombed, but only one casemate was blown open. On 11–12 April, four fighter-bomber missions were attempted; on one occasion a bomber mission of twenty-four planes attacked the bunkers.[32] The bombing missions were unsuccessful because they took too long to strike their target, and the guns would be hidden behind their blast doors again.

Now the 92nd Infantry Division had advanced enough that the guns came in range of the 3-inch guns of the 679th Tank Destroyer Battalion. At a range of approximately nine kilometers [six miles], each company aimed at one of the three targets and stood by to deliver indirect fire. The companies also possessed the ranges of the other two batteries, so that they could swiftly fire at any target that presented itself. To ensure a quick response, a direct link was established between the platoons and the observation post. A round was always kept in the chamber of each 3-inch gun and a gunner remained at the lanyard.

Special codenames were assigned for the specific targets: Sugar, Love, and Mike; as soon as one of the codenames was called, a company would fire five rounds at their designated target. There was an additional codename: Geronimo; when this was called, all companies would engage their targets with five rounds. This meant within forty-five seconds of calling a target, a round would strike that battery. The smoke generator of the enemy was destroyed twice, and to boost the firing power of the Tank Destroyer Battalion an 8-inch howitzer was assigned to help neutralizing the Punta Bianca guns.[33] Although the batteries weren't destroyed, the eastern batteries ceased firing on 19 April. The guns on the western side continued to fire. Although it had taken a while to neutralize the hostile guns, they had achieved their task. The 92nd Infantry Division had been held up by these batteries, allowing other defenders time to fortify their positions.[34]

Other targets also fell victim to the guns of the 679th. A convoy of eight trucks was engaged and had to leave two vehicles behind, while the rest sped away. On 15 April a self-propelled 88mm gun took up position at the extreme end of the La Spezia peninsula and fired at the observation post through which the tank destroyers received their fire directions. The gun fired over and under their intended target, but didn't hit it. In reply the entire 679th Tank Destroyer Battalion fired back. Swiftly the vehicle was set on fire, which exploded when the ammunition cooked off. A total of 144 rounds had been fired during this fire mission.

On 16 April a platoon of six guns were pulled from the line and used in Aulla. These were put in position on Mount Grigola to fire on the network of roads near Aulla. The men slipped into positions on top of a ridge with their guns during the night; the cliffs descended steeply on both sides, which meant the men were visible on the skyline when they fired, allowing the enemy to return fire with mortars and artillery. According to their own estimations, 250 mortar and 400 88 mm rounds were fired back by the Germans. The platoon suffered three casualties: two men were killed and one wounded, but they continued to fire.

Between 17 and 24 April, 7,220 rounds were fired on Aulla. According to partisans, and judging by the wreckage left behind by the Axis forces, the action had been very effective. Aulla fell on 25 April 1945, when it was taken by the 442nd Infantry Regiment, a unit made up of Japanese American troops that had been attached to the 92nd Infantry Division in March that year.

On 14 April casualties were sustained by the battalion. Technician Fifth Grade Hulie Nix and Technician Fifth Grade Lively Leftwich were wounded in action at the HQ rear. Two days later Leftwich would die of his wounds. On 19 April Sergeant Louis Newton of B Company was wounded by shell fragments at 16:50, he died from these injuries just eighty minutes later. On 22 April, Lieutenant R.A. Smith, of C Company, was killed in action and the next day Private John O. Lane, of B Company, was struck by the recoil of the 3-inch gun and died from his injuries.

Although the Third Reich was crumbling, some troops held out and several coastal defense batteries were still offering resistance in Genoa. On 26 April, the batteries had even fired on the city, causing several casualties. By 28 April, the Monte Maro battery, which consisted of two 381 mm guns, three 152 mm guns, and four 90 mm guns, still hadn't surrendered.[35] Negotiations with the remaining German troops to convince them to give up their struggle had failed.

To force the Germans into submission, A Company would be put in position in front of them. After midnight on 28 April, Captain Kenneth B. Stark, company commander of A Company, was given the mission of reconnoitering the places he would put his guns. It was a dark night with no moon and steady rain. The streets were so narrow the halftracks could barely pass through and at the last turn the guns needed to be manhandled into position. From there they could deliver direct fire on the emplacements. Machine guns were also deployed and aimed at the gun ports. The coastal guns couldn't be depressed far enough to return fire and at 14:30 the battery surrendered.

For the 679th there would be no more combat, but casualties were still sustained. On 29 April, Frank Allen died during an accident; James Kirk told about this and another incident:

> I remember one young fellow who was the driver [Frank Allen], he was cleaning the .50 caliber machine gun and he was standing in front of it and moving the gun around. The Sergeant who was in charge got in the vehicle and stepped on a pedal, and there was still one round in the chamber of the .50 caliber machine gun and it caught him right in the head. Splattered his head everywhere.[36]
>
> [Another incident was when] we had one very studious soldier in our group that was blown up in the library. They had ammunition stored in the library and they accidentally blew it up, and he was blown up in the library of all places.[37]

The incident Kirk refers to happened on 18 July, when stored enemy mines exploded in Viareggio. A nearby Red Cross Club was caught in the blast and twenty-four soldiers, twenty-three black, one white, perished. Among the twenty-four soldiers who died, there were three members of the 679th Tank Destroyer Battalion: Sergeant William E. Forster and technicians Fifth Grade James Alford and Clarence Smith.[38]

On 2 May the German troops in Italy surrendered and Hitler was declared dead. Almost a week later, on 8 May, the war in Europe ended. Most of the troops were given a day off on 11 May and many men attended churches within the vicinity. On 15 May, when moving to Bolzanetto to the north of Genoa, a halftrack and 3-inch gun overturned and injured seven men. The next day the men watched the movie *Two Down and One to Go!* a documentary short film explaining that although Hitler and Mussolini had been defeated, the war in the Pacific wasn't over.[39]

However, the 679th Tank Destroyer would take no part in this combat. For the 679th, the cessation of combat meant that they would be used to guard abandoned hostile munition depots, train, and be used as a show of force to the Italians. Throughout its duration in combat, between 18 March and 2 May 1945, a total of 47,404 shells had been fired. The unit was eventually shipped back to the United States and disbanded on 27 October 1945.

Chapter 9

The Dusk of the Tank Destroyers

The end of the 614th Tank Destroyer Battalion

As the war was ending, it became obvious that the original tank destroyers were nearly obsolete. Instead of the envisioned 220 battalions, the force was downsized throughout the war and only sixty-one tank destroyer battalions served in combat. Doctrinal confusion, changes in weaponry and unrealistic expectations plagued the branch throughout its existence.

Although the guns were versatile, they didn't excel in their task. Tanks, which the tank destroyers were supposed to eliminate, themselves became the primary means to destroy other tanks. Patton was proven right in his prediction that 'the tank destroyer is predestined to become just another tank'.[1] In terms of firepower the M10 and 3-inch tank destroyers were outmatched, and improved communications led to better cooperation between tanks. The latest tank destroyer, the M36, was mounted with a 90 mm gun, the same as the M26 Pershing tank. In both offensive and defensive warfare, tanks outclassed the tank destroyers. Among senior commanders there was confusion about the tank destroyer doctrine and their employment in combat. Perhaps most damning of all was that the supposed threat, a mass assault of German tanks, failed to materialize. However, interest in lightly armored, but heavily armed vehicles remained. On 10 November 1945 the Tank Destroyer Center was discontinued and less than a year later, on 1 November 1946, the last Tank Destroyer Battalion, the 656th, was deactivated in Camp Campbell, Kentucky.

Towed tank destroyers proved in particular to be an antiquated concept, despite numbering half of the battalions. They couldn't compete with the self-propelled guns, which could rapidly move, fire, and relocate. The towed weapons needed to be manhandled into position or moved by a prime mover. Although the gun shield offered some protection, the crew was much more vulnerable than their comrades in the self-propelled variants. The fighting in the Ardennes made it painfully obvious that the towed units were superseded by their more mobile counterparts.[2]

In North Africa the towed guns were favored by senior commanders, as the terrain suited the combat. They could be dug in, exposing little of themselves, whereas the higher profile of the self-propelled variants made them more vulnerable to retaliation, although they couldn't be moved in combat. The desert also allowed combat to take place at a greater range than in Europe. Infantry posed a lesser risk, because in Europe they could entrench themselves in cities and villages. However, this clashed with the Tank Destroyer doctrine, which encouraged them to strike at the enemy, reposition, and strike again. The panzers encountered in 1942 and 1943 in Africa were less armored than the hostile tanks encountered in 1944 or 1945.

Despite being inadequate, the tank destroyers offered a reply to the supremacy of the tanks, which weren't invincible. The mobile anti-tank guns became a component of the infantry division, while the artillery was given the task of anti-tank defense and the Armored Force took over some parts of the tank destroyer doctrine. The tank destroyers themselves ceased to exist.[3]

Overall, the tank destroyers were a rushed reply to the threat from the German armored divisions. In this they suffered from all plans that are made in haste. The tank destroyer tactics were impractical, as the circumstances in which they could be used almost never arose. This was either due to a lack of German armor, or the lack of knowledge about tank destroyer tactics, which resulted in tank destroyers being employed incorrectly by the senior commanders. For example, tank destroyer companies might be spread out along the front, so that if the enemy made an armored breakthrough, they couldn't be used effectively. However, this could also be an adaptation to the circumstances, as the German commanders were less willing to commit large scale armored forces.

Just as the tank destroyers weren't needed anymore once the war was over, so too fewer soldiers were needed. Men were transferred to other units or sent back to the United States. One of the people that was transferred was Frank S. Pritchard:

HEADQUARTERS 614th
TANK DESTROYER BATTALION
Hofheim, Germany 16 October 1945

To the officers and enlisted men of the 614th Tank Destroyer Battalion: After having served with you for exactly two years, I am about to be relieved of command and return to the United States.

I repeat here what I have said many times before, that I am proud to have served with you and to have had a place in a military organization that made such a wonderful record. I hope that, in the future, I hear of the wonderful things you have done as civilians just as I have often heard from others of your wonderful work as soldiers.

You have done a wonderful job.

Frank S. Pritchard
Lieutenant Colonel, Infantry.[4]

Major Richard K. James became the new commanding officer in October, replaced by Major Floyd E. Rees later that same month. What remained of the battalion eventually went back to America on the ship SS *Mahanoy City Victory*, and was deactivated on 31 January 1946 at Camp Kilmer, NJ.

The Dusk of the Tank Destroyers 139

However, it wouldn't be the end. After the fall of Japan, Korea became independent again, although it was divided in a northern and southern sphere of influence. The north was occupied by the Soviet Union, while America occupied the south. Local troubles and diplomatic conflicts caused tension over the American occupation and a conflict loomed. To prepare for a potential war, a number of units were reactivated. One of them was the 614th Tank Destroyer Battalion on 30 June 1946, in the same place where they had fought their pretend wars for so long: Camp Hood, Texas. Their new commander was Lieutenant Colonel Delmer P. Anderson. This time the destroyers of tanks were equipped with the self-propelled M18 instead of the towed 3-inch guns.

The unit received its first soldiers the next day, when re-enlisted soldiers arrived from the Overseas Replacement Depot, Camp Kilmer, New Jersey, who were originally supposed to go to Europe. Two more groups of 280 men arrived on 2 July, they were joined on the 6th by another two groups consisting of 171 men each, of which one group was made up of Selective Service inductees. On 11 August more men arrived, again from Camp Kilmer and again Selective Service inductees. On 19 August, Lieutenant Colonel Henry W. Allard assumed command and replaced Lieutenant Colonel Delmer Anderson. Allard had previously served with the 2nd Armored Division and later served as a commander of a prisoner of war camp. In the third week of July the soldiers already present started a thirteen-week individual weapons training program. However, the unit didn't last long, because on 1 November the 614th was deactivated yet again.

While the journey of the 614th had started on 25 July 1942 in Camp Carson, Colorado, it had taken the soldiers throughout America, across the ocean to Europe, where they saw England, France, Germany, and Austria before returning to the U.S. Pritchard reflected on the unit's performance:

> Looking back at the record, what had this battalion done? First, it again proved to the world that the negro soldier could and

would fight. Other battalions had done more in this war than the 614th, but the 614th had done, and done well, everything that had been asked of it. It had won the esteem and affection of the 103d Infantry Division, with which it was associated for so long. It had won the respect of corps and army commanders and their staffs. It had merited a visit from the Commanding General of the Seventh Army, Lieutenant General Alexander M. Patch, who had watched its record develop: Its exploits had been publicized in the pages of *Time, Yank, The Stars and Stripes*, and many other magazines and newspapers. It had also proved that, when men demonstrate their worth, that racial troubles are largely ended, and the colored man is accepted. No friendship could be stronger between groups of men than the friendship that existed between the colored gamecocks of the 614th TDs and the white officers and soldiers of the 103d Division.[5]

The men of the 614th had experiences that were common among U.S. soldiers regardless of race or creed in the Second World War, such as eating their food out of helmets or discussions about life, survival, and death. Lawrence Johnson once posed the question to a chaplain as to why some men got killed, while others survived. The chaplain answered that those left behind hadn't fulfilled their mission yet. This wasn't merely in a military sense, but also concerned life in general.

Indeed, the battalion had demonstrated that black soldiers were equally as capable of fighting and dying as their white compatriots. While the men were originally intended to thwart the blitzkrieg of the Germans, there were few tanks for them to destroy in 1944 and 1945. However, in the fight against Jim Crow, they did destroy the prejudices that some white Americans held.

The soldiers of the 614th had won the esteem of the 103d Division, with whom they had traveled and shared so much while moving across Europe. They participated in the triumphs and losses of the division, such as Schillersdorf, where half of the third platoon of C Company was captured, or in the nightly withdrawal on 21 January 1944. However, they were there too when the 103d Division linked up with the 88th Infantry Division, linking the Seventh and Fifth army on the Austrian-Italian border.

Equally remarkable is what happened to Lieutenant George Mitchell, who wasn't just captured once, but twice. After being captured, he was sent to the officers' camp XIII-B at Hammelburg.[6] The camp had once been used as a training site, before it was used to harbor captured soldiers. There were two camps, Stalag XIII-C for enlisted men, where some of the 614th men were detained, and another one for officers: Stalag XIII-B.

In spring 1945 the camp was getting full, with prisoners coming in from other camps that were too close to the front lines, and recently captured American soldiers from the Battle of the Bulge. One of the prisoners who had recently arrived was Lieutenant Colonel John K. Waters, the son-in-law of General Patton, who had been captured in February 1943 in Tunisia. At the camp the conditions were bad, as there was a lack of food and heating. There were over 1,500 Americans at the camp, as well as 3,000 Serbians. At the camp for enlisted men there were 5,000 men.

In March the 4th Armored Division was around 100 kilometers [60 miles] away from the camp and Patton came up with a daring plan to strike deep into the enemy's rear and liberate the camp. The prisoners, estimated around 300, could be brought back with the task force. The attempt was hastily planned, resulting in errors and oversights. In total, sixteen tanks, twenty-eight halftracks, and thirteen other vehicles carried the eleven officers and 303 men, dubbed 'Task Force Baum', after their commander Abraham Baum, left in the evening of 26 March and fought their way to the camp, running into counterfire and being forced to reorient along the road. On the 27th the column arrived at the camp, although John Waters was shot by a German soldier when approaching the task force, and the Serbians were fired upon by the Americans, mistaking their uniforms for the German feldgrau.[7]

More problems arose; instead of taking back an estimated 300 prisoners, there were too many men. For a while Mitchell and the others were liberated, but during the trip back, the men ran into Hetzers, German tank destroyers, and the column disintegrated. Mitchell was captured again, and later marched to the east by his captors to stay out of Allied hands, eventually moving to Nuremberg.

As he was leaving Nuremberg, the city was attacked by American airplanes. During this raid forty American officers were killed, while another forty were wounded. Mitchell was the only black American among them and suffered a head injury. Despite being wounded, he was forced to move on. Medics offered assistance as best as they could on the way, but couldn't offer much. He was eventually liberated on 3 May 1945 by the 4th Armored Division and the 86th Infantry Division when he was fifty kilometers from Munich. After being liberated, he was sent to Rheims, France, where he could recover, before being shipped to the United States on the hospital ship *George Washington*.[8]

Back home

While the men of the 614th established good relations with the soldiers of the 103d Infantry Division, there were only limited attempts at integrating the Armed Forces. The few white soldiers that did fight alongside African Americans had a favorable opinion, as racial prejudices were challenged and overcome under fire. However, due to the small size of the integration and the few black American combat units, most white soldiers remained unchallenged in their world views. As Christopher Sturkey encountered when he came home:

> When I returned to the States I went down to the defense plant where my wife worked, to surprise her. I had on all of my paraphernalia: battle stars, campaign ribbons, the works. I was early so thought I'd have a hamburger at the White Tower around the corner. I ordered it and the counter girl told me, 'We don't serve niggers in here.' Now this is where I thought

> the battle should have begun, in all of the little places where little people get their pleasure in telling us we are not good enough to eat in, drink in, shop in, the whole bit, their little places of business. Here I was supposed to be some kind of a hero returned from the war and the first thing I hear from some poor white hash-slinging bitch I've been fighting for, is 'We don't serve niggers in here.'[9]

An unpleasant surprise awaited the men, as not all were given the hero's welcome they had hoped for. They had strived for a double victory, fighting against the Axis and for equal rights, but the circumstances to which they returned seemed to have remained the same.

Pritchard continued his career with the *Lansing State Journal* as a reporter and as an editor. Besides a career in the media, he continued to serve his country in the army reserve, spending a total of forty-two years in service. He retired from the *State Journal* in 1964 and died in 1975.[10]

George Mitchell returned to his hometown of Gary, Indiana, in September 1945. He returned to his wife and 13-month-old son, whom he had seen mere days after his birth. He had a silver plate installed in his skull, because of his injuries. After the war he stayed in the service, although he spent a year-and-a-half recovering. He eventually managed to rise to captain and left the service on 5 April 1950.[11]

After the war in Europe was resolved Joseph Awkard went to the Philippines, deploying with a quartermaster unit. In Manilla the segregation was a lot stricter than in Europe, and the black and white soldiers hadn't fought side by side. Since there were few opportunities to relax, the black officers started a club called the Cosmocrat, where Awkard met Julita Castro, whom he married. He would become the first black man to receive a PhD from the University of Virginia. They moved to Tallahassee, Florida, where he worked at the Florida A&M University. He passed away in 2006.

Lawrence Johnson reenlisted after the war, so that he could spend time in Europe, which he would never be able to do otherwise. He even went skiing in the Alps. He eventually returned to the US and attended college, majoring in Architectural Engineering. As an architect he designed and built houses and churches. He married Bertha Mae Robinson in 1949, and had two children. He encouraged them to keep learning and studying throughout their lives, so they would grow as individuals. While working as an engineer for the army in St Louis, Missouri, he always ate lunch at his desk; he was the only black engineer and none of his colleagues would eat with him. This only changed when he got a Jewish coworker who would eat with him; with the passing of time these habits gradually changed. In later years, he spoke at his grandson's school about his wartime experiences. He was involved in local civic and church activities, being an Elder at the time of his death in 2010.

Now that the war was over, the men of the 614th went back to their old lives, changed by the experiences in Europe. Walter S. Coleman returned to New York and worked there as a train conductor. Later in life, he moved to North Carolina, where he eventually became a minister. He passed away on 15 May 2018. Lun Arrington returned home after the war and worked as a mechanic. Later he worked as an iron worker in a factory. He passed away in 2009.

Alger Gillespie met Rosa Stroud, with whom he lived in Sacramento. He finished his high school education after the war and studied sociology at the California State University, Sacramento. He earned a license for a private practice in marriage, family and child counseling. His service had given him a lot of self-confidence.[12]

Near the end of the war Charles Branson, of the 827th Tank Destroyer Battalion, was guarding prisoners in Arles, France, where he did outside security. Two days after the war ended, a commanding officer ordered him and other soldiers to dispose of any foreign weapons they had acquired. They were told to tag the weapons with their name and serial number and put them in the designated box, so they could be returned later. Branson put in two Berettas, thinking: 'I've come this far. I don't want to do anything now that's going to prevent me from getting out of here as soon as possible.'[13] The weapons were never returned. He was discharged from the service on 3 October 1945 and committed himself to public service after war, eventually becoming a patient advocate in a veterans' hospital. He passed away in 2005.[14]

James Kirk, of the 679th Tank Destroyer Battalion, which fought in Italy, was shipped back to the USA in August 1945 and, while he was preparing for the struggle in the Pacific, the Japanese surrendered after two atomic bombs were dropped. He too, despite being a veteran, suffered from segregation upon his return. As he recounted:

> [We] went to a movie, and they ushered us up into the balcony. In [Cheyenne,] Wyoming, in 1945. [I] just took it with a grain of salt, and went up in the balcony.[15]

He explained he felt that, as a black man, it was unwise to resist against the existing system. In December 1945 he was discharged with the rank of Private First Class. He recounted this time:

> I know that I was glad to be out of the service. I laid around the house for so long drawing that 52-20 [unemployment benefit for servicemen], my mother finally said, 'Son, you're going to have to get out of here and get yourself a job!' I knew some friends of mine said they were hiring on the Chicago Northwestern [railway], so I went over there and got a job.[16]

James Kirk returned to St Paul, divorced the wife he had married in 1941, and remarried in 1946. He continued to work on dining cars until 1962. He retired in 1982. For him, his service had taught him respect for others, although he joked that he was also the best bedmaker in town. The war allowed him the chance to see countries that he would never have seen otherwise. He passed away in 2011.

Reuben Yelding, was ordered to remain in Italy while the rest of the 679th Tank Destroyer Battalion shipped back to the States. While his friends returned home, he couldn't go with them. Heartbroken, he watched them leave; he would never see them again and it would bring him to tears to think about it. He was proud of the Tuskegee airmen; he considered the Army Air Corps to be the most prestigious branch of the services, and the fact that they had served proved to him that black people could, and would, be equal to white people.

Despite fighting for freedom, he had to take a segregated ship and a segregated bus back to a segregated life in Alabama. He resented this so much that he moved from Alabama to South Haven, Michigan. Here he met and married Alma Bowers, with whom he raised a family. He worked in a foundry and stressed to his children the importance of education. He became the first black American to be elected to the South Haven Board of Education. He passed away on 20 January 2013.

The Medal of Honor

Although the war, was over, the struggle for equal rights and representation remained. As soon as the war was over, and the dust had settled, the black press noted that although black soldiers and sailors participated in the war, none had been awarded the highest honor that an American soldier can get: the Medal of Honor. Perhaps best summed up with the title 'Not One Out of a Million' in the editorial of *The Crisis* in December 1945:

> Brave white heroes in our armed services have been awarded the nation's highest decoration, the Congressional Medal of Honor, literally in batches by President Truman. The Crisis would not take one ounce of credit from these men whose citations suggest that the honor they have won, high as it is, is not adequate thanks for their sacrifices and heroism. Yet it does seem strange to Negro Americans that out of the nearly one million of their men in the armed services not one should have performed in such a manner as to be cited for the Congressional Medal of Honor.[17]

Indeed, in past wars black Americans had fought and earned the Medal of Honor, from its inception during the Civil War, up to the First World War. However, during the Second World War none had been awarded. The belief was that this was either the result of explicit or implicit racism, a refusal to recognize the contribution of black American servicemen.

In 1992 this feeling resulted in a commission from the Department of Defense to examine what had happened and if indeed any Medal of Honor recommendations were improperly handled. In this study, a couple of factors were noted in the handling of the awards, as well as circumstances during that time.

Partially this was due to the nature of segregation and the lack of black combat units, which meant that they were less likely to earn the Medal of Honor. Since they were kept out of combat, there were less opportunities for them to distinguish themselves in action, which is a requirement for the Medal of Honor. Prevailing attitudes among some senior officers, which believed that black people were inferior to white people, further complicated the matter. The process of handling recommendations was different in the battle theaters in Europe, the Pacific and the Mediterranean.

To complicate the matter even further, similar wording in the award criteria, and the impossibility of measuring heroism, meant that errors in judgement could be made. As a contemporary noted: 'There is no sharp cleavage between acts meriting Medal of Honor, Distinguished Service Cross, or Silver Star.'[18] Even among senior officers there were differences in perception. In the case of the 761st Tank Battalion, their commander Lieutenant Colonel Bates admitted after the war that his expectations were so high for all of his men that it resulted in few decorations.[19] Similar errors slipped into the handling process, for example when commanders disapproved of a recommendation and didn't forward it, even though they should do so.

Out of the list of distinguished service cross holders, seven were awarded the Medal of Honor. Vernon Baker, Edward A. Carter,

John R. Fox, Willy F. James, Ruben Rivers, George Watson and Charles L. Thomas were awarded the Medal of Honor by President Bill Clinton in the White House. Vernon Baker was the only living veteran attending, the others had passed away in the intervening years or perished during their heroic actions. On behalf of Charles Thomas, who had passed away in 1980 from cancer, Sandra Johnson, his niece, accepted the medal.

When the smoke dissipates

While the 614th Tank Destroyer Battalion might not have been the most glorious Tank Destroyer Battalion of the Second World War, the unit did fight well. When examining its history, a few factors stand out for its success. However, further examination is needed to cement these arguments within the historical debate.

First, as identified before, the segregated American units needed the best officers. Like any other army unit, good officers are needed for it to excel. So too did segregated units need good commanders. The black combatants were regarded as special and the status of the black troops even extended to the German soldiers, who according to Lawrence Johnson, feared the black American soldiers more than their white counterparts. Due to the prevailing racism and segregation, the men needed not only a good military leader, but also someone that could manage the racial issues prevailing at that time. Pritchard, as seen during the unit's history and afterwards, was certainly capable of this. In fact, his skill as a commander of black soldiers was recognized by General Haffner. In a message on 5 February 1945 from General George Marshall to General Eisenhower it was mentioned that 'Lieutenant Colonel Frank S. Pritchard, Infantry, presently commanding 614th Tank Destroyer Battalion (colored), is reported to be highly successful as a commander of colored troops in combat.' The message went on to state that 'the 614th Tank Destroyer Battalion was attached to [Haffner's] division and was the equal to any white battalion in courage, stamina and training.' It was suggested that Pritchard might be transferred to the 92nd Infantry Division, where his skill could be employed on a larger scale.[20] However, luckily for the 614th Tank Destroyer Battalion, he remained with his outfit.

Pritchard would show the men how proud he was of them and more than once his men expressed their gratitude to him. If indeed Pritchard created, or ordered the creation of, the unit history, it's a testament of the love he had for his men, as well as the pride in them and their unit. In this the 614th had luck as for example the 827th Tank Destroyer Battalion changed commanders regularly and not all of them were suited for their task.

The second factor is pride, or rather confidence. The 614th had been adequately trained for the task which they had to perform. They knew their weapons and could handle them with skill. Moreover, this was demonstrated to others and recognized in return. Many praises have been expressed towards the 614th, from both high ranking officers, as well as enlisted men. The black soldiers might have started as another unwanted, ignored unit, but it developed into a valuable asset of the American army that the men of the 103d Infantry Division could take pride in, perhaps best summed up when Pritchard related what Major General Charles Haffner, the former commander of the 103d Infantry Division, told him: 'Pritch, I didn't want your outfit. Now if they try to take them away, they will have a fight on their hands.'[21] The next commander of the 103d, Anthony McAuliffe, similarly praised the 614th Tank Destroyer Battalion, making the soldiers proud.[22] This would motivate the men to fight on, and as Dr Thomas M. Campbell recalled: 'We had wounded men fighting despite their wounds because they didn't want to leave the outfit.'[23]

The 614th was also an example and the men knew this. They would be judged years later by their actions. They weren't just a statistic or a number, but they were a unit whose exploits were written about. The audience at home, as well as fellow soldiers learned of their actions in the newspapers and magazines. The 614th were leading the way together with others, as they paved the way for an equal military and an equal society, as expressed in the newspapers:

> But it was the soldiers with the machine guns, the cannon, the howitzers and the 'Long Toms' who put on the greatest show of them all and forever dispelled any possible doubts about the combat ability of the American Negro soldier. Of course there had never been any such doubt in their own minds, but some time back critics had ventured the opinion that Negro soldiers wouldn't make good combat soldiers. Gone forever is that mistaken idea and here to stay forever is the glorious record of units like the 761st Tank [battalion], the 614th TDs, the 452nd ack ack [anti-aircraft artillery], the 578th [field artillery], the 969th [field artillery], and other kindred units.[24]

Another factor, related to the 103d, is that the 614th was attached to them for a long period of time. It allowed the units to get attuned to one another, and familiarization between the men developed. Tank Destroyer Battalions that were frequently attached and detached, suffered from these rapid movements in morale and material.[25] The 614th was attached to the 103d and remained with them to the end of the war. The confidence of the units was boosted during the combat at Climbach, where the 614th showed what it was capable of to the 103d and the world. Having established their reputation as fierce fighters, and shown their value, it facilitated further cooperation.

It's unknown if race influenced the decision not to convert the 614th to a self-propelled unit. In June 1945, out of the twenty-six tank destroyer battalions serving in the Third Army, they remained the only towed outfit.[26] To make a better comparison, the three Tank Destroyer Battalions that were activated on the same day as the 614th can be examined: the 821st, the 822nd, the 823rd.

The Dusk of the Tank Destroyers 151

Tank Destroyer Battalions activated on 25 July 1942 and their conversions.

Unit	Towed?	When arrived on European mainland?	When committed to combat?	When converted to M10/M18?
614th	Yes	8 October 1944	November 1944	Never converted
821st	Yes	26 June 1944	July 1944	M10, December 1944
822nd	Yes	23 January 1945	February 1945	M18, March/April 1945
823rd	Yes	24 June 1944	June 1944	M10, December 1944

When comparing these four battalions, it stands out that the 614th is the only outfit that never converted to a self-propelled battalion. While they arrived late in Europe, they weren't the last to land. The 822nd arrived later than the 614th, but was converted to the M18 Hellcat in the last weeks of the war. Although the feeling is understandable that the soldiers felt that they were treated as a second-rate unit, the sample group is small and other factors might have influenced these decisions.

However, Lieutenant Christopher Sturkey's remark about the 614th being a towed unit and the others being self-propelled is incorrect. Although he stated: 'all of the white outfits I saw had the new self-propelled jobs which you just had to swing into action. Ours was towed by a truck, but that's all right, we could still split trail, beat them to the draw, and hit the target.'[27] This is incorrect, as on 27 January 1945 the battalion commander of the 807th Tank Destroyer Battalion, which was a white towed outfit, visited the 614th battalion command post.[28] Two days later an overlay of the 807th's gun positions was given to the 614th. The 807th was converted to a self-propelled unit in April 1945.

In fact, that the 614th remained a towed outfit, might have been a blessing in disguise. Indeed, the towed 3-inch guns weren't the best anti-tank weapons in the American arsenal, but the men of the

614th were skilled in their use and they had been training with them for years. They had confidence in their weapons. Other units were converted during combat and not allowed enough time to train or adapt to their new weapons, before being sent into battle.[29] This resulted in loss of men and materiel, as they had to familiarize themselves with their weapons in the field. Since the 614th remained with the same weapons throughout the war, they have been spared any casualties that might have resulted from this.

The 614th Tank Destroyer Battalion's glory is elusive and not always has it been properly identified. Horace Evans, a member of the 761st Tank Battalion, mentions that as a unit the 761st weren't credited for their actions, because they were frequently attached and detached, while units would get the glory, but 'a few isolated tanks, no matter whether they saved the day or not, are overlooked.'[30] Curiously enough, when the 761st fought together with the 614th as they moved towards Klingenmünster, the same process occurred. The 761st is often mentioned and remembered by the men of the 103d in Task Force Rhine, but the reconnaissance platoon of the 614th is often forgotten. On the other hand, the tanks of the 761st were misidentified as belonging to the 614th Tank Destroyer Battalion in the history of the 103d Infantry Division.[31]

Although the unit credited is the 761st tank destroyer, the action involved also included the reconnaissance platoon during the attack on Klingenmuster. As Private Cefkin, a white soldier, recounted from the 103d Infantry Division,

> I do believe that they [the 761st Tank Battalion] saved my life in a hazardous situation. [...] It is also worth noting that after the war, there were many veterans who favored an end to segregation in the Armed Forces. When I returned to civilian life in Los Angeles, I joined the American Legion, and we WWII veterans tried to desegregate our American Legion post. We were a few votes short and that effort failed. However,

many of us then abandoned the Legion and formed a post of the American Veterans Committee (AVC). That organization – 'We are citizen's first and veterans second' – included African Americans and also women. In this respect, the struggles of the 761st gained success on both fronts, in the ETO in the struggle against the Nazis and for first-class citizenship for African American servicemen.[32]

Although not mentioned explicitly by name, the 614th were there too and, beyond doubt, they too contributed towards a better future for all Americans. They too shared in the struggle of the infantry and more than one man of the 103d was proud of having the 614th as their tank killers.

More explicitly mentioned was the combat at Climbach, which had a lasting influence on the lives of some people. John Thornton Dorsey Jr., an infantry soldier of the 103d Division, remembered it well, 'Very bad scene. Many dead black men—blood, carnage, mangled bodies.' He was struck by the skin color of the victims: 'Why are you here? What stake do you have in this?' The wounded and dead of the third platoon made such an impression on him, that on his return in America he decided to be involved in civil rights.[33]

While the skin color of the men might have caused them problems before, during, and after the war, at least once it was in their benefit. When Dr Campbell, the head of the medical detachment in the 614th Tank Destroyer Battalion, entered a restricted combat area, he was stopped by a soldier of the 103d Infantry Division and didn't know the appropriate password. When that man wanted to take him to headquarters at gunpoint, Dr Campbell blurted out: 'Good God, man when was the last time you ever saw a black German?' The soldier shrugged and told him that 'Yankee' was the password and allowed him to carry on.[34]

Overall, the 614th fought bravely and distinguished themselves both on and off the battlefield during the Second World War, earning the respect of their fellow countrymen. Several factors made this possible, such as confidence and pride in themselves and their commanders. By being attached to a single division for a long time, they knew the strengths and limitations of each other. They fought, bled, and died for freedom. Not only the freedom of people in occupied Europe, but also their own freedom. Due to their actions, they challenged the prejudices that their fellow countrymen might have. Thus, they fought and helped achieve victory on both fronts.

Appendix A

List of men in the unit

Although the list covers many men in the battalion, a few people might be missed. Neither Lieutenant Williams and Technician Fifth Grade McGee, who made up the advance detachment together with Claude Ramsey, appear on the list of people who served in the unit, according to Pritchard. Claude Ramsey served with the maintenance and communication platoon, while the other two men are unmentioned. Lieutenant Williams is present on the officer roster in December. It could be that the other two men were liaisons, and no organic part of the unit, representing the unit in the United Kingdom.[1] Furthermore, reinforcements that arrived in December 1944 aren't presented in this appendix. The reason is that the replacements were properly processed after 1 January 1945 and those that came before them have been missed.

614th Tank Destroyer Battalion
Headquarters and headquarters company

Rank	Name	
Lt Col	Frank S.	Pritchard
Maj	Leroy H.	Sample
Capt	Charles W.	Ogelsby
Capt	Robert J.	O'Leary
Capt	Gordon P.	Maloche
Capt	Charles J.	Richard
Capt	James H.	Carn
WOJG	Arnie E.	Hollins
1st Lt	Leonard I.	Burch
2nd Lt	Milton B. Co.	Deas
1st Sgt	George E.	Russell

Rank	Name	
S/Sgt	Chester L.	Perry
S/Sgt	James H.	Holley
Tec 4	Floyd	Guioe
Tec 4	Oscar Jr.	Ruffin
Cpl	Lawrence K.	Williams
Tec 5	Roy T.	Odem
Tec 5	William M.	Johnson
Tec 5	James T.	Smith
Tec 5	Alvin R.	Holmes
Pfc	Sterling	Lutz
Pfc	Willie E.	Wirts
Pvt	Milton M.	Bell
Pvt	Il. C.	Williams
Pvt	John A.	Robertson
Pvt	Ezekiel	Moffitt
Pvt	Willie	Magby
T/Sgt	Gordon	Brown
Sgt	Ben Jr.	Evans
Pfc	Matthew	Mckines
Pvt	Euel	Russell
Pvt	Eddie L.	Pates
Pvt	Douglas	Young
Tec 5	Carl B.	Bush
Pvt	George	Bass
M/Sgt	Willard L.	Hill
T/Sgt	Charles E.	Tenry
Tec 5	Ronald	Pollard
Tec 5	Joseph G.	Williams
T/Sgt	Clinton T. Jr.	Walker
T/Sgt	Giles W.	Pearson
Tec 4	Louis D.	White
Tec 4	John G.	Rush
Tec 5	Walter S.	Coleman
Tec 5	James W.	Smith
Tec 5	William D.	Parker
Tec 5	Elias	Prince
Tec 5	John A.	King

Appendix A: List of men in the unit   157

Rank	Name	
Tec 5	Benjamin	Boydd
Tec 5	Richard C.	Weeks
Tec 5	Anthony	Powell
Pfc	Reuben O.	Wiggins
Pfc	Herman	Rivera
Pvt	Sears	Warren
T/Sgt	Isaac	Thomas
S/Sgt	Smiley T.	Easley
Tec 4	Clarence H.	Dudley
Tec 5	John Jr.	Robinson
Tec 5	George M.	Robinson
Tec 5	Raymond	Stansberry

First Reconnaissance Platoon

Rank	Name	
1st Lt	Ormond A.	Forte
S/Sgt	John O.	Weir
Tec 5	Carl	Roberts
Tec 5	Richard	Perry
Tec 5	Nathaniel	Oliver
Pfc	Paul	Bland
Sgt	Robert E.	Fuller
Tec 5	James W.	McNair
Pfc	Tom	Massey
Pfc	Freeman Jr.	Whitfield
Pfc	James B.	Williams
Pfc	Chester	Davis
Pfc	Thomas D.	Ingram
Pfc	William H.	Foster
Pvt	Willie T.	Wright
Pvt	Joseph	Gwyn
Pvt	Mark H.	Ray
Pvt	Lester L.	Latson
Pvt	Charlie	Coleman
Pvt	James C.	Harper
Pvt	Walker	Lee
Pvt	Maryland	Williams

Rank	Name	
Second Reconnaissance Platoon		
1st Lt	Serreo S.	Nelson
S/Sgt	Leroy	Williams
Sgt	Matthew	Spencer
Tec 5	Robert L.	Smith
Tec 5	Norah	Marshall
Tec 5	Leroy R.	Watson
Tec 5	Leonard	Truesdale
Pfc	Kenneth C.	Johnson
Pfc	Clarence L.	Clark
Pvt	John T.	Smith
Pvt	Argusta	Mims
Pvt	Austin L.	Johnson
Sgt	Samuel	Booker
Tec 5	Wylon	Davis
Pfc	George F.	Ogletree
Pfc	Lloyed R.	Mable
Pfc	Lawrence H.	Floyd
Pvt	Booker T.	Steward
Pvt	Sterling J.	Denney
Pvt	Leo O.	Greer
Pvt	Henry	Weaver
Pvt	Samuel	Adams
Maintenance and communications platoon		
2nd Lt	Andrew J.	Favors
WOJG	Raymond	Lambs
M/Sgt	John W. Jr.	Hurns
S/Sgt	Henry	Evans
S/Sgt	Richard H.	Irvin
Sgt	Harry M.	Butler
Sgt	Fred L.	McCain
Tec 4	Thomas O.	McNeal
Tec 4	William A.	Adams
Tec 4	Henry L.	Toomer
Tec 4	Rubin	Patterson
Tec 4	Melvin L.	Thomas
Tec 4	William A.	Strait

Appendix A: List of men in the unit   159

Rank	Name	
Tec 4	Rufus	McGlothin
Tec 4	James	Spain
Tec 5	Hubert	Jackson
Tec 5	William A.	Clarkson
Tec 5	John C.	Pitts
Tec 5	Leon	Singleton
Tec 5	Birnie W.	Neal
Pfc	William A.	Cane
Pfc	Dalmond	Boyd
Pvt	Allen L.	Anthony
2nd Lt	Claude W.	Ramsey
T/Sgt	Charles I.	Anderson
Sgt	Charles E.	Smith
Tec 4	Nehemiah	Stubbs
Cpl	Vincent E.	Perches
Tec 5	John	Epps
Tec 5	James A.	Moore
Tec 5	T. H.	Henley
Pfc	William C.	Barker
Pvt	McKinley Jr.	Richmond
Pvt	John C.	Cunningham
Pvt	Harvey T.	McCarter
Pvt	Elijah A.	Gibson
Transportation Platoon		
2nd Lt	Preston Jr.	Helm
S/Sgt	George W.	Tumey
Sgt	Julius W.	Wiggins
Pfc	James Jr.	McKinney
Pfc	Bennie L.	Bailey
Pfc	Rogers	Pollard
Tec 5	James O.	McClain
Tec 5	Johnnie	Permint
Tec 5	Buster	Williams
Pvt	Paul	Reynolds
Pvt	Samuel H.	Collins
Pvt	Macon L.	Morrisey
Pvt	Alexander	McRimmon

Rank	Name	
Pvt	Rory	Bullock
Pvt	Joseph L.	Hedgepeth
Pvt	John W.	Morrison
Pvt	Frank	Newman
Pvt	James	Davis
Tec 5	Cylester V.	Nunnally
Pfc	Luther	Porter
Pvt	Lenyer	Lataker
Pvt	Cullen	Hunter

Company 'A'
Company Headquarters

Capt	Beauregard	King
2nd Lt	Lloyd A.	Gregory
1st Sgt	Oliver S. Jr.	Cox
S/Sgt	James C.	Colbert
S/Sgt	Lazarus L.	Garrett
S/Sgt	Garfield	Gladden
S/Sgt	Warren J.	Glapion
Sgt	Charles E.	Parks
Tec 4	Henry Jr.	Clay
Tec 4	James	Dunbar
Tec 4	L. C.	Hendley
Tec 4	James T.	Mayoy
Tec 4	Eugene	Outterbrider
Tec 4	Ernest	Rogers
Tec 4	James H.	Roundtrea
Cpl	Alvin	Alexander
Tec 5	D.	Fleming
Tec 5	Otis V.	Buckner
Tec 5	Marvin L.	Demery
Tec 5	J. C.	Foster
Tec 5	Howard H.	Freeman
Tec 5	James F.	House
Tec 5	Walter B.	McGummings
Sgt	Tubal C.	Temberfeld
Tec 5	Alto	White
Pfc	Ira	Chavis

Appendix A: List of men in the unit

Rank	Name	
Pfc	Milton L.	Jenkins
Pfc	Obie J.	Rogers
Cpl	Curtis O.	Scott
Pfc	Ambric Jr.	Bridgeforth
Pfc	James W.	Parker

First platoon

Rank	Name	
1st Lt	Joseph L.	Keeby
S/Sgt	Columbus	Bryant
Pvt	Roy	Craine
Pvt	Henry L.	Bass
Sgt	Hallet L.	Jones
Cpl	Horace E.	Banks
Pfc	James C.	Brown
Pvt	Elige	Loper
Pfc	Piper W.	Coleman
Pvt	Henry L.	Keener
Pfc	Charlie	Smith
Pvt	Walter	McKenzie
Pvt	Asta M.	Baldwin
Pvt	George E.	Carson
Cpl	James C.	Colford
Pfc	Hermon	Body
Pfc	Cary	Stepter
Tec 5	Russell J.	Austin
Pvt	Shirley L.	Phillips
Pvt	John T.	Bynum
Pvt	Daniel	Buford
Sgt	Rayford T.	Calloway
Cpl	Edward J.	Carter
Tec 5	Northea	Butler
Pfc	Lycurgus	Brothers
Pvt	A. Z.	Smith
Pvt	John	Eason
Pvt	John W.	Everitt
Pvt	Charlie Jr.	Smith
Cpl	John Jr.	Stacy
Sgt	Thomas	Shelby

Rank	Name	
Tec 5	Samuel P.	Baker
Pfc	Jack	Lame
Pfc	Cornelius	Fortune
Pvt	Carol	Fultz
Pvt	Guy	Dean
Pvt	Franklin	Gates
Pvt	James D.	Johnson
Pvt	Louis V.	Moore
Pvt	Otto Jr.	Parker
Sgt	Lewis D.	Cullum
Pfc	Phillip	Allen
Pvt	Celesius A.	Thorne
Pfc	Johnnie	Boyd
Sgt	Eddie L.	Jakes
Cpl	Walter Jr.	Dawson
Tec 5	Isaac	Lee
Pfc	James R.	Figgs
Pvt	James	Cozart
Pvt	Everet	Morris
Pvt	Nathaniel D.	Ford
Pfc	James E.	Ray
Pfc	Grady	Martin
Pfc	Curlin	Fearrington

Second Platoon

2nd Lt	Edward J.	Carey
S/Sgt	Lewis H.	Marns
Pfc	Charles L.	Corother
Pvt	Robert	Barnes
Cpl	James Jr.	Gilmore
Pfc	Lester B.	Green
Pfc	Robert	Winbush
Sgt	George W.	Evans
Pfc	William A.	Walker
Pfc	Robert	Beamon
Cpl	James Jr.	Brown
Pfc	Gilbert	Linebarger
Pfc	Charlie P.	Taylor

Appendix A: List of men in the unit

Rank	Name	
Pvt	Hugh S.	Washburn
Sgt	Wilson	Davis
Pvt	William T.	Young
Pfc	C. L.	Berry
Pvt	James W.	Pressley
Pvt	Eleazer	Wilson
Pvt	William W.	Perry
Pfc	William	Savage
Pfc	William T.	King
Pvt	Peter L.	Willis
Tec 5	Isaac F.	Brewer
Sgt	Robert C.	Garnett
Pvt	William J.	McBrayer
Pfc	Raymond B.	Booker
Pfc	M. G.	Mickles
Pvt	Clifton L.	Moody
Pvt	Algernon B.	White
Pvt	Leroy	Bocker
Pvt	Walter L.	Davenport
Pvt	Eddie L.	Barker
Tec 5	Ernest	Fleming
Sgt	John D.	Grace
Cpl	Nathaniel	Bass
Pfc	Samuel	Durham
Pvt	Banks	Alderman
Pfc	Macon	Guyton
Pvt	Arthur M.	Layne
Pfc	Frank J.	Williams
Pvt	Thurston B.	Smith
Pvt	Arthur Jr.	Mixon
Tec 5	Avery L.	Blackey
Sgt	Erdis A.	Alfred
Cpl	Charles H.	Purvis
Pfc	Willis	Ballerd
Pvt	Eulis	Halbert
Pvt	Leonard G.	Bernett
Pvt	Christopher C.	Robinson

Rank	Name	
Pvt	Preston O.	Porter
Pvt	Leo A.	Turner
Pvt	Levitus A.	Deloney
Tec 5	Henry L.	Holloway

Third Platoon

2nd Lt	Charles C.	Robinson
S/Sgt	Johnnie	King
Pfc	Clark	Moore
Pvt	Albert	Rone
Sgt	Henry B.	Fletcher
Cpl	Joseph W.	Greenlee
Pfc	Arthur	Smith
Pvt	Eli M.	Edwards
Pfc	Acie	Barnes
Pfc	Nathaniel	Williams
Pvt	Judson L. O.	Coleman
Pvt	Garrett	Williams
Tec 5	Morris D.	Grigsby
Pvt	Luther B.	Holley
Sgt	Laforce	Nelson
Cpl	Nelson	Rasberry
Tec 5	Willie T.	Breeze
Pfc	William A.	Sarten
Pvt	Frank L.	Martin
Pfc	Richard	Hargrove
Pfc	Isaiah	Cotton
Pvt	Ardis O.	Moore
Pvt	Lewis	Morris
Pvt	John W.	Taylor
Sgt	Sam B.	Williams
Cpl	George	Hill
Pvt	Carl	Busch
Pvt	Wavery	Blue
Pvt	Waders C.	Hathaway
Pvt	Charles D.	Johnes
Pfc	Walter W.	Noewel
Pfc	Freddie	Hankins

Appendix A: List of men in the unit   165

Rank	Name	
Pfc	Charlie B.	Walters
Pvt	Wilson	Pearson
Pvt	Linard W.	Jessup
Sgt	Jeff	Rockett
Cpl	Lewis Deal	Gregory
Pvt	David	Savage
Pvt	Harry	Hazel
Pfc	George W. Jr.	Harrell
Pfc	George P.	Jones
Pvt	Cleave	Frison
Pvt	Lawrence L. C.	Johnson
Pvt	Bennie	Grimes
Sgt	Avery V.	Williams
Cpl	Richard Jr.	Parker
Tec 5	James E.	Barbee
Pfc	Jim	Speight
Pfc	Theodore R.	Patron
Pfc	Willie	Welis
Pfc	Willie	Moore
Pvt	Clifford I. Jr.	Baker
Pfc	William H.	Adams
Pfc	John H.	Brooks
Pvt	Horace O.	Guest

Company 'B'
Company Headquarters

Capt	Robert L.	Finley
1st Lt	Raymond H.	Powell
1/Sgt	Sloan	King
S/Sgt	Amos A.	Dashiell
S/Sgt	Ernest E.	Joynes
S/Sgt	James F.	McDougald
S/Sgt	Chester	Thomas
Sgt	Gordon B.	McGinnis
Tec 5	George L.	Brockman
Tec 5	George C.	Donaldson
Tec 5	Arthur D.	Hayes
Tec 5	Donald E.	Newman

Rank	Name	
Tec 5	Jessie J.	Ragland
Tec 5	Wylvester J.	Thompson
Tec 5	William G.	Williams
Cpl	Joseph L.	Hall
Tec 4	Eldridge W.	Buford
Tec 4	Thomas S.	Carlisle
Tec 4	Jim E.	Hunter
Tec 4	Eldrigde C.	McGlendon
Tec 4	Isiah	Polk
Tec 4	Leonza	Smith
Tec 4	Clarence R.	Wilson
Tec 5	Francois M.	Beasley
Cpl	James	Morrison
Pfc	James	Brunson
Pfc	James J.	Higgins
Pfc	Harry L.	Walton
Pvt	Vilia	Allen
Pvt	Charlie E.	Melton
Pvt	Henry L.	Partin

First platoon

1st Lt	Charles	Nelson
S/Sgt	Esther T.	Mays
Sgt	John T.	Briggs
Pvt	Lodis T.	Brewington
Pfc	Jessie W.	Blanton
Pfc	Frank	Burnett
Pfc	Johnnie B.	Ceasar
Pfc	Ernest L.	White
Pvt	James R.	Bannerman
Pvt	Ollie	Hammiel
Pvt	Lonza E.	Lawrence
Pvt	Wilbur C.	Quattlebaum
Pvt	Abnon	Robinson
Pvt	Curtis F.	Swinger
Sgt	David F.	Duncan
Cpl	Elmer J.	Kelley
Tec 5	Harvey L.	Modica

Appendix A: List of men in the unit

Rank	Name	
Pfc	Aggie	Brown
Pvt	Arthur H.	Carter
Pvt	William A.	Danner
Pvt	David	Robinson
Pvt	Raymond	Roundtree
Pvt	Reynold L.	Ward
Pvt	Johnnie M.	White
Sgt	Adolphus	Lyons
	John J.	Sims
Cpl	Raymond E.	Evans
Tec 5	James	Curry
Pfc	Charlie Jr.	Bynum
Pvt	John C.	Clark
Pvt	Leander	Gipson
Pvt	Thomas E.	Holliday
Pvt	George W.	Reddicks
Pvt	William D.	Sellars
Pvt	Clarence A.	Alston
Cpl	Theados L.	Paysour
Tec 5	Frank	Jackson
Pfc	Lewis L.	Belle
Pfc	Bradie	Bogan
Pfc	George R.	Green
Pvt	John L.	Davis
Pvt	Abie	Hodge
Pvt	Nelson	Webb
Pvt	Curtis A.	Young
Sgt	Theodore R.	Hudson
Cpl	Lewis	Bryant
Tec 5	Shellie	Seymore
Pfc	Cornelius G.	Bender
Pfc	William C.	Bradshaw
Pfc	Henry R.	Hart
Pvt	Clifford A.	Costley
Pvt	Henry T.	Gibbs
Pvt	James	Watkins

Rank	Name	
Second Platoon		
1st Lt	Ulysses	Watkins
S/Sgt	Wilbur	Turner
Sgt	Adolphus	Newton
Cpl	Ralph	Savage
Pfc	J. C.	Cheatham
Pfc	Aubrey	Morris
Pfc	James	Mason
Pfc	George	Wright
Tec 5	Albert	Dobey
Pfc	Lewis	Booker
Pfc	Hosie	Hamilton
Pvt	Jarvis	Majette
Pfc	Grady	Marsh
Pfc	Lloyd	Wooland
Pvt	Hurley	English
Pvt	Gunney	Huggins
Pvt	Prince	Davis
Pvt	Moses	Smallwood
Sgt	William	Scruggs
Cpl	Joseph	Allen
Tec 5	Horace	Clark
Pvt	William H	Dewar
Pvt	Samuel	Haley
Pvt	Leonza	Ford
Pvt	Roy	Hamrick
Pvt	Wilbord	Henderson
Pvt	Stacy	Halloman
Pvt	Fletcher	Pope
Sgt	Simuel	Pruitt
Cpl	Andrew	Wells
Pfc	Junicus	Baskerville
Pfc	Cebe	Young
Pfc	Robert	Russell
Sgt	Theodore	Strong
Cpl	George	Winchester
Tec 5	James	Williams

Appendix A: List of men in the unit

Rank	Name	
Pvt	Johnnie	Hebron
Pvt	Roy	Jackson
Pvt	Edward	Lawrence
Pvt	Elbert	Morris
Pvt	Jemmie	Perry
Pfc	William	Raynor
Pvt	Warner	White
Sgt	Carl	Gibson
Cpl	John	Bolling
Tec 5	Johnnie	Mathews
Pfc	Andrew	Morris
Pfc	Andrew	Palmer
Pvt	Ruebin	Burns
Pvt	Harry	Jones
Pvt	Charlie	Murphy
Pvt	Harry	Gore
Pvt	Evan	Stanback
Third platoon		
1st Lt	Forest A.	Walker
S/Sgt	John E. Jr.	Stubbs
Sgt	Daniel A.	Beeks
Pfc	Ralph R.	Washington
Pvt	Elbred R.	Malone
Pfc	Waverly A.	Crawford
Pvt	Lynnette E.	Haywood
Pfc	Grady L.	Lyles
Pfc	Floyd	Reid
Pfc	John H.	Walker
Pvt	W. D.	Coleman
Pvt	Eddie	Corbett
Pvt	Remus	Franklin
Pvt	Alger C.	Gillespie
Sgt	Willard	Herbert
Pfc	James	McKinney
Pvt	Ernest V.	Tatum
Pfc	Herbert	Overton
Pfc	Willie A.	Southerland

Rank	Name	
Pvt	Llewellyn	Samuels
Pvt	Reuben C.	Scott
Sgt	Ira W.	Lockey
Cpl	William N.	Greenlee
Tec 5	James	Moore
Pfc	Eddie N.	Alston
Pfc	George R.	Birch
Pfc	Robert L.	Winbush
Pvt	George	Embry
Pvt	Archie L.	Jackson
Pvt	Joseph	McCulluch
Sgt	Mitchell	Wheeler
Tec 5	George C.	Knox
Cpl	Robert L.	Bullock
Pfc	James D.	Ellison
Pfc	Derwin	Moore
Pvt	William H.	Grasty
Pvt	Joseph E.	Johnson
Pvt	Herbert E.	Peterson
Pvt	Joyce T.	Shepherd
Sgt	Alexander	Bonner
Pfc	James P.	Green
Tec 5	Luell J.	Love
Pfc	Walter P.	McKnight
Pfc	Horace L.	Nesbitt
Pfc	Tommie	Hill
Pfc	George W.	Owens
Pvt	Willie D.	Adair
Pvt	Henry L.	Bennett
Pvt	Finley	Cunningham
Pvt	Claude	Moore
Pvt	John A.	Hales
Pvt	Otis Jr.	Woody
Tec 5	Sylvester L.	Jackson

Company 'C'
Company Headquarters

1st Lt	Charles L.	Thomas
1st Lt	Floyd J.	Stalling

Appendix A: List of men in the unit

Rank	Name	
1/Sgt	Jesse J. W.	McCorry
S/Sgt	Harvey	Claybrook
S/Sgt	Johnnie	Johnson
S/Gt	Ulyesses N.	Love
S/Sgt	Arthur	Page
Tec 4	Warren G.	Anderson
Tec 4	John E.	Jones
Tec 4	George H.	Punch
Tec 4	Paul	Warner
Tec 4	Russel E.	Wright
Tec 4	Herschel S.	Kirk
Cpl	Elbert	Moss
Tec 5	John	Foster
Tec 5	Thomas J.	Hanebel
Tec 5	Menlin H.	Jeffries
Tec 5	Emsey S.	Lindsey
Tec 4	Hubbert	Phillips
Pfc	Arthur	McCloud
Pfc	Lacy L.	Murchison
Pfc	Bradley L.	Norman
Pfc	Walter	Wallace
Pfc	Riley	Weeks
Pvt	Strakard	McKinney
Pvt	Sam J.	Woode
Pvt	Joseph E.	Hawkins

First Platoon

Rank	Name	
1st Lt	Walter S.	Smith
S/Sgt	Christopher J.	Sturkey
Sgt	Clarence	Owens
Pfc	Dave	Ratliff
Pvt	Robert L.	Jones
Pfc	Moses	Hopkins
Sgt	Chesterfield	Jones
Pvt	Otis	Pettigrew
Tec 5	Colford	Cutler
Pvt	Thomas J.	Waddell
Pvt	Fred	Clements

Rank	Name	
Pfc	George H.	Johnson
Pvt	Roy	Griffin
Sgt	Charlie B.	Crump
Cpl	Frank	Ivey
Tec 5	Jim C.	Collier
Tec 5	Hezekiah	Shaw
Pfc	Henry B.	Griffin
Pfc	Eddie L.	Banks
Pvt	Robert L.	Kearney
Pvt	David W.	Campbell
Pfc	Delgar	Ford
Pvt	Harrold E.	Blaine
Pvt	Arthur	Reeves
Sgt	Lepoleon	Cotton
Cpl	James E.	Palin
Pvt	Luther J.	Hall
Pvt	Roosevelt	Ruffin
Pvt	Lincoln	Sterling
Sgt	Lonnie	Summers
Cpl	Arteria	Whelers
Pfc	Johnnie	Barbee
Pfc	Frank M.	Miller
Pfc	John W.	Spencer
Pfc	Govenor V.	McLeod
Pvt	Willie	Scott
Pfc	Robert L.	Walker
Cpl	William E.	Allen
Pvt	Thurston C.	Honeyblue
Pvt	Russell P.	Proctor
Tec 5	Stacey	Cummings
Pvt	James L.	Gary
Pvt	Harey W.	Hawkinds
Pvt	Ray	Dempson
Pvt	Jermiah	Lynch
Pvt	Phelix	Smith
Pvt	Lloyd	Milis
Pfc	Frederick	Tucker

Appendix A: List of men in the unit   173

Rank	Name	
Pvt	Arlis	Tarkington
Pfc	Samuel	Jenkins
Pvt	Joseph N.	Slaughter
Pfc	Roosevelt	Jones
Pvt	Herman	Mitchell

Second Platoon

Rank	Name	
1st Lt	Thomas H.	Shaw
S/Sgt	George W.	Sims
Tec 5	J. C.	Martin
Pfc	Prince	Alexander
Pfc	Willie B.	Bostick
Pfc	Henry	Eaton
Tec 5	Arthur E.	Nelson
Pvt	Simuel	McGleen
Pvt	James	Morrison
Pvt	Chester A.	Williams
Cpl	Robert G.	Lee
Pvt	Horace L.	Whitfield
Sgt	Benjamin W. Jr.	Bryant
Pvt	Bonnie O. Jr.	Harris
Tec 5	Henry	Griffin
Pvt	Charlie G.	Brooks
Pvt	Frank Jr.	Canty
Tec 4	Nathaniel	Crouch
Tec 4	Robert L.	Davis
Tec 4	Lonnie	Hinton
Cpl	Otis	May
Tec 5	William	McClerkin
Tec 5	Joseph Jr.	Simms
Tec 5	Charles H.	McGowan
Tec 5	Paul	Williams
Pfc	Carl	Hunter
Pvt	Elijah	Hawkins
Pvt	Lewis Jr.	Lee
Pvt	John A.	Loving
Pvt	Willie	Thompson
Pvt	Nathaniel	Varner

Rank	Name	
Sgt	Otis M.	Barnes
Cpl	Armstead	Sharp
Tec 5	Plummer	Massenburg
Pfc	Scott	Jarrett
Pfc	John A.	Burnett
Pfc	Moses H.	Wesley
Pvt	Martin	Mongriff
Pvt	Walter	Sharp
Pvt	Roy	Harris
Pvt	Rufus	Sims
Sgt	Weldon D.	Freeman
Cpl	Henry T.	Rhone
Tec 5	Alfonzo	Norfleet
Pfc	Jonathan	Cureton
Pfc	John H.	Evans
Pfc	James E.	Fenner
Pfc	John	Gilliam
Pfc	Fred	Terley
Pvt	Rema	Giles
Pvt	Norman E.	Smith
Pvt	James J.	Albricht
Pvt	Willie L.	Downey
Pvt	George	Elam

Third platoon

Rank	Name	
1st LT	George W.	Mitchell
S/SGT	Robert	Cannon
Tec 5	Robert W.	Harris
Tec 5	Henry J.	Smith
Pfc	William H.	Phipps
Pfc	Benjamin W.	Shinhoster
Pvt	James E.	Nesby
Pvt	Silvester V.	Solomon
Sgt	Walter	West
Cpl	Blease	Spell
Pvt	Vandy Jr.	Evans
Pfc	Howard	Kenneth

Appendix A: List of men in the unit

Rank	Name	
Pvt	Hayward	McKnight
Pvt	Charlie B.	Rattler
Sgt	William L.	Tabron
Pvt	Shelton	Murph
Pfc	Charlie	Hester
Pfc	Walter H. Jr.	Milis
Pfc	Luther Jr.	Moore
Tec 5	James A.	Perry
Cpl	Peter	Simmons
Sgt	Thomas J.	Phillips
Cpl	Al Jr.	Hockaday
Pfc	Whit L.	Knight
Pfc	Willie	Modlin
Pvt	Thomas C.	McDaniel
Pvt	Sam	Patraeck
Pvt	Leon	Tobin
Pvt	Dave	Smith
Sgt	Roosevelt	Robertson
Pvt	Plato	King
Pfc	Barnett W.	Brown
Pfc	Jack	Childs
Cpl	Daniel	James
Tec 5	Odell	Jeffries
Pvt	Linwood	Johnson
Pvt	Vernon W.	Higgs
Sgt	Dillard L.	Booker
Tec 5	James J.	Robeson
Pfc	Robert L.	Bullock
Pvt	Willie J.	Gordon
Pfc	Delmon B.	Glasco
Pvt	Jesse L.	Speight
Pfc	Jesse T.	Sturvident
Pvt	Samuel	Williams
Pvt	Robert	Green
Pvt	John	Cooper
Pvt	Lucius	Riley
Pvt	Burnie	Swindell

Rank	Name	
Pvt	Eugene J.	Detiege
Cpl	Lennon L.	Whitlow
Pvt	Reed Jr.	Jones
Pvt	Leonard	Wheeler
Pvt	Wilbert	Welch
S/SGT	Silvester	Harrington

Medical Detachment

Capt	Thomas M.	Campbell
S/SGt	Dale A.	Richardson
Tec 5	Julius C. Jr.	Highe
Tec 4	John J.	Lee
Tec 4	Calvin W.	Williams
Cpl	Rockey	Williams
Tec 5	Robert C.	Harris
Tec 5	Jethro	Thompson
Tec 5	Lonnie	Torian
Tec 5	Selesta	Whitehead
Pfc	Joseph S.	Wynn
Pfc	Thomas L. Jr.	Kilgo
Pfc	Calvin	Lassiter
Pvt	Aubry L.	Rollins
Pfc	Edward W.	Wilkerson
Pvt	William	Wilkins

Replacements received since 1 Jan 1945

Officers

1st Lt	Jesse S.	Hickman
2nd Lt	Robert C.	Brooks
2nd Lt	Adam W.	Berry
2nd Lt	Alfonso T.	McArthur
2nd Lt	Joseph C.	Awkard

Enlisted men

M/Sgt	Stonewall	Jackson
T/Sgt	James W.	Early
S/Sgt	Leo S. Jr.	Smoot
Pfc	Henry P.	Ford
Pvt	Ollie L.	Williams

Appendix A: List of men in the unit   177

Rank	Name	
Pvt	David E.	Woods
Pvt	James	Young
Pvt	James	Williams
Tec 5	Edgar W.	Reeves
Tec 4	William E.	Davis
Pfc	John E.	Strahorne
Sgt	Earl L	Martin
Pfc	Sam	Campbell
Pfc	Joseph	Falk
Pfc	Charlie E.	Giles
Pvt	Percy	Chamber
Pvt	Allen B.	Cooper
Pvt	Solomon	Cunningham
Pfc	Colas O.	Bland
Pfc	Claudie L.	Cheatum
Pfc	William E.	Ferguson
Pfc	Amos	Bartie
Pvt	Joseph L.	Coleman
Pvt	Fred	Cowser
Pvt	William L.	Dark
Pvt	Harold H.	Gordon
Cpl	Clinton E.	Jiggetts
Cpl	Alvin	Mixon
Tec 5	Elonzo	Danforth
Pvt	Hugh S.	Smith
Pvt	David	Leatio
Pvt	James A.	Greene
Cpl	William T.	Nash
Tec 4	Roy D.	Jones
Pfc	James	Moore
Pvt	Charles C.	Hughes
Pvt	John	Copeland
Pvt	Robert L. Jr.	Cunningham
Pvt	Leroy	Crisp
Pvt	William H.	Dancey
Pvt	James	Duncan
Pfc	Julian R.	Frye

Rank	Name	
Pvt	Bennett F.	Garner
Pvt	Herman	Green
Tec 5	Jerome A.	Hauck
Tec 5	Johnnie	Holland
Pvt	Clarence E. Jr.	James
Pvt	Frank L.	Johnson
Pvt	Arthur	Littles
Tec 5	Jamie	Lovett
Pvt	Tolbert	Miles
Pvt	Joseph	Mitchell
Tec 5	Alfred	Nichols
Cpl	Willie B.	Nunley
Pvt	Blanchard L.	Parker
Pvt	James W.	Pinckney
Pvt	Clarence	Reese
Sgt	John A.	Saulter
Pfc	Sam Jr.	Thomas
Tec 4	Joseph Jr.	Thomas
Pvt	Lawrence W.	Weaver
Pvt	Lott D.	Williams
Pvt	Dudley	Williams
Pvt	Charles A.	Williams
Pvt	Willie	Wilson
Pvt	Linnie B.	Bonner
Pvt	Joseph L.	Carr
Pvt	Felix A.	Bowers
Pvt	Richard C.	Gore
Pvt	Lloyd	Jackson
Tec 5	George H. Jr.	Johnson
Pfc	William H.	Tillery
Pfc	Paul A.	Young
Pvt	John D.	Leek
Pvt	Alfred J.	McDade
Pvt	Thomas	Mitchell
Pvt	Thomas L.	Moore
Pvt	James O.	Parker
Pvt	Nathaniel	Smith

Appendix A: List of men in the unit

Rank	Name	
Pvt	Solomon	Walker
Pvt	Alfred T.	Williams
Pvt	Charles E.	Wilson
Pfc	John H.	Wise
Pfc	George E.	York
Pfc	George B.	Wilson
Pvt	Eldrege	Massey
Pvt	Arthur E.	Millner
Pvt	Charles E.	Ogburn
Pvt	Willie	Patrick
Pvt	Edward R.	Thompson
Pvt	George	Willhite
Pvt	Leroy	Williams
Pvt	Napoleon L.	King
Pvt	Joseph W. Jr.	Wilkerson
Pvt	Charles M.	Williams
Pvt	Sampson	Roberts
Pfc	Arthur	Dunlap
Pvt	Vincent Jr.	Edwards
Pfc	John T.	Fox
Cpl	Noah	Folks
Pfc	Charlie R.	Green
Pvt	William H.	Hartsfield
Pvt	Walter	Harris
Pfc	John E.	Leath
Pvt	Robert	Morris
Pvt	Robert	Doxon
Tec 5	John R.	McAllister
Tec 5	Richard S.	Freeman
Pfc	James R.	Mosley
Pfc	Joe	Rascoe
Pfc	Ed	Skrine
Pfc	Jack	Moore
Pfc	Steve V.	Poston
Pfc	Donald B.	Richardson
Pvt	Arthur W.	Green
Pvt	Jake	Hall

Rank	Name	
Pvt	Willie	Garrett
Pvt	Fox	Hall
Pvt	Samuel	Lamb
Cpl	Ned	Combs
Tec 5	Bernard	Collins
Pfc	Earnest	Bartee
Pfc	Murray	Carter
Pvt	Edward L.	Archer
Pvt	Willie	Armstrong
Pvt	Eddie L.	Bond
Pvt	Earl J.	Burgess
Pvt	M. B.	Buckley
Pvt	Clyde L.	Cannon
Pvt	Leonard E.	Clerk
Pvt	James	Brantley
Pvt	Hanford Jr.	DeGroat
Cpl	Oliver	Blissitt
Pfc	Benjamin F. Jr.	Hale
Pfc	James	Hardaway
Pfc	Edward C.	Hughes
Pfc	Isiah H.	Landrum
Pfc	John A.	McKeever
Pvt	Ralph	Dean
Pvt	Cerena	Edmond
Pvt	Charles	Farley
Pvt	Lawrence K.	Finch
Pvt	Edward J.	Gale
Pfc	Jay D.	Hudson
Pvt	Billie W.	Wilcox
Pvt	Cleveland H.	Mosley

Appendix B

List of casualties

Casualties sustained by the 614th Tank Destroyer Battalion

Rank	Name		Date	Cause
Pfc	Clarence	Clark	11/22/1944	Died, non-battle
Pvt	Guilford	Cutler	11/30/1944	KIA
Cpl	Lincoln	Sterling	11/30/1944	LWA
Pfc	Frederick	Tucker	11/30/1944	LWA
Pvt	Arlis	Tarkington	11/30/1944	LWA
Cpl	Lewis	Gregory	12/10/1944	KIA
Tec 5	Odell	Jeffries	12/14/1944	KIA
Tec 5	James J.	Robeson	12/14/1944	LIA
Pfc	Howard	Kenneth	12/14/1944	LIA
Pfc	Jesse T.	Sturdivant	12/14/1944	SWA
1st Lt	Charles L.	Thomas	12/14/1944	LWA
Cpl	Peter	Simmons	12/14/1944	SWA (Died later)
Pfc	William H.	Phipps	12/14/1944	KIA
Pfc	Lucius	Riley	12/14/1944	KIA
Cpl	Al Jr.	Hockadey	12/14/1944	LWA
Tec 5	James A.	Perry	12/14/1944	LWA
Pfc	Willie	Modlin	12/14/1944	LWA
Pvt	Sam	Patrick	12/14/1944	LWA
Pvt	Linwood	Johnson	12/14/1944	LWA
Pvt	Shelton	Murph	12/14/1944	KIA
Pvt	Leon	Tobin	12/14/1944	SWA
Pvt	Horace L.	Whitfield	12/14/1944	LWA
Sgt	Roosevelt	Robertson	12/14/1944	LWA
Sgt	Dillard L.	Booker	12/14/1944	LWA
Pfc	Paul	Bland	1/6/1945	LWA
1st Lt	Ormond A.	Forte	1/20/1945	LIA
Pvt	Martin	Moncrief	1/22/1945	LWA
Pfc	Scott	Jarrett	1/25/1945	KIA
Pfc	Henry	Eaton	1/25/1945	LWA

Rank	Name		Date	Cause
Sgt	Bonnie O.	Harris	1/25/1945	SWA
1st Lt	George W.	Mitchell	1/27/1945	MIA
S/Sgt	William L.	Tabron	1/27/1945	MIA
Sgt	Wilbert	Welch	1/27/1945	MIA
Sgt	Walter	West	1/27/1945	MIA
Cpl	Whit L.	Knight	1/27/1945	MIA
Cpl	Plato	King	1/27/1945	MIA
Tec 5	Thomas J.	Hanebel	1/27/1945	MIA
Pfc	Robert L.	Bullock	1/27/1945	MIA
Pvt	Reed Jr.	Jones	1/27/1945	MIA
Pvt	George H.	Punch	1/27/1945	MIA
Pvt	Charlie B.	Rattler	1/27/1945	MIA
Cpl	Blease	Spell	1/27/1945	MIA
Pvt	Clarence	Reese	1/27/1945	LWA
Pvt	Blancard L.	Parker	2/14/1945	Died, non battle
Tec 5	James E.	Barbee	2/15/1945	LWA
Pvt	Curtis F.	Swinger	2/16/1945	LWA
Pfc	Albert T.	Dobey	2/19/1945	LIA
Pfc	Riley	Weeks	2/28/1945	LWA
Capt	Beauregard	King	3/15/1945	SWA
Tec 5	Letster L.	Latson	3/16/1945	SWA
Sgt	Elijah A.	Gibson	3/19/1945	SWA
Pvt	Henry R.	Hart	3/23/1945	DOI
Pfc	Robert B.	Russell	3/23/1945	LIA
Pfc	Aubrey	Harries	3/23/1945	LIA
Pfc	Albert T.	Dobey	3/23/1945	LIA
Pvt	George A.	Wright	3/23/1945	LIA
Pvt	James	William	3/23/1945	LIA
Pfc	Carol	Fultz	4/4/1945	LIA
Pfc	John H.	Evans	4/9/1945	LIA
Pvt	Thomas	Mitchell	4/17/1945	Died Non-battle
S/Sgt	James F.	McDougald	4/22/1945	KIA
Sgt	Ernest	Joynes	4/22/1945	LWA
2nd Lt	Adam	Berry	4/23/1945	SWA
Tec 4	Hubbert	Phillips	4/23/1945	SWA
Cpl	James W.	Parker	4/23/1945	SWA
Tec 5	Levitus A.	Deloney	4/23/1945	SWA

Appendix B: List of casualties 183

Rank	Name		Date	Cause
Pfc	Robert B.	Beamon	4/23/1945	LWA
Pfc	Thurston B.	Smith	4/23/1945	SWA
Pfc	Charlie P.	Taylor	4/23/1945	SWA
Pvt	Leroy	Booker	4/23/1945	SWA
Pvt	Earl J.	Burgess	4/23/1945	SWA
Pvt	Arthur Jr.	Mixon	4/23/1945	KIA
Pvt	Frank J.	Williams	4/24/1945	LWA
Tec 5	Luell J.	Love	4/25/2020	LWA
Pfc	Freeman J.	Whitfield	4/25/1945	KIA
1st Lt	Joseph L.	Keeby	5/2/1945	KIA
Sgt	Leroy	Williams	5/2/1945	KIA
Tec 5	Austin L.	Johnson	5/2/1945	KIA
Tec 5	Robert L.	Smith	5/2/1945	KIA
Pfc	James C.	Harper	5/2/1945	KIA
Pfc (Med Det)	Jerome W.	Whitfield	5/2/1945	KIA
Pfc	Samuel	Durham	5/2/1945	KIA
Pvt	Thomas J.	Phillips	5/2/1945	LWA
Cpl	Elmer J.	Kelley	5/3/1945	Died Non-battle
Pvt	James O.	Parker	5/4/1945	DOI
Tec 4	Willie Jr.	Thompson	5/4/1945	SIA
Pfc	James L.	Gary	5/4/1945	LIA
Pfc	Roy	Harris	5/4/1945	LIA
Pfc	George H.	Johnson	5/4/1945	LIA
Pvt	Tolbert	Miles	5/4/1945	LIA
Pvt	Arthur	Littles	5/4/1945	LIA
Pvt	Bennett F.	Garner	5/4/1945	LIA
Sgt	Samuel	Booker	5/5/1945	LWA
Tec 5	Wylon	Davis	5/5/1945	LWA
Pfc	Alfred W.	Nichols	6/22/1945	Died Non-battle
Pvt	Eddie L.	Bond	7/19/1945	Died Non-battle

Appendix C

Medals and citation

Throughout its history, many of the soldiers distinguished themselves, both inside and outside of combat. A platoon of the battalion and individual soldiers received the following awards: one Distinguished Unit Citation, one Distinguished Service Cross, which was later upgraded to the Medal of Honor, eight Silver Star Medals and thirty Bronze Star Medals. These have all been compiled here.

Citation: Distinguished Unit Citation

The 3d Platoon, Company 'C', 614th Tank Destroyer Battalion is cited for outstanding performance of duty in action against the enemy on 14 December 1944, in the vicinity of Climbach, France. The 3d Platoon was an element of a task force whose mission was to storm and capture the strategically important town of Climbach, France, on the approaches to the Siegfried Line. Upon reaching the outskirts of the town, the task force was halted by a terrific hail of fire from an enemy force firmly entrenched in the surrounding woods and hills overlooking the route of approach. The only position available for direct fire upon the enemy was an open field. As the 3d Platoon moved into position, its commander and several men were wounded. Undeterred by heavy enemy small arms, mortar and artillery fire, which was now being directed against their position. The men of the 3d Platoon valiantly set up their three inch guns and delivered accurate and deadly fire into the enemy positions. Casualties were mounting; two of their four guns were knocked out; nevertheless the remaining crew members heroically assisted in the loading and firing of the other guns. At the height of the battle, enemy infantry converged on the position from the surrounding woods, threatening to wipe out the platoon's position. While a few members of the gun crews remained firing the three inch guns, others manned machine guns and individual weapons, laying down a devastating curtain of fire which inflicted numerous casualties on the enemy and successfully repulsed the attack. During the fire-fight an ammunition shortage developed, and gun crews were reduced to skeleton size, one man loading, aiming and firing, while the other men repeatedly traveled a distance of fifty yards through a hail of mortar and small arms fire, to obtain shells from a halftrack which had been set on fire by a direct hit from an enemy mortar shell. Heedless of possible injury men continuously exposed themselves to enemy fire to render first aid to the wounded. In this engagement, although the Platoon suffered over fifty percent casualties and lost considerable material, its valorous conduct in the face of overwhelming odds enabled the task force to capture its objective. The grim determination, the indomitable fighting spirit and the esprit de corps displayed by all members of the 3d Platoon reflect the highest traditions of the Armed Forces of the United States.

Citation: Distinguished Service Cross

Charles L. Thomas, 01824391, First Lieutenant, Field Artillery, Company 'C', 614th Tank Destroyer Battalion (towed), for extraordinary heroism in action on 14 December 1944, near Climbach, France. While riding in the lead vehicle of a task force organized to storm and capture the village of Climbach, France, Lieutenant Thomas's armored scout car was subjected to intense enemy artillery, self-propelled gun, and small arms fire. Although wounded by the initial burst of hostile fire, Lieutenant Thomas signaled the remainder of the column to halt and, despite the severity of his wounds, assisted the crew of the wrecked car in dismounting. Upon leaving the scant protection which the vehicle afforded, Lieutenant Thomas was again subjected to a hail of enemy fire which inflicted multiple gunshot wounds in his chest, legs and left arm. Despite the intense pain caused by these wounds, Lieutenant Thomas ordered and directed the dispersion and emplacement of two anti-tank guns which in a few moments were effectively returning the enemy fire. Realizing that he could no longer remain in command of the platoon, he signaled to the platoon commander to join him. Lieutenant Thomas then thoroughly oriented him on enemy gun dispositions and the general situation. Only after he was certain that his junior officer was in full control of the situation did he permit himself to be evacuated. Entered military service from Detroit, Michigan.

Citation: Silver Star
First Lieutenant Walter S. Smith, 01824931, FA (TD), Tank Destroyer Battalion (Towed), for gallantry in action in Germany on 22 November 1944. Lieutenant Smith was directing the movement of his 3-inch towed guns across open, exposed terrain near Mittel when the column was heavily shelled by enemy artillery. Under fire for the first time, his men left their vehicles and sought cover. Realizing that the valuable pieces of equipment must be moved if they were to escape total destruction, Lieutenant Smith, by fearless example, rallied his platoon, ordered an immediate resumption of the march and brought all guns, vehicles and men through the hail of fire without loss. His aggressiveness, inspiring courage and loyalty to duty are worthy of the highest praise. Entered Military Service from Kansas.

Citation: Silver Star
Second Lieutenant (then Staff Sergeant) Christopher J. Sturkey, 02000693, FA (TD) Tank Destroyer Battalion (Towed) for gallantry in action in Germany on 22 November 1944. Lieutenant Sturkey was helping to direct the movement of 3-inch towed guns across terrain which was heavily pounded by hostile artillery fire. When his comrades left their vehicles and sought cover, Lieutenant Sturkey, perceiving that the valuable pieces of equipment must immediately be moved if they were to escape total destruction, braved the bombardment and, by courageous example, encouraged the men to return to their vehicles and resume the march. By his action, he brought all weapons and men

to safety without loss. Lieutenant Sturkey's gallantry and leadership reflect the highest credit upon himself and the army. Entered Military Service from Michigan.

Citation: Silver Star
Private First Class Leon Tobin, 34311075, Field Artillery, Company 'C', 614th Tank Destroyer Battalion. For gallantry in action. During the daylight hours of 14 December 1944, in the vicinity of Climbach, France, Private Tobin, a member of a task force in the attack, went into position in open terrain under severe enemy artillery and small arms fire to man a 3-inch gun. Although his position was in direct line of enemy fire and full observation he brilliantly and skillfully directed fire into enemy strongpoints. The intensity of the fire became so severe that the area was blasted by hostile fire wounding and killing his comrades on all sides of him. In the face of certain self-destruction he gallantly stood at his post manning the gun with the assistance of one other comrade. He continued to pour fire into the enemy with such relentless furor and utter disregard for his life, that they became confused. When his comrade was killed he remained at his post unassisted until he was cut down by direct fire suffering excruciating pain from severe wounds. Private Tobin's display of gallantry and superior calmness in the face of devastating fire materially assisted the attacking infantry in reaching their objective successfully. Residence: Monroe, Louisiana.

Citation: Silver Star
First Lieutenant George W. Mitchell, 01822712, Field Artillery, Company 'C', 614th Tank Destroyer Battalion. For gallantry in action. During the daylight hours of 14 December 1944, Lieutenant Mitchell as second in command of a tank destroyer platoon, with a task force attacking Climbach, France, took command of the platoon, when his platoon leader was wounded. Constantly exposed to intense enemy artillery, mortars and small arms fire, he magnificently and efficiently directed the fire of his guns against enemy positions. Numerous

times, with utter disregard for his life, he moved from gun to gun supplementing the gun crews as the complement of gun positions were reduced by enemy action. In one instance, Lieutenant Mitchell gallantly manned a gun, loading, sighting and firing it single-handedly. He courageously exposed himself, to aid in the evacuation of the wounded from the front line to places of safety and many lives were saved by this action. Lieutenant Mitchell's display of coolness under fire and magnificent courage, was an inspiration to all and contributed to a large degree in the successful capture and occupation of Climbach, with a minimum of casualties to the task force. Residence: Gary, Indiana.

Citation: (Posthumous) Silver Star

Corporal Peter Simmons, 34513288, Field Artillery, Company 'C', 614th Tank Destroyer Battalion. For gallantry in action. During the daylight hours of 14 December 1944, in the vicinity of Climbach, France, Corporal Simmons, a member of a task force in the attack, went into position in open terrain under severe enemy artillery and small arms fire to man a 3-inch gun. Although his position was in direct line of enemy fire and in full observation, he brilliantly and skillfully directed fire into enemy strongpoints. The intensity of the fire became so severe that the area was blasted by hostile fire wounding and killing his comrades on all sides. In the face of certain self-destruction he gallantly stood at his post manning the gun with the assistance of one other comrade. He continued to pour fire into the enemy with such relentless furor and utter disregard for his life, that they became confused. An enemy bullet found its mark and Corporal Simmons fell mortally wounded. As a result of his display of outstanding gallantry and superior calmness in the face of devastating fire he materially assisted the attacking infantry in reaching their objective. Throughout this entire action Corporal Simmons' display of valor was in accordance with the highest traditions of the military service. Residence: Silver Street, South Carolina. Next of kin: Mrs. Maneuia Simmons (mother), Route 1, Box 12, Silver Street, South Carolina.

Citation: (Posthumous) Silver Star

Private First Class William H. Phipps, 34459324, Field Artillery, Company 'C', 614th Tank Destroyer Battalion. For gallantry in action. On 14 December 1944, in the vicinity of Climbach, France, Private Phipps was seriously wounded while driving his quarter ton truck through an artillery barrage. Private Phipps, with utter disregard for his life, on his own initiative, drove his platoon leader to a gun position without revealing his bitter wounds. He courageously drove forward in face of the intense enemy artillery and bazooka fire, firing his weapon until he collapsed from his mortal wound. His valiant action assisted materially in the success of the infantry's mission. Private Phipps's outstanding valor and spirit of duty were in accordance with the highest traditions of the military service. Residence: Littleton, North Carolina. Next of kin: Mr. Wiley Phipps (uncle) Route 2, Box 276, Littleton, North Carolina.

Citation: Silver Star

First Lieutenant Serreo S. Nelson, 01823192, Field Artillery, Second Reconnaissance Platoon, 614th Tank Destroyer Battalion. For gallantry in action. On 23 March 1945, when a reconnaissance party of a task force was ambushed by fifty of the enemy and ordered to surrender, Lieutenant Nelson opened fire with his light machine gun, enabling the group to withdraw without loss. Retracing their route, the party was stopped by a wagon placed as a hasty roadblock and covered by automatic weapon fire. Lieutenant Nelson dismounted, opened fire, assisted in moving the wagon from the road and led his men safely to the rear of the task force. A short time later, the task force was subjected to enemy fire from high ground and a hostile attempt was made to free prisoners in the rear of the column. Lieutenant Nelson organized his men, returned the fire and broke up the hostile attempt. His actions reflected the highest traditions of the military service. Residence: Omaha, Nebraska.

Citation: (Posthumous) Silver Star

First Lieutenant Joseph L. Keeby, 01823168, Field Artillery, First Reconnaissance Platoon, 614th Tank Destroyer Battalion. For gallantry in action. On 2 May 1945, near Scharnitz, Austria, when the leading vehicle of a task force was hit by enemy fire, Lieutenant Keeby immediately took the lead position in his armored car. Disregarding heavy enemy anti-tank, small arms and machine gun fire, he moved forward to seize critical bridges located in the town. When an anti-tank shell knocked out his armored car he was fatally wounded by machine gun fire. His aggressive actions which disclosed the enemy gun positions and led to the capture of the town reflected the highest traditions of the military service. Residence: Chicago, Illinois. Next of kin: Mrs. Quarcia M. Keeby, (Wife), 6120 Eberhart Avenue, Chicago, Illinois.

Citation: Bronze Star

Private First Class Whit L. Knight, 34450873, Field Artillery, Company 'C', 614th Tank Destroyer Battalion. For heroism in action. During the day of 14 December 1944, in the vicinity of Climbach, France, Private Knight, a member of a task force in the attack, skillfully sighted, loaded and fired his 3-inch gun single-handedly directly into approaching enemy forces. The area surrounding him was constantly blasted by intense enemy small arms and artillery fire but with undaunted courage and with utter disregard for his life, he remained at his post. Realizing his gun was inadequate to impede the progress of the onrushing enemy, he dashed courageously to a nearby machine gun directing devastating fire into their midst. Private Knight's outstanding valor assisted immeasurably in forcing the enemy to withdraw, enabling our infantry to push forward successfully toward their objective. Residence: Kingston, North Carolina.

Citation: Bronze Star

Technician Fifth Grade Robert W. Harris, 37376570, Field Artillery, Company 'C', 614th Tank Destroyer Battalion. For heroism in action.

During the daylight hours of 14 December 1944, in the vicinity of Climbach, France, Technician Harris, a member of a task force in the attack, fully cognizant that his gun crews were running out of ammunition, brilliantly drove his truck over fire-swept roads to obtain vitally needed ammunition. When the truck was fully loaded with ammunition, he courageously drove forward toward his gun positions. About halfway to his objective, he was stopped by the task force commander and informed that if he went farther he was certain to be hit by enemy fire. With utter disregard for his life and displaying magnificent courage, he skillfully drove his vehicle to within 25 yards of his gun positions as intense enemy small arms, mortar and artillery fire blasted his path. He unloaded the truck, uncrated the ammunition boxes and valiantly carried the ammunition forward to each gun emplacement. Technican Harris' outstanding valor in the face of devastating enemy fire materially assisted the attacking infantry troops in reaching their objective successfully. Residence: Marcelline, Missouri.

Citation: Bronze Star

Technician Fifth Grade James A. Perry, 34460951, Field Artillery, Company 'C', 614th Tank Destroyer Battalion. For heroism in action. During the daylight hours of 14 December 1944, in the vicinity of Climbach, France, Technician Perry, a member of a task force in the attack, skillfully manned his gun from an exposed position in order to fire accurately and efficiently into enemy strongpoints. The area surrounding his position was constantly blasted by enemy machine gun, mortar and artillery fire. In the face of this withering action he continued to fire directly into enemy positions with utter disregard for his life. In addition to neutralizing ferocious enemy activity to his front, he brilliantly directed fire on an enemy machine gun nest close by, wiping it out. As a result of Technician Perry's magnificent courage, attacking infantry troops were materially assisted in advancing successfully to their objective. Residence: Louisburg, North Carolina.

Citation: Bronze Star
Private Thomas C. McDaniel. 34321721, Field Artillery, Company 'C', 614th Tank Destroyer Battalion. For heroism in action. During the daylight hours of 14 December 1944, Private McDaniel was a member of a task force assigned the mission of capturing the town of Climbach, France. The platoon of which he was a member, moved into positions in open terrain exposed to intense enemy machine gun and artillery fire. Keenly observing enemy grenadiers attempting to outflank his section, he, with utter disregard for his life, courageously manned a .30 caliber machine gun and successfully stopped their attack, inflicting several casualties. His heroic action, in the face of heavy enemy fire, materially assisted the accomplishment of the task force's mission. Residence: Chattanooga, Tennessee.

Citation: Bronze Star
Sergeant Dillard L. Booker, 32811587, Field Artillery, Company 'C', 614th Tank Destroyer Battalion. For heroism in action. During the daylight hours of 14 December 1944, in the vicinity of Climbach, France, Sergeant Booker, on his own initiative, brought his 3-inch gun forward into an advantageous, but exposed position. Being in advance of our infantry lines, he and his crew was unable to obtain supporting fire, but disregarding personal safety advanced forward. He was afforded excellent observation of the enemy by placing his gun in an open field but it enabled strong enemy forces to lay down an intense artillery and small arms barrage around the gun position. Undaunted by these harassing conditions, he courageously carried out his mission and destroyed numerous enemy strongpoints. His heroic actions so disrupted the opposing forces that our infantry was able to deploy around the flanks of the enemy and overwhelmed them. This resulted in our forces successful advance and entry into Climbach, France. Residence: New York, New York.

Citation: Bronze Star

Sergeant William L Tabron, 34460307, Field Artillery, Company 'C', 614th Tank Destroyer Battalion. For heroism in action. During the day of 14 December 1944, Sergeant Tabron was a member of task force whose mission was to capture the town of Climbach, France. While approaching their objective the entire task force was pinned down by heavy small arms and artillery fire emanating from enemy pillboxes. Disregarding the intense enemy fire, Sergeant Tabron, with his crew, went forward with their towed gun and set up in an open field exposed to hostile fire. With utter disregard for his life, he courageously manned his .50 caliber machine gun to protect his crew, some of which were wounded, from enemy grenadiers attempting to flank their position. Unnerved by the wounds received in this action, he remained at his post until the infantry successfully pressed forward its attack. His devotion to duty and self-sacrifice was an inspiration to all. Residence: Wilson, North Carolina.

Citation: Bronze Star

First Lieutenant Floyd J. Stallings, 01824814, Field Artillery, Company 'C', 614th Tank Destroyer Battalion. For heroism in action. During the daylight hours of 14 December 1944, in the vicinity of Climbach, France, Lieutenant Stallings, as a member of a task force in the attack, observed his company commander lying in an exposed position, wounded, the victim of enemy fire. With utter disregard for his life he courageously dashed 100 yards over open terrain under a severe enemy machine gun, mortar and artillery concentration. Completely oblivious of the withering fire that raked his path, he succeeded in reaching his wounded commander's side. At great personal risk, he valiantly assisted his commanding officer to the nearest aid station. As a result of Lieutenant Stallings's display of magnificent courage, prompt and efficient medical attention was administered expeditiously. Residence: San Francisco, California.

Citation: Bronze Star

Corporal Al Hockaday, Jr., 34459213, Field Artillery, Company 'C', 614th Tank Destroyer Battalion. For heroism in action. During the daylight hours of 14 December 1944, in the vicinity of Climbach, France, Corporal Hockaday, a gun commander, successfully placed his gun in a forward position where excellent observation was available on the entrenched enemy forces. The enemy, realizing the serious threat facing them, laid down a murderous artillery barrage about him. This terrific onslaught of enemy fire knocked out a nearby gun crew. With utter disregard for his safety, he fearlessly began sighting and firing the nearby gun. Despite the severity of the enemy action about him he courageously manned both guns single-handedly and successfully disrupted the enemy forces to such an extent that our infantry was able to move forward and seize their objective. Residence: Roanoke, North Carolina.

Citation: Bronze Star

Technician Fourth Grade Paul Warner, 33316456, Field Artillery, Company 'C', 614th Tank Destroyer Battalion. For heroism in action. During the daylight hours of 14 December 1944, in the vicinity of Climbach, France, Technician Warner, a member of a task force in the attack, observed his company commander lying in an exposed position wounded, the victim of enemy fire. Realizing that immediate evacuation was necessary, he dashed to his vehicle and sped across 75 yards of fire-swept terrain to rescue his commanding officer. As he maneuvered the vehicle out into open terrain, enemy small arms and artillery fire blasted his path but he continued on with undaunted courage and with utter disregard for his life. He remained under this devastating fire for over fifteen minutes while he assisted in placing the officer in the vehicle. He again skillfully crossed the area of concentrated fire and reached the nearest aid station quickly. As a result of Technician Warner's outstanding valor in the face of intense enemy fire, medical attention was rendered expeditiously to his commanding officer. Residence: Crestmont, Pennsylvania.

Citation: Bronze Star
First Lieutenant Joseph L. Keeby, 01823168, Field Artillery, First Reconnaissance Platoon, 614th Tank Destroyer Battalion. For heroism in action. On the night of 4 February 1945, Lieutenant Keeby was in command of a raiding party whose mission was to capture the enemy located in a mill between Bitcholtz and Mulhausen, France. Lieutenant Keeby brilliantly planned and executed the raid, maintaining the enthusiasm of the raiding party throughout the entire action. He led his patrol to the mill and was with the initial assault elements when they entered the enemy strongpoint. In the fight that followed, Lieutenant Keeby quickly disposed of one of the enemy by a well placed hand grenade. His resourcefulness materially assisted in capturing six of the enemy and in obtaining valuable information. His actions were in accordance with the highest traditions of military service. Residence: Chicago, Illinois.

Citation: Bronze Star
Private First Class Henry Weaver, 33199728, Field Artillery, Second Reconnaissance Platoon, 614th Tank Destroyer Battalion. For heroism in action. During the night of 4 February 1945, in the vicinity of Bitcholtz, France, Private Weaver was a member of an assault group whose mission was to enter an enemy held building on the outskirts of town and capture the occupants. As they approached the objective, enemy automatic rifle fire was directed at them. Private Weaver, quickly observing the source of fire, killed the enemy rifle man before he was able to inflict casualties upon the group. As a result of this raid, six enemy prisoners were taken and valuable information obtained. Private Weaver's heroic action in this engagement was in accordance with the highest traditions of the military service. Residence: Baltimore, Maryland.

Citation: Bronze Star

Private First Class, Thomas Ingram, 18213303, Field Artillery, First Reconnaissance Platoon, 614th Tank Destroyer Battalion. For heroism in action. During a raid by our forces in the vicinity of Bitcholtz, France, on 4 February 1945, Private Ingram was assigned to a security group with the mission of protecting the assault group. As the men moved out, the enemy opened fire with a machine gun temporarily halting further progress. Firing with deadly accuracy, Private Ingram killed the enemy machine gunner, allowing the assault group to proceed. As a result of the raid, six enemy prisoners were taken and valuable information obtained. Private Ingram's heroic action in this engagement was in accordance with the highest traditions of the military service. Residence: Fort Worth, Texas.

Citation: Bronze Star

Private Leo Greer, 38137617, Field Artillery, Second Reconnaissance Platoon, 614th Tank Destroyer Battalion. For heroism in action. During a raid by our forces in the vicinity of Bitcholtz, France, on 4 February 1945, Private Greer was assigned to a security group with the mission of protecting the assault group. As he moved forward to his position, he discovered a machine gun nest manned by two of the enemy about to open fire on the assault group. He attacked the machine gun position, killed the two enemy soldiers and moved on to his assigned post. As a result of this raid, six enemy prisoners were taken and valuable information obtained. Private Greer's heroic action was in accordance with the highest traditions of the military service. Residence: St Augustine, Texas.

Citation: Bronze Star

Private George Bass, 14019371, Field Artillery, First Reconnaissance Platoon, 614th Tank Destroyer Battalion. For heroism in action. During a raid by our forces in the vicinity of Bitcholtz, France, on 4 February 1945, Private Bass was a member of a six-man assault group whose mission was to enter a building occupied by the enemy, and either kill or capture them. Bravely preceding his group into the building, Private Bass sprayed the room with fire from his automatic rifle, creating an element of surprise and pinning down the enemy. The assault group proceeded to successfully accomplish its mission and as a result of the raid six of the enemy were taken prisoner and valuable information obtained. Private Bass's action in this engagement was in accordance with the highest traditions of the military service. Residence: Columbus, Georgia.

Citation: Bronze Star

Captain Beauregard King, 0412501, Field Artillery, Company A, 614th Tank Destroyer Battalion. For heroic achievement in action. On 15 March 1945, Captain King planned and organized a small task force for an attack on Kindwiller, France. Leading his men in the attack, Captain King was severely wounded by enemy automatic weapon fire. After falling to the ground, he called his second in command and urged him to continue the attack, which resulted in the capture of the village and the taking of a number of prisoners. Captain King's outstanding leadership reflected the highest traditions of the military service. Residence: Tabuco, Alabama.

Citation: Bronze Star

Private First Class Thomas L. Kilgo, Jr., 34461097, Medical Department, Medical Detachment, 614th Tank Destroyer Battalion. For heroism in action. On 15 March 1945, Private Kilgo, medical aid man, was attached to a small task force attacking Kindwiller, France, when heavy enemy automatic weapon fire wounded the task force commander. Disregarding the enemy fire, Private Kilgo made his way over the open ground and administered aid to the fallen officer. Private Kilgo's actions, resulting in the prompt evacuation of a wounded man, reflected the highest traditions of the military service. Residence: Asheville, North Carolina.

Citation: Bronze Star

Staff Sergeant Charles E. Parks, 34459861, Field Artillery, Company A, 614th Tank Destroyer Battalion. For heroic achievement in action. On 15 March 1945, Sergeant Parks assisted in planning and organizing an attack by a small task force. When the task force commander was wounded, Sergeant Parks took command and led the group over open ground in the face of heavy enemy automatic weapon fire to take the village and capture a number of the enemy. Sergeant Park's display of courage and leadership reflected the highest traditions of the military service. Residence: Charlotte, North Carolina.

Citation: Bronze Star

Private First Class Mark H. Ray, 34302120, Field Artillery, Headquarters Company, 614th Tank Destroyer Battalion. For heroism in action. On 19 March 1945, near Nothweiler, Germany, when a blown bridge prevented a reconnaissance platoon from moving forward in their vehicles, Private Ray advanced on foot, carrying his machine gun. The platoon was immediately pinned down by heavy enemy machine gun fire from four well concealed emplacements, which wounded his section Sergeant. Disregarding the enemy fire, Private Ray assisted the wounded man to the platoon command post, where he aided in pointing out on a map, the exact location of the enemy positions. This information proved to be of valuable assistance in the planning of future operations. Private Ray's actions reflected the highest traditions of the military service. Residence: Franklin, North Carolina.

Citation: Bronze Star

Sergeant Elijah Gibson, 34550577, Field Artillery, Headquarters Company, 614th Tank Destroyer Battalion. For heroism in action. On 19 March 1945, near [CENSORED] Germany, when a blown bridge prevented a reconnaissance platoon from moving forward in their vehicles, Sergeant Gibson proceeded forward to a position to observe enemy dispositions. He opened fire on three of the enemy that he observed on the road and the enemy immediately fired upon the platoon from well concealed positions. Disregarding the enemy fire, Sergeant Gibson continued firing and observing enemy positions, until he was wounded. Before being evacuated beyond the platoon command post, Sergeant Gibson pointed out on a map the exact locations of the enemy positions. This information proved to be of valuable assistance in the planning of future operations. Sergeant Gibson's actions reflected the highest traditions of the military service.

Citation: Bronze Star
Private First Class Ronald Pollard, 38063301, Field Artillery, Headquarters Company, 614th Tank Destroyer Battalion. For heroism in action. During the night of 22 March 1945, a motorized reconnaissance platoon was ambushed by the enemy and further progress was halted by a wagon placed as a temporary roadblock. Private Pollard immediately fired his light machine gun until it jammed, then using his sub-machine gun until he expended the ammunition, he picked up a machine gun from a member of the platoon and continued firing. Disregarding heavy enemy fire, he led a small group of men and directed the removal of the wagon, permitting the platoon to escape and continue its mission. Private Pollard's actions reflected the highest traditions of the military service. Residence: Sweetsprinqs, Missouri.

Citation: Bronze Star
Sergeant Matthew Spencer, 35479070, Field Artillery, Second Reconnaissance Platoon, 614th Tank Destroyer Battalion. For heroism in action. During the night of 22 March 1945, a motorized task force reconnaissance section was halted by heavy enemy automatic weapon fire from both sides of the road. In the action that followed, an enemy officer armed with a submachine gun attempted to shoot Sergeant Spencer's platoon leader. Sergeant Spencer knocked the enemy officer off balance with the butt of his carbine, deflecting the enemy officer's

fire. After the enemy soldier was killed Sergeant Spencer assisted in the direction of fire into the hostile positions, enabling the section to proceed on its mission. His actions reflected the highest traditions of the military service. Residence: Louisville, Kentucky.

Citation: (Posthumous) Bronze Star
Staff Sergeant James F. McDougald, 32801434, Field Artillery, Company B, 614th Tank Destroyer Battalion. For meritorious service in action from 7 September 1944 to 21 April 1945 in France and Germany. Sergeant McDougald, Company Supply Sergeant worked long hours and performed his duties in a highly commendable manner. His devotion to duty amazed the company at all times to be supplied with critical items. In pursuit of his duties he was mortally wounded by enemy small arms fire. His actions reflected the highest traditions of the military service. Residence: New York, New York. Next of kin: Mrs. Monai McDougald (wife), 1890 Seventh Avenue, New York, New York.

Citation: Bronze Star
Lieutenant Colonel Frank S. Pritchard, 0139855, Infantry, Headquarters 614th Tank Destroyer Battalion. For meritorious service in connection with military operations against the enemy during the period 10 December 1944 to 13 April 1945, in France and Germany. Residence: Lansing, Michigan.

Citation: Bronze Star
Start Sergeant John J. Lee, 12085416, Medical Department, Medical Detachment, 614th Tank Destroyer Battalion, from 10 March to 1 April 1945, in France and Germany. Residence: Brooklyn, New York.

Citation: Bronze Star
Staff Sergeant Lazarus Garrett, 38048785, Field Artillery, Company A, 614th Tank Destroyer Battalion, from 1 December 1944 to 28 February 1945, in France. Residence: Fort Worth, Texas.

Citation: Bronze Star
First Sergeant Robert Cannon, 13079356, Field Artillery, Company C, 614th Tank Destroyer Battalion, from 27 January to 8 May 1945, in France, Germany and Austria. Residence: Philadelphia, Pennsylvania.

Citation: Bronze Star
Technician Fifth Grade Isaac Brewer, 34167052, Field Artillery, Company A, 614th Tank Destroyer Battalion from 7 September 1944 to 8 May 1945, in France, Germany and Austria. Residence: Birmingham, Alabama.

Citation: Bronze Star
Major Robert J. O'Leary, 01166577, Field Artillery, Headquarters 614th Tank Destroyer Battalion, from 10 March to 1 May 1945 in France and Germany. Residence: Glenburn, North Dakota.

Citation: Bronze Star
First Lieutenant Ormond A. Forte Jr., 01822983, Field Artillery, Headquarters 614th Tank Destroyer Battalion, from 10 December 1944 to 15 February 1945 in France. Residence: Chicago, Illinois.

Citation: Bronze Star
Major Leroy H. Sample, 0285690, Infantry, Headquarters 614th Tank Destroyer Battalion, from 10 March to 1 May 1945 in France and Germany. Residence: Mt Clemens, Michigan.

Literature and sources

'95TH VICTORY DIVISION, SAARLAUTERN, GERMANY; NEGRO TANK DESTROYERS, BITSCHOFEN, GERMANY', 16687, 111-ADC-2884, Department of Defense. Department of the Army. Office of the Chief Signal Officer. (9/18/1947 – 3/1/1964), Series: Moving Images Relating to Military Activities, 1947 – 1964 Record Group 111: Records of the Office of the Chief Signal Officer, 1860 – 1985.

'Arsenal of Democracy', President Roosevelt, December 29, 1940, accessed through: https://www.mtholyoke.edu/acad/intrel/WorldWar2/arsenal.htm.

'AWARDED DISTINGUISHED SERVICE CROSS', *The Dayton Forum*, 30 March 1945.

'Black, White Men Shed the Same Color Tears', *Lansing State Journal*, 22 March 1971.

'Col. Frank Pritchard, Lansing Newsman', *Detroit Free Press*, 28 January 1975.

'Col. Pritchard Feted on Eve of Retirement as Journal Editor', *Lansing State Journal*, 29 May 1964.

'Fighters Shifted to Service Units', *Jackson Advocate*, 23 October 1943.

'Growing up black in Shepherdstown', Congressional Record Volume 144, 20, 4 March 1998.

'James Knight Killed When Mine Explodes', *The Michigan chronicle*, 11 August 1945.

'Many Negro Combat Troops Prove Heroes in France; First Full Report on GI's in Battle', *The Daily Bulletin*, 12 March 1945.

'Lt. Mitchell: Gary's 'One Man Army' Home on Sick Leave', *The Indianapolis Recorder*, 22 September 1945.

'Negro Soldiers' Historic Role Recalled', *Lansing State Journal*, 18 February 1968.

'People', *The Sacramento Bee*, 13 July 2000.

'Soldier dies in gun accident at Custer', *Battle Creek Enquirer*, 19 September 1942.
'Tank Killers', *Fortune*, November 1942, 116-120.
'The troops were segregated; bullets were colorblind', *Southside Sentinel*, 21 February 2002.
'Three Inch Fury', n.d.
409th Infantry Regiment, accessed through: http://103divwwii.usm.edu/.
410th Regimental Journal, accessed through: http://103divwwii.usm.edu/.
411th Infantry Regiment, accessed through: http://103divwwii.usm.edu/.
614th Tank Destroyer Battalion, accessed through: www.tankdestroyer.net.
669th Tank Destroyer Battalion, accessed through: www.tankdestroyer.net.
679th Tank Destroyer Battalion, accessed through: www.tankdestroyer.net.
813th Tank Destroyer Battalion, accessed through: www.tankdestroyer.net.
827th Tank Destroyer Battalion, accessed through: www.tankdestroyer.net.
829th Tank Destroyer Battalion, accessed through: www.tankdestroyer.net.
Baddeley, Alan, Michael W. Eysenck, Michael C. Anderson, *Memory* (New York, 2015).
Barrios, Willie W.J., 'The Operations of 'F' Company, 411th Infantry (103d Infantry Division) Near Climbach, France, (Alsace), 14 December 1944 (Rhineland Campaign) (Personal Experience of a Rifle Company Commander)'.
Baily, Charles M., *Faint Praise: American Tanks and Tank Destroyers during World War II* (North Haven, 1983).
Battistelli, Pier Paolo, *Panzer Divisions 1944-45* (Oxford 2009).
Charles T. Boyle, 'Operations of an advance command post party 411th Infantry, 103d Infantry Division in the vicinity of Marktwald, Germany, 27 April 1945 (Personal Experience of Regimental Staff Officer – S-1)', Cactus Division newsletter, February 2011, 27.
Cameron, Robert, *Mobility, Shock, and Firepower: The Emergence of the U.S. Army's Armor Branch, 1917–1945* (Washington D.C., 2008).
Cefkin, J., E Company, 409th Infantry Regiment, accessed through: http://103divwwii.usm.edu/.
Center of Military History United States Army, *Biennial Reports of the Chief of Staff of the United States Army to the Secretary of War 1 July 1939 – 30 June 1945* (Washington, 1996).

Chronik der Gendarmerie von Leutasch, 8 May 1945.

Clarke, Jeffrey, & Robert Smith, *Riviera to the Rhine* (Washington D.C., 1993).

Converse, Elliott, e.a., *The Exclusion of Black soldiers from the Medal of Honor in World War II* (Jefferson, 2008).

Diana, Leonard, Company A, 410th Infantry Regiment, accessed through: http://103divwwii.usm.edu/.

Dorsey, John Thornton Jr., 'An account by a World War II Combat Infantryman'.

East, William, and William Gleason, *The 409th Infantry Regiment in World War II*, Washington, 1947.

E.T.O Board of Review, Opinions, CM ETO 10616 – CM ETO 11987, volume 23–24.

Family Archive, Lawrence Johnson.

Family Archive, Reuben Yelding.

Fifth Army History, Part IX, Race to the Alps, 1947.

Gabel, Christopher, *Seek, Strike, and Destroy: U.S. Army Tank Destroyer Doctrine in World War II*, Fort Leavenworth, 1985.

Gibran, Daniel K., *The 92nd Infantry Division and the Italian Campaign in World War II* (Jefferson, 2017).

Greenfield, Kent Roberts e.a., *The Army Ground Forces: The organization of Ground Combat Troops* (Washington D.C., 1987).

Gregory, David, 'Charles Branson (served 1942–1945)', Florida State University Special Collections & Archives, OHPCN 1148.

Hammelburg Lager, Roster of American Prisoners of War interned at Oflag XIII-B, Hammelburg, US National Archives File.

Haythornthwaite, Philip, *The World War One Sourcebook* (London, 1998).

Hood, John Bell, *Advances and Retreat* (1880).

Jefferson, Robert, 'African Americans in the U.S. Army During World War II', in: Steven D. Smith and James A. Zeidler (eds), *A Historic Context for the African American Military Experience*, Champaign, 1998.

Lankford, Jim, 'Gamecocks at War: The 614th Tank Destroyer Battalion', *On Point* (website) 2012.

Lee, Ulysses, *The Employment of Negro Troops*, Washington D. C., 2001.

Martin, Ralph, 'Negroes in Combat', *Yank: The Army Weekly*, vol. 3, 36, 23 February 1945.

Matloff, Maurice, *Command Decisions: The 90 Division Gamble* (Washington D.C. 1990) 366, 374.

Mollo, Andrew, *The Armed Forces of World War II: Uniforms, Insignia and Organization* (Hong Kong, 1981).

Montgomery, James, *B Company 776 Tank Destroyer Battalion in Combat* (Baltimore, 1983).

Mueller, Ralph, and Jerry Turk, *Report After Action: The story of the 103d Infantry Division*, Innsbruck, 1945.

Negro Digest, April 1946, volume IV, 6.

Office of Judge Advocate General of the Army, Board of review, Holdings Opinions Reviews, volume 27, 1943–1944.

Office of Judge Advocate General of the Army, Board of review, Holdings Opinions Reviews, volume 81, 1949.

Penick Motley, Mary, *The Invisible Soldier: The Experience of the Black Soldier, World War II*, Detroit, 1987.

Philips, Kimberley, *War! What's it good for? Black Freedom Struggles and the U.S. Military from World War II to Iraq* (Chapel Hill, 2012).

Rogers, Frank, 'My World War II: Company G, 409th Infantry, 103d Division', n.d.

Rusiecki, Stephen M., *In final defense of the Reich: The Destruction of the 6th SS Mountain Division 'Nord'*, (Annapolis, 2010).

Saylor, Thomas, 'Oral History Project World War II Years, 1941–1946 – James Kirk' (2003), *Oral History Project: World War II Years, 1941–1946*, 129. Accessible through: https://digitalcommons.csp.edu/oral-history_ww2/129.

Sproesser, William D., '40 days of Combat and one Day in Hell: L-Company, 411th Infantry Regiment, 103d Division'.

Stubbs, Mary Lee, and Stanley Russell Connor, *Armor-Cavalry, Part I: Regular Army and Army Reserve* (Washington, D.C., 1969) accessed through: https://history.army.mil/books/Lineage/arcav/arcav.htm.

The Crisis, December 1945.

The Cross Of Lorraine: A Combat History Of The 79th Infantry Division, June 1942-December 1945 (1986).

The General Board, United States Forces, European Theater, 'Report on Study of Organization, Equipment, and Tactical Employment of Tank Destroyer Units', n.d.

The Making of the Modern U.S., Louisiana Separate Car Act, 1890, accessed through: http://projects.leaDrmsu.edu/makingmodernus/exhibits/show/plessy-v--ferguson-1896/louisiana-separate-car-act--18.

The National WWII Museum, 'The Rise of the Panzer Division', (version: 19 July 2018) Accessible through: https://www.nationalww2museum.org/war/articles/rise-panzer-division (checked: 10 November 2020).

The 3rd Cavalry Reconnaissance Squadron (Mecz.) In World War II, 9 August 1944 To 9 May 1945, 1946.

Thorne, Robert, Journal, 17 January 1945, accessed through: https://www.trailblazersww2.org/.

White, Walter, 'It's Our Country Too: The Negro Demands the Right to Fight For It', *The Saturday Evening Post*, 213, 63.

Whiting, Charles, *48 hours to Hammelburg* (New York, 1982).

Wilson, Dale, 'The Army's Segregated Tank Battalions in World War II', *Army History*, (Fall, 1994).

Williams, Robert L., *History of the Association of Black Psychologists: Profiles of Outstanding Black Psychologists* (Bloomington, 2008).

Endnotes

Chapter 1
1. 'Three Inch Fury', n.d.
2. Mary Penick Motley, *The Invisible Soldier: The Experience of the Black Soldier, World War II* (Detroit, 1987); Thomas Saylor, 'Oral History Project World War II Years, 1941–1946 – James Kirk' (2003), *Oral History Project: World War II Years, 1941–1946*, 129. Accessible through: https://digitalcommons.csp.edu/oral-history_ww2/129; Gregory, David, 'Charles Branson (served 1942–1945)', Florida State University Special Collections & Archives, OHPCN 1148.
3. Dr Christopher Gabel, *Seek, Strike, and Destroy: U.S. Army Tank Destroyer Doctrine in World War II*, Fort Leavenworth, 1985; Robert Cameron, *Mobility, Shock, and Firepower: The Emergence of the U.S. Army's Armor Branch, 1917–1945* (Washington D.C., 2008).
4. Ralph Mueller and Jerry Turk, *Report After Action: The story of the 103d Infantry Division*, Innsbruck, 1945.
5. Jeffrey Clarke & Robert Smith, *Riviera to the Rhine* (Washington D.C., 1993).
6. Robert Jefferson, 'African Americans in the U.S. Army During World War II', in: Steven D. Smith and James A. Zeidler (eds), *A Historic Context for the African American Military Experience* (Champaign, 1998). Ulysses Lee, *The Employment of Negro Troops* (Washington D.C., 2001).
7. Elliott Converse, e. a., *The Exclusion of Black soldiers from the Medal of Honor in World War II* (Jefferson, 2008); Andrew Mollo, *The Armed Forces of World War II: Uniforms, Insignia and Organization* (Hong Kong, 1981).
8. 'Three Inch Fury', 36.
9. Alan Baddeley, Michael W. Eysenck, Michael C. Anderson, *Memory* (New York, 2015) 339-340.
10. Motley, *The Invisible Soldier*, 174.

Chapter 2

1. Philip Haythornthwaite, *The World War One Sourcebook* (London, 1998) 96.
2. The National WWII Museum, 'The Rise of the Panzer Division', (version: 19 July 2018) Accessible through: https://www.nationalww2museum.org/war/articles/rise-panzer-division (checked: 10 November 2020).
3. Gabel, *Seek, Strike, and Destroy*, 7-8, 18.
4. Cameron, *Mobility, Shock, and Firepower*, 293-294.
5. Kent Roberts Greenfield e. a., *The Army Ground Forces: The organization of Ground Combat Troops* (Washington D.C., 1987).
6. Cameron, *Mobility, Shock, and Firepower*, 305, 309.
7. Gabel, *Seek, Strike, and Destroy*, 19.
8. Gabel, *Seek, Strike, and Destroy*, 24.
9. 'Tank Killers', *Fortune*, November 1942, 116.
10. Gabel, *Seek, Strike, and Destroy*, 22.
11. 'Tank Killers', *Fortune*, 116-117.
12. 'Tank Killers', *Fortune*, 116.
13. 'Tank Killers', *Fortune*, 119.
14. Cameron, *Mobility, Shock, and Firepower*, 408.
15. Cameron, *Mobility, Shock, and Firepower*, 414.
16. Cameron, *Mobility, Shock, and Firepower*, 414; Gabel, *Seek, Strike, and Destroy*, 27.
17. Gabel, *Seek, Strike, and Destroy*, 26.
18. The General Board, 'Report on Study of Organization, Equipment, and Tactical Employment of Tank Destroyer Units', 17.
19. Gabel, *Seek, Strike, and Destroy*, 43.
20. 'Arsenal of Democracy', President Roosevelt, December 29, 1940, accessed through: https://www.mtholyoke.edu/acad/intrel/WorldWar2/arsenal.htm.
21. The Making of the Modern U.S., Louisiana Separate Car Act, 1890, accessed through: http://projects.leaDrmsu.edu/makingmodernus/exhibits/show/plessy-v--ferguson-1896/louisiana-separate-car-act--18.
22. Kimberley Philips, *War! What's it good for? Black Freedom Struggles and the U.S. Military from World War II to Iraq* (Chapel Hill, 2012) 24.
23. Philips, *War!*, 24.

Endnotes   209

24. Walter White, 'It's Our Country Too: The Negro Demands the Right to Fight For It', *The Saturday Evening Post,* 213, 63.
25. Jefferson, 'African Americans in the U.S. Army During World War II', 222-223.
26. Dale Wilson, 'The Army's Segregated Tank Battalions in World War II', *Army History,* (Fall, 1994) 15.
27. Motley, *The Invisible Soldier,* 172.
28. Office of Judge Advocate General of the Army, Board of Review, Holdings Opinions Reviews, volume 27, 1943–1944, 232.
29. Office of Judge Advocate General of the Army, Board of Review, Holdings Opinions Reviews, volume 27, 1943–1944, 233.
30. Center of Military History United States Army, *Biennial Reports of the Chief of Staff of the United States Army to the Secretary of War 1 July 1939 – 30 June 1945* (Washington, 1996) 24.
31. Lee, *The Employment of Negro Troops,* 180.
32. Special orders, 5 March 1943, 614th Tank Destroyer Battalion, accessed through: www.tankdestroyer.net.
33. Lee, *The Employment of Negro Troops,* 122.
34. 'Fighters Shifted to Service Units', *Jackson Advocate,* 23 October 1943.
35. Family Archive, Lawrence Johnson.
36. Special orders, 28 December 1942, 829th Tank Destroyer Battalion, accessed through: www.tankdestroyer.net.
37. Special orders, 21 April 1943, 829th Tank Destroyer Battalion, accessed through: www.tankdestroyer.net.
38. Unit Journal October-November 1944, 669th Tank Destroyer Battalion, accessed through: www.tankdestroyer.net.
39. Mary Lee Stubbs and Stanley Russell Connor, *Armor-Cavalry, Part I: Regular Army and Army Reserve,* (Washington, D.C., 1969) 69, accessed through: https://history.army.mil/books/Lineage/arcav/arcav.htm
40. Maurice Matloff, *Command Decisions: The 90 Division Gamble* (Washington D.C. 1990) 366, 374.
41. 'Soldier dies in gun accident at Custer', *Battle Creek Enquirer,* 19 September 1942.
42. 'Fighters Shifted To Service Units', *Jackson Advocate,* 23 October 1943.

Chapter 3

1. In a letter Hood to General Sherman made his opinion very clear: 'You came into our country with your Army, avowedly for the purpose of subjugating free white men, women, and children, and not only intend to rule over them, but you make negroes your allies, and desire to place over us an inferior race, which we have raised from barbarism to its present position, which is the highest ever attained by that race, in any country in all time. [...] Better die a thousand deaths than submit to live under you or your Government and your negro allies!' John Bell Hood, *Advances and Retreat* (1880) 235.
2. Gabel, *Seek, Strike, and Destroy*, 47-48.
3. Motley, *The Invisible Soldier*, 167.
4. Motley, *The Invisible Soldier*, 167-168.
5. 'Col. Pritchard Feted on Eve of Retirement as Journal Editor', *Lansing State Journal*, 29 May 1964.
6. Motley, *The Invisible Soldier*, 168.
7. 'Black, White Men Shed the Same Color Tears', *Lansing State Journal*, 22 March 1971.
8. 'Black, White Men Shed the Same Color Tears', *Lansing State Journal*, 22 March 1971.
9. 'Three Inch Fury', 6.
10. 'Three Inch Fury', 6-7.
11. 'Three Inch Fury', 7.
12. 'Three Inch Fury', 7.
13. 'Three Inch Fury', 7.
14. 'Three Inch Fury', 7.
15. 'Three Inch Fury', 38.
16. 'Three Inch Fury', 8.
17. 'Three Inch Fury', 8-9.
18. 'Negroes in Combat', *Yank: The Army Weekly*, volume 3, 26, 23 February 1945, 7.
19. Pier Paolo Battistelli, *Panzer Divisions 1944-45* (Oxford 2009) 17.
20. Cameron, *Mobility, Shock, and Firepower*, 318.
21. Charles M. Baily, *Faint Praise: American Tanks and Tank Destroyers during World War II* (North Haven, 1983) 112.

22. Baily, *Faint Praise*, 113.
23. Mollo, *The Armed Forces of World War II*, 186
24. Gabel, *Seek, Strike, and Destroy*, 55.
25. Gabel, *Seek, Strike, and Destroy*, 58.

Chapter 4

1. Mueller and Turk, *Report After Action*, 54.
2. Mueller and Turk, *Report After Action*, 54-55.
3. 'Three Inch Fury', 11. The enemy is misidentified as the 20th Panzer Grenadier Division. This is unlikely, as that division was on the Eastern Front at that time. It should be the 21st Panzer Division.
4. Sturkey misidentifies the enemy, as at that time the German 6th Corps, the *VI. Armeekorps*, was operating on the Eastern front. The enemy consisted of the 82nd, LXXXII. *Armeekorps*.
5. Motley, *The Invisible Soldier*, 169.
6. 'Three Inch Fury', 10.
7. Private Chester Jones, 614th Tank Destroyer Battalion, accessed through: www.tankdestroyer.net.
8. The film is present in the National Archives: '95TH VICTORY DIVISION, SAARLAUTERN, GERMANY ; NEGRO TANK DESTROYERS, BITSCHOFEN, GERMANY', 16687, 111-ADC-2884, Department of Defense. Department of the Army. Office of the Chief Signal Officer. (9/18/1947 – 3/1/1964), Series: Moving Images Relating to Military Activities, 1947 – 1964 Record Group 111: Records of the Office of the Chief Signal Officer, 1860 – 1985.
9. 'Three Inch Fury', 11.
10. *The 3rd Cavalry Reconnaissance Squadron (Mecz.) In World War II, 9 August 1944 To 9 May 1945, 1946.*
11. Mueller and Turk, *Report After Action*, 1, 18.
12. Cactus Division newsletter, February 2011, 27, 6.
13. 'Three Inch Fury', 11.
14. Sergeant Charles McGowan, 614th Tank Destroyer Battalion, accessed through: www.tankdestroyer.net.
15. 'The troops were segregated; bullets were colorblind', *Southside Sentinel*, 21 February 2002.

16. 409th Infantry Regiment, 2nd Battalion, Journal – December 1944, 13 December, accessed through: http://103divwwii.usm.edu/
17. Willie W. J. Barrios, 'The Operations of 'F' Company, 411th Infantry (103d Infantry Division) Near Climbach, France, (Alsace), 14 December 1944 (Rhineland Campaign) (Personal Experience of a Rifle Company Commander)', 8-9.
18. Barrios, 'The Operations of 'F' Company', 22-23.
19. Sergeant Dillard Booker, 614th Tank Destroyer Battalion, accessed through: www.tankdestroyer.net.
20. Barrios, 'The Operations of 'F' Company', 11.
21. Jim Lankford, 'Gamecocks at war: The 614th Tank Destroyer Battalion', *On Point*, 2010, 3.
22. Motley, *The Invisible Soldier*, 174.
23. Motley, *The Invisible Soldier*, 174.
24. Sergeant Dillard Booker, 614th Tank Destroyer Battalion, accessed through: www.tankdestroyer.net.
25. Sergeant Dillard Booker, 614th Tank Destroyer Battalion, accessed through: www.tankdestroyer.net.
26. Barrios, 'The Operations of 'F' Company', 14-15.
27. Barrios, 'The Operations of 'F' Company', 18.
28. 'Negroes in Combat', *Yank*, 6.
29. There are different versions of what was said. Booker's version has been used, although *Yank* and *Report After Action* present other accounts: Blackshear said: 'You can't go up there right now. The artillery fire is too heavy.' Harries replied: 'Get the hell out of my way. I'm taking this up to my buddies.' Negroes in Combat', *Yank*, 6. 'Can't go up there, it's coming in too heavy.' 'The hell I can't, the boys need it up there.' Mueller and Turk, *Report After Action*, 49. Booker's version from: Sergeant Dillard Booker, 614th Tank Destroyer Battalion, accessed through: www.tankdestroyer.net.
30. Barrios, 'The Operations of 'F' Company', 22.
31. Mueller and Turk, *Report After Action*, 49.
32. Barrios, 'The Operations of 'F' Company', 24.
33. 'AWARDED DISTINGUISHED SERVICE CROSS', *The Dayton Forum*, 30 March 1945.
34. 'Negroes in Combat', *Yank*, 7.

35. Sergeant Weldon Freeman, 614th Tank Destroyer Battalion, accessed through: www.tankdestroyer.net.
36. Mueller and Turk, *Report After Action*, 43.
37. 'Three Inch Fury', 39-40.
38. The General Board, United States Forces, European Theater, 'Report on Study of Organization, Equipment, and Tactical Employment of Tank Destroyer Units', n.d., 15-16.

Chapter 5

1. Clarke and Smith, *Riviera to the Rhine*, 493-495.
2. Clarke and Smith, *Riviera to the Rhine*, 498.
3. Clarke and Smith, *Riviera to the Rhine*, 499.
4. Clarke and Smith, *Riviera to the Rhine*, 504; Mueller and Turk, *Report After Action*, 60.
5. James Montgomery, *B Company 776 Tank Destroyer Battalion in Combat* (Baltimore, 1983) 77.
6. 411th Infantry Regiment, Regimental Journal January 1945, 2 January, accessed through: http://103divwwii.usm.edu/.
7. Private Chester Jones, 614th Tank Destroyer Battalion, accessed through: www.tankdestroyer.net.
8. 103d Infantry Division, General Orders, 11 January 1945, accessed through: http://103divwwii.usm.edu/.
9. 411th Infantry Regiment, Regimental Journal January 1945, 13 January, accessed through, http://103divwwii.usm.edu/
10. Robert Thorne, Journal, 17 January 1945, accessed through: https://www.trailblazersww2.org/.
11. Motley, *The Invisible Soldier*, 170.
12. Leonard Diana, Company A, 410th Infantry Regiment, accessed through: http://103divwwii.usm.edu/.
13. Mueller and Turk, *Report After Action*, 67.
14. Clarke and Smith, *Riviera to the Rhine*, 526.
15. Frank Rogers, 'My World War II: Company G, 409th Infantry, 103d Division', n.d., 39.
16. Sergeant Dillard Booker, 614th Tank Destroyer Battalion, accessed through: www.tankdestroyer.net.

17. Unknown, 614th Tank Destroyer Battalion, accessed through: www.tankdestroyer.net.
18. 410th Regimental Journal, 23 January. Accessed through: http://103divwwii.usm.edu/.
19. 'Three Inch Fury', 39.
20. Sergeant Dillard Booker, 614th Tank Destroyer Battalion, accessed through: www.tankdestroyer.net.
21. Stephen M. Rusiecki, *In final defense of the Reich: The Destruction of the 6th SS Mountain Division 'Nord'*, (Annapolis, 2010) 43.
22. Daily Reports, 20-29 January, 614th Tank Destroyer Battalion, accessed through: www.tankdestroyer.net.
23. Clarke and Smith, *Riviera to the Rhine*, 526-527.
24. Clarke and Smith, *Riviera to the Rhine*, 527.

Chapter 6

1. Mueller and Turk, *Report After Action*, 74.
2. Sergeant Thomas Ingram, 614th Tank Destroyer Battalion, accessed through: www.tankdestroyer.net.
3. Sergeant Thomas Ingram, 614th Tank Destroyer Battalion, accessed through: www.tankdestroyer.net.
4. Sergeant Thomas Ingram, 614th Tank Destroyer Battalion, accessed through: www.tankdestroyer.net.
5. 411th Infantry Regiment, 411th Regimental Journal, 15 March 1945, accessed through: http://103divwwii.usm.edu/.
6. Mueller and Turk, *Report After Action*, 86.
7. 410th Infantry Regiment, 3rd Battalion Journal, 16 March 1945, accessed through: http://103divwwii.usm.edu/.
8. 'Three Inch Fury', 38-39.
9. Sergeant Dillard Booker, 614th Tank Destroyer Battalion, accessed through: www.tankdestroyer.net.
10. Sergeant Dillard Booker, 614th Tank Destroyer Battalion, accessed through: www.tankdestroyer.net.
11. 'Three Inch Fury', 27.
12. William East and William Gleason, *The 409th Infantry Regiment in World War II*, Washington, 1947, 122.

Endnotes 215

13. East and Gleason, *The 409th Infantry Regiment in World War II*, 122.
14. East and Gleason, *The 409th Infantry Regiment in World War II*, 123-124.
15. East and Gleason, *The 409th Infantry Regiment in World War II*, 124.
16. East and Gleason, *The 409th Infantry Regiment in World War II*, 124.
17. East and Gleason, *The 409th Infantry Regiment in World War II*, 126.

Chapter 7

1. 'Three Inch Fury', 30.
2. Charles T. Boyle, 'Operations of an advance command post party 411th Infantry, 103d Infantry Division in the vicinity of Marktwald, Germany, 27 April 1945 (Personal Experience of Regimental Staff Officer – S-1)', 3.
3. 411th Infantry Regiment, Narrative of Operations April, accessed through: http://103divwwii.usm.edu/.
4. 411th Infantry Regiment, Narrative of Operations April, accessed through: http://103divwwii.usm.edu/.
5. 'Three Inch Fury', 30-31.
6. Sergeant Dillard Booker, 614th Tank Destroyer Battalion, accessed through: www.tankdestroyer.net.
7. 614th Tank Destroyer Battalion, Battalion Journal April 1945, 25 April, accessed through: www.tankdestroyer.net.
8. Mueller and Turk, *Report After Action*, 130.
9. Sergeant Thomas Ingram, 614th Tank Destroyer Battalion, accessed through: www.tankdestroyer.net.
10. Sergeant Dillard Booker, 614th Tank Destroyer Battalion, accessed through: www.tankdestroyer.net.
11. William D. Sproesser, '40 days of Combat and one Day in Hell: L-Company, 411th Infantry Regiment, 103d Division', 23.
12. Private Chester Jones, 614th Tank Destroyer Battalion, accessed through: www.tankdestroyer.net.
13. Sergeant Thomas Ingram, 614th Tank Destroyer Battalion, accessed through: www.tankdestroyer.net.
14. 'Three Inch Fury', 33.
15. Periodical Medical Report, 614th Tank Destroyer Battalion, 19 June 1945, Eisenhower Presidential Library, Museum & Boyhood Home.
16. *Chronik der Gendarmerie von Leutasch*, 8 May 1945.

Chapter 8

1. Robert L. Williams, *History of the Association of Black Psychologists: Profiles of Outstanding Black Psychologists* (Bloomington, 2008) 161.
2. Lee, *The Employment of Negro Troops*, 375.
3. Gregory, 'Charles Branson (served 1942–1945)', 1-2.
4. Lee, *The Employment of Negro Troops*, 680.
5. Lee, *The Employment of Negro Troops*, 681; Gregory, 'Charles Branson (served 1942–1945)', 2.
6. Gregory, 'Charles Branson (served 1942–1945)', 4.
7. Clarke and Smith, *Riviera to the Rhine*, 520.
8. 'Growing up black in Shepherdstown', Congressional Record Volume 144, 20, 4 March, 1998.
9. Battalion history, January 1945, 813th Tank Destroyer Battalion, accessed through: www.tankdestroyer.net.
10. 'Three Inch Fury', 38.
11. *The Cross Of Lorraine: A Combat History Of The 79th Infantry Division*, June 1942 – December 1945 (1986) 108.
12. Negro Digest, April 1946, volume IV, 6, 46.
13. Lee, *The Employment of Negro Troops*, 682.
14. E.T.O Board of Review, Opinions, CM ETO 10616 – CM ETO 11987, volume 23 – 24, 18.
15. E.T.O Board of Review, Opinions, volume 23 – 24, 19.
16. E.T.O Board of Review, Opinions, volume 23 – 24, 19.
17. E.T.O Board of Review, Opinions, volume 23 – 24, 19-20.
18. Office of Judge Advocate General of the Army, Board of Review, Holdings Opinions Reviews, volume 81, 1949, 412-414.
19. The M8 was a six-wheeled vehicle that employed a four-man crew: a commander, a gunner, a radioman and a driver. Saylor, Thomas, 'Oral History Project World War II Years, 1941–1946 – James Kirk' (2003). Oral History Project: World War II Years, 1941–1946, 129, 14.
20. Family Archive, Reuben Yelding.
21. Various orders, 2 April 1945, 679th Tank Destroyer Battalion, accessed through: www.tankdestroyer.net.
22. Battalion Diary, 7 February 1943, 679th Tank Destroyer Battalion, accessed through: www.tankdestroyer.net.

23. Battalion Diary, 16 December 1943, 679th Tank Destroyer Battalion, accessed through: www.tankdestroyer.net.
24. Battalion Diary, 20 – 26 March 1944, 679th Tank Destroyer Battalion, accessed through: www.tankdestroyer.net.
25. Battalion Diary, 14 May 1944, 679th Tank Destroyer Battalion, accessed through: www.tankdestroyer.net; Battalion Diary, 18 May 1944, 679th Tank Destroyer Battalion, accessed through: www.tankdestroyer.net.
26. *Fifth Army History, Part IX, Race to the Alps*, 1947, 'Chapter III: Diversion and Break-Through', 38.
27. Daniel K. Gibran, *The 92nd Infantry Division and the Italian Campaign in World War II* (Jefferson, 2017) 62.
28. Saylor, 'Oral History Project World War II Years, 1941–1946 – James Kirk', 16.
29. Saylor, 'Oral History Project World War II Years, 1941–1946 – James Kirk', 16.
30. Battalion Diary, 18 March 1945, 679th Tank Destroyer Battalion, accessed through: www.tankdestroyer.net.
31. *Fifth Army History*, 'Chapter III: Diversion and Break-Through', 37.
32. *Fifth Army History*, 'Chapter III: Diversion and Break-Through', 40.
33. *Fifth Army History*, 'Chapter III: Diversion and Break-Through', 43.
34. *Fifth Army History*, 'Chapter III: Diversion and Break-Through', 43.
35. Lee, *The Employment of Negro Troops*, 587.
36. Saylor, 'Oral History Project World War II Years, 1941–1946 – James Kirk', 15.
37. Saylor, 'Oral History Project World War II Years, 1941–1946 – James Kirk', 15.
38. 'James Knight Killed When Mine Explodes', *The Michigan Chronicle*, 11 August 1945.
39. Battalion History, May 1945, 679th Tank Destroyer Battalion, accessed through: www.tankdestroyer.net.

Chapter 9

1. 'Tank Killers', *Fortune*, 116-117.
2. Gabel, *Seek, Strike, and Destroy*, 63.
3. Gabel, *Seek, Strike, and Destroy*, 64-65.

4. Farewell letter Pritchard, 614th Tank Destroyer Battalion, accessed through: www.tankdestroyer.net.
5. 'Three Inch Fury', 35.
6. Hammelburg Lager, Roster of American Prisoners of War interned at Oflag XIII-B, Hammelburg, US National Archives File.
7. Charles Whiting, *48 hours to Hammelburg* (New York, 1982) 133.
8. 'Lt. Mitchell: Gary's 'One Man Army' Home on Sick Leave', *The Indianapolis Recorder*, 22 September 1945.
9. Motley, *The Invisible Soldier*, 171-172.
10. 'Col. Frank Pritchard, Lansing Newsman', *Detroit Free Press*, 28 January 1975.
11. 'Lt. Mitchell: Gary's 'One Man Army' Home on Sick Leave', *The Indianapolis Recorder*, 22 September 1945.
12. 'People', *The Sacramento Bee*, 13 July 2000.
13. Gregory, 'Charles Branson (served 1942–1945)', 5-6.
14. 'Growing up black in Shepherdstown', Congressional Record Volume 144, 20, 4 March, 1998.
15. Saylor, 'Oral History Project World War II Years, 1941–1946 – James Kirk', 3.
16. Saylor, 'Oral History Project World War II Years, 1941–1946 – James Kirk', 22.
17. *The Crisis*, December 1945, 345.
18. Converse e. a., *The Exclusion of Black soldiers from the Medal of Honor in World War II* 39.
19. Converse e. a., *The Exclusion of Black soldiers from the Medal of Honor in World War II* 74.
20. U.S. Army, U.S. Forces, European Theater, Historieal Division: Records, 1941–1946, National Archives and Records Administration, 407, Cables – In Log, ETOUSA (Gen Lee), Feb 1-10,1945.
21. 'Negro Soldiers' Historic Role Recalled,' *Lansing State Journal*, 18 February 1968.
22. 'Black, White Men Shed the Same Color Tears', *Lansing State Journal*, 22 March 1971.
23. 'Black, White Men Shed the Same Color Tears', *Lansing State Journal*, 22 March 1971.

24. 'Many Negro Combat Troops Prove Heroes in France; First Full Report on GI's in Battle', *The Daily Bulletin*, 12 March 1945.
25. Cameron, *Mobility, Shock, and Firepower*, 497-498.
26. 614th Tank Destroyer Battalion, Various documents 1945, accessed through: www.tankdestroyer.net.
27. Motley, *The Invisible Soldier*, 170.
28. 614th Tank Destroyer Battalion, Battalion Journal January 1945, 27 January & 29 January, accessed through: www.tankdestroyer.net.
29. The General Board, 'Report on Study of Organization, Equipment, and Tactical Employment of Tank Destroyer Units', 28.
30. Motley, *The Invisible Soldier*, 163.
31. Mueller and Turk, *Report After Action*, 102.
32. J. Cefkin, E Company, 409 Infantry Regiment, accessed through: http://103divwwii.usm.edu/.
33. John Thornton Dorsey Jr., 'An account by a World War II Combat Infantryman', 1.
34. 'Black, White Men Shed the Same Color Tears', *Lansing State Journal*, 22 March 1971.

Appendix 1
1. 'Three Inch Fury', 7.s.

Index

NAMES

Albright, James J., 60
Alford, James, 134
Allard, Henry W., 139
Allen, Frank, 134
Anderson, Delmer P., 139
Arrington, Lun, 144
Awkard, Joseph, 115, 143

Baker, Herschel D., 115
Baker, Vernon, 131, 147
Barbee, James, 89
Barda, James, 62
Barrios, Willie, 61-2, 68
Bates, Paul L., 23, 96, 147
Baum, Abraham, 141
Berry, Adam W., 96
Black, Asa C., 32
Blackshear, John, 61, 63-4, 67-8
Blaskowitz, Johannes, 74
Bond, Eddie L., 113
Booker, Dillard, 62-3, 65, 67-8, 80-1, 84, 88, 94-5, 106, 109
Booker, Samuel, 111
Boswell, Dan, 25, 116
Bowers, Alma, 146

Boynton, William, 33
Branson, Charles, 116-7, 119, 144
Braun, Eva, 108
Brookers, Robert, 19
Bruce, Andrew D., 12-5, 17, 78
Bryant, Benjamin W., 59, 69, 96
Bullock, Robert, 85
Burch, Leonard I., 92, 120
Burke, Clarence, 24
Burnett, John A., 60

Campbell, David, 54
Campbell, Thomas, 36-7, 43, 51, 149, 153
Campbell, William A., 36
Cannon, Robert, 58, 95-6
Carey, Edward J., 96
Carn, James H., 96
Carter, Edward A., 147
Castro, Julita, 143
Cefkin, 152
Clark, Clarence, 49
Clarks, Mark W., 110
Clements, Fred, 55
Clinton, Bill, 148

Index 221

Coleman, Walter S., 144
Cureton, Jonathan, 70
Cutler, Guilford, 55

Darrah, John W., 115
Davis, George, 24
Davis, Wylon, 111
Detwiller, James W., 122-3
Devers, Jacob L., 82
Diana, Leonard, 78
Dietrich, Marlene, 105
Disney, Walt, 31
Dobey, Albert T., 96
Donaldson, George, 104
Dorsey, John Thornton, 153
Douglas, Alonzo, 19

Eaton, Henry, 85
Eisenhower, Dwight, 148
English, Hurley, 104
Evans, Horace, 152
Evans, John H., 70

Fenner, James E., 70
Flowers, Joe, 122-3
Forster, William E., 134
Forte, Ormond, 44, 113
Fox, John R., 148
Freeman, Weldon, 69-70

Gibson, Elijah, 87, 93
Giles, Rema, 70
Gill, George Jr., 25
Gillespie, Alger, 144

Glover, Clifton T., 23-4
Golds, Westley, 24
Greer, Lee D., 88-9
Gregory, Lewis, 60
Griffin, Henry B., 54
Griffin, Roy, 55

Haffner, Charles C., 57, 76, 148-9
Hall, Felix, 18
Hall, Luther J., 55
Hanebel, Thomas J., 85
Harper, James, 109, 112
Harris, Bonnie O., 85
Harris, Robert, 67-8
Harrod, Dennette, 129
Hart, Henry, 96
Hastie, William H., 21
Hennighausen, 97
Henrikson, Charles, 66
Hester, John H., 39
Hightower, Jefferson, 22
Hitler, Adolf, 10, 74, 81, 108
Hockaday, Al, 63, 65
Hood, John Bell, 14, 35
Hudson, George, 115

Ingram, Thomas, 87-9, 108, 111

Jackson, Frank, 104
James, Daniel, 109-10
James, Richard K., 138
James, Willy F., 148
Jarrett, Scott, 85
Jeffcoat, Robert, 24

Johnson, 43
Johnson, Austin, 87, 109, 112
Johnson, Harry, 121
Johnson, Lawrence, 34, 61, 140, 143, 148
Johnson, Sandra, 148
Jones, Chesterfield, 51, 54-5, 75, 111
Jones, Reed Jr., 85
Jones, Robert F., 120-1
Jones, Victor, 80
Joynes, Ernest, 105

Keeby, Joseph L., 75, 89, 93-4, 109, 112
Kennon, Blaisdell, 34, 37
Kilgo, Thomas, 91-2
King, Beauregard, 44-5, 56, 71-2, 81, 91-2, 96
King, Lester, 24
King, Napoleon, 94
King, Plato, 85
Kirk, James, 124-5, 130, 134, 144
Knight, Eddie, 127
Knight, Whit, 65, 85

Lane, John O., 133
Latson, Lester, 92
Leftwich, Lively, 133
Lloyd, Claudius, 97
Love, Luell L., 107

Magby, Willie, 57, 92-3, 120
Mann, Theophilus, 26, 33

Marshall, George C., 12, 148
McAfee, Ray F., 122-3
McAuliffe, Anthony, 72, 76-7, 90, 95, 102, 113, 149
McCloud, Andrew, 33
McDaniel, Thomas, 65
McDougald, James, 104
McGee, 39, 42
McGowan, Charles, 58
McGrayne, Donald, 127
McKaine Oliver, Francis, 115
McNair, Lesley, 12-13, 15, 35
Meloy, Guy S., 102
Michel, Joseph, 70
Miller, Doris, 19
Mitchell, George, 62, 65, 73, 85, 91, 141-3
Moody, Clifton, 109
Morrison, James, 104
Murph, Shelton, 64
Murphy, Robert O., 23
Myers, Richard, 66

Nelson, Serreo, 96, 99-100, 112
Newton, Louis, 133
Nichols, Alfred W., 113
Nix, Hulie, 133
Nolan, Beecher R., 122-3
Norfleet, Alphonso, 70
Nunley, Robert, 94

Ogelsby, Charles, 40
Ogletree, George, 111
O'Leary, Robert J., 92-3, 113

Oliver, Joe, 122
Owens, George W., 104

Parker, Blanchard L., 89
Parker, James, 111-12
Parks, Charles, 91, 92
Patch, Alexander, 74, 90, 140
Patraeck, Sam, 73
Patton, George, 13, 45, 98
Perry, Arthur, 64
Pettigrew, Otis, 55
Phillips, Thomas, 87, 109
Phipps, William H., 65
Pierce, John T., 73, 102
Plessy, Homer, 18
Polk, Isiah, 104-106
Pollard, Ronald, 100
Pritchard, Frank S., 29, 35, 37-8, 39, 41-4, 49, 69, 72, 83, 85, 90, 92-3, 107, 113, 138-9, 143, 148-9
Punch, George, 85

Ramsey, Claude, 23, 39, 42
Rattler, Charlie, 85
Ray, Mark, 93
Rees, Floyd E., 138
Reese, Clarence, 94
Rhone, Henry T., 59, 69
Richard, Charles J., 43, 71
Riley, Lucius, 65
Rivers, Ruben, 148
Robertson, Roosevelt, 63, 65, 95
Robinson, Bertha Mae, 144
Robinson, Jackie, 22-3

Rogers, Frank, 80
Rommel, Erwin, 81
Roosevelt, Franklin Delano, 17, 103
Ruffin, Roosevelt, 55
Rundstedt, Gerd von, 74
Ryder, Frederick, 115

Sample, Leroy, 113
Sargent, Chester, 113
Saxton, Willie R., 123
Shaw, Thomas, 69, 82
Simmons, Peter, 64
Simpson, Jessie N., 122
Sims, Rufus, 60
Smith, Clarence, 134
Smith, R. A., 133
Smith, Robert L., 109, 112
Smith, Walter, 45, 50-1, 55, 68, 75, 94, 112
Spell, Blease, 85
Spencer, Matthew, 99, 100
Sproesser, William, 110
Stallings, Floyd, 67
Stark, Kenneth B., 133
Sterling, Lincoln, 56
Strayhorne, John, 111
Stroud, Rosa, 144
Stubbs, John E. Jr., 112
Sturkey, Christopher, 36, 38, 51-2, 68, 75, 78, 112, 142, 151
Summer, Lonnie, 75
Swindell, Burnie, 65
Swinger, Curtis, 89

Tabron, William, 63-5, 68, 85
Tarkington, Arlis, 56
Taylor, Maxwell, 72
Thomas, Amos, 25
Thomas, Charles L., 36, 52, 54, 61-4, 67-8, 75, 148
Thompson, James G., 20
Thorne, Robert, 77
Tindall, Richard, 115
Tobin, Leon, 64, 73
Truman, Harry, 103
Tucker, Frederick, 56
Turner, J. H., 31

VanderZwiep, Philip J., 115
Vann, Robert L., 21

Walker, L. C., 104
Ward, Orlando, 39
Warner, Paul, 67
Washington, Henry, 24

Washington, Joseph, 24
Waters, John K., 141
Watson, George, 68, 148
Weaver, Henry, 89
Weeks, Riley, 90
Weir, John O., 40, 111
Welch, Wilbert, 85
Wesley, Moses H., 70
West, Key, 78-9
West, Walter, 85
White, Walter, 21
Whitfield, Jerome, 109
William, John, 70
Williams, James B., 94
Williams, Leroy, 108-109
Williams, Robert, 39, 42
Williams, Samuel, 94
Wilson, Otis, 25, 116

Yelding, Reuben, 124-5, 130, 145

PLACES
Alethausen, 107
Antwerp, 70
Arles, 144
Aschaffenburg, 102
Aulla, 132-3
Avonmouth, 42

Bensheim, 102
Berlin, 108
Bernstadt, 107

Birkenhordt, 98
Bischholtz, 87, 92
Bitschhoffen, 60, 88
Bobenthal, 94
Bohringen, 106
Bollenborn, 97
Bolzanetto, 134
Bristol, 42
Brussels, 113
Buren, 56

Burlafingen, 107
Burley, 42
Buschdorf, 50-1, 53

Camp Bowie, 25, 27, 34
Camp Breckinridge, 23
Camp Campbell, 136
Camp Carson, 27, 34, 139
Camp Claiborne, 57
Camp Forrest, 27, 114
Camp Gruber, 27, 29
Camp Hood, 15, 22-5, 27, 30, 33, 35-9, 41-2, 115-16, 124-5, 139
Camp Kilmer, 27, 138-9
Camp Livingston, 27
Camp Patrick Henry, 22
Camp Shanks, 41, 128
Camp Swift, 27, 33
Camp Wheeler, 124
Camp Wolters, 34
Cherbourg, 44-5
Cheyenne, 145
Climbach, 61-3, 67-9, 76, 93, 153
Colmar, 122

Darmstadt, 103

Eberbach, 81-2
Eft, 56
Elmstein, 102
Eschbach, 58

Farschviller, 72
Folpersviller, 75

Forbach, 76
Fort Benning, 18
Fort Custer, 27, 33
Fort Devens, 34
Fort Huachuca, 27, 31
Fort Knox, 19, 27
Fort Stotsenberg, 19

Gary, 143
Gaubiving, 76
Genoa, 133-4
Gerslingen, 107
Goersdorf, 93
Gumbrechtshoffen, 92
Gundershoffen, 92

Haguenau, 61, 78-9
Hall, 109
Hammelburg, 140
Hampton Roads, 27
Hatten, 118-20
Hegenlohe, 104
Hiroshima, 113
Hofheim, 113, 138
Huntsville, 39

Impflingen, 102
Indiantown Gap Military Reservation, 27
Ingwiller, 82, 90
Innsbruck, 104, 109-10

Killeen, 40
Kindwiller, 91

Kirchberg, 108
Kircheim, 104
Klingenmünster, 97-8, 100, 152
Kuttolsheim, 57

La Spezia, 129
Lampersloch, 92
Las Vegas, 116
Lauterbach, 76
Lauterschwan, 96
Le Havre, 128
Leghorn; *see* Livorno
Lembach, 62
Leutasch, 112
Livorno, 128
Lixhausen, 85
Lixing, 75
London, 113
Lunéville, 55, 57

Manilla, 143
Marseille, 57, 123, 128-9
Massa, 129, 131
Menchhoffen, 91
Metz, 45
Metzingen, 104, 106
Mietesheim, 58-9
Mitschdorf, 93
Mulhausen, 87
Münchweiler, 98-9

Nagasaki, 113
Neufvillage, 72
New York, 27, 144
Niederbronn, 81, 92

Nittenwald, 110
Nothweiler, 93-4
Nuremberg, 103, 142

Oberau, 108
Oberhofen, 103
Obermodern, 82
Oberperl, 49, 55
Offwiller, 92

Paris, 113
Partenkirchen, 108
Pearl Harbor, 19, 124
Perl, 49
Pisa, 128-30
Pluderhausen, 104
Portland, 124
Printzheim, 80, 82-3
Punta Bianca, 129, 131,
Puttenlange, 76

Reichshoffen, 77, 93
Reisdorf, 97
Rheims, 142
Rittershoffen, 118, 120
Rothbach, 92

Sacramento, 144
Saint-Sylvain, 128
Scharnitz, 108
Schillersdorf, 83-5, 140
Schlierbach, 107
Schongau, 108
Selestat, 57
Silz, 98

Soultz, 61
South Haven, 146
Southhampton, 42
St Jean Rohrbach, 72
St Louis, 144
St. Paul, 124, 145
Stafferied, 113
Strass, 108
Stuttgart, 103
Surtainville, 44

Tallahassee, 143

Uhwiller, 83

Viareggio, 134

Waldsee, 102
Warm Springs, 103
Wingen, 62, 93
Woerth, 60, 81
Worgel, 111

Zinswiller, 81-2
Zutzendorf, 85